IBSEN

Letters and Speeches

Edited by EVERT SPRINCHORN

A DRAMABOOK
HILL AND WANG · NEW YORK

FIRST EDITION JANUARY 1964

Manufactured in the United States of America
by The Colonial Press Inc., Clinton, Massachusetts

IBSEN

Letters and Speeches

PREFACE

PREFACE

The first collection of Ibsen's letters, edited by Halvdan Koht and Julius Elias, was published in simultaneous Danish and German editions in 1904 while Ibsen was still alive. The English edition, translated by J. N. Laurvik and Mary Morison, appeared the following year. A supplementary volume, *Speeches and New Letters,* translated by Arne Kildal, came out in 1911. Since then a number of additional letters have come to light, many of which have been translated into English in various books on the playwright. But there has been no major English edition of his letters since that of 1905, a situation that the present volume seeks to remedy.

The task of selecting the letters is made relatively easy by the fact that Ibsen was not a voluminous correspondent. Though his career stretched over fifty years, and though he acted as his own literary agent, the total number of extant letters is less than fifteen hundred, and about nine hundred of these are business letters.* (Strindberg, who lived to be only sixty-three, wrote about seven times as many letters.) I have selected 276 letters for this new edition, and I have also included thirteen speeches, four prefaces, and one autobiographical fragment. Of the 238 letters in the 1905 edition, 155 have been included in whole or in part. The translations have been thoroughly revised and some errors corrected. One hundred twenty-nine letters that are not in the 1905 edition are printed here, and of these over fifty have not previously been translated.

The strict chronological order is violated in a few instances in order to make the book easier to read as a kind of autobiography. But in each case a cross-reference has been made in the proper chronological place.

* Else Høst, "Brev fra Henrik Ibsen," *Edda,* LVI (1956), p. 2. The centennial edition of Ibsen's works, edited by Bull, Koht, and Seip (Oslo, 1928–1957), contains 1404 letters, but there are known to be other extant letters.

For sake of convenience, the letter headings are in the same style throughout ("Rome, June 18, 1881") and do not necessarily follow Ibsen's own headings.

Footnotes are the editor's unless otherwise indicated.

The three dots of ellipsis (. . .) indicate the omission of anything from a word to several paragraphs. Dashes are usually Ibsen's. Passages in brackets [ ] are the editor's; those in parentheses ( ) are Ibsen's.

I have generally expressed the value of foreign money in terms of the American dollar of that time, but since the dollar has changed so much in purchasing power, the figures may not have much meaning. It might help to bear in mind that the average workingman's wage in the 1880's in Scandinavia amounted to eight hundred kronor a year, that is, about two hundred 1880 dollars.

I wish to thank Professor Leif Sjöberg of Columbia University, who looked up some material that was not easily available to me, and Mrs. Elisabeth Blair, who typed the final manuscript.

E. S.

Letters (*cont'd.*)

ACKNOWLEDGMENTS

The following letters were translated by Gerik Schjelderup in Bergliot Ibsen's *The Three Ibsens* (The Hutchinson Group, London and New York, 1952):

June 25, 1873
September 12, 1877
  (to Sigurd Ibsen)
September 12, 1877
  (to Suzannah Ibsen)
August 30, 1880
September 18, 1880
July 20, 1884

August 19, 1884
August 30, 1884
September 17, 1884
December 22, 1886
March 5, 1889
April 10, 1891
June 13, 1897
June 15, 1897

The Preface to *The Feast at Solhaug* was translated by William Archer in *The Collected Works of Henrik Ibsen,* Vol. II (London and New York, 1908), pp. 183–92.

The following speeches, articles, and letters were translated by the present editor from *Henrik Ibsens samlede verker: Hundreårsutgave* (Centennial Edition), edited by Francis Bull, Halvdan Koht, and Didrik Arup Seip, 21 vols. (Gyldendal Norsk Forlag, Oslo, 1928–1957):

Memories of Childhood
Preface to *Catiline*
Preface to *Love's Comedy*
Speech at the Unveiling of the Memorial Statue on P. A. Munch's Grave in Rome
Speech at the Danish Students' Banquet, Copenhagen, October 3, 1885
Speech to the "Gnistan" Literary Society in Göteborg, September 12, 1887
Speech at the Private Party Given by Frederik Hegel, October 5, 1887
Speech at the Banquet in Copenhagen, April 1, 1898
Preface to Collected Works, "To the Reader," March, 1898
Letters of:

May 20, 1844
October 6, 1845
July 23, 1857

September 2, 1865
November 16, 1865
March 16, 1866

The two letters to H. Lassen of October 24, 1872, and November 14, 1872, which came to light after the Centennial Edition was completed, were translated by the present editor from Øyvind Anker, "Omkring Førsteoppførelsen av *Kjærlighedens Komedie* på Christiania Theater 1873," *Edda*, LXI (1961), pp. 64, 68.

The two notes to Hildur Andersen of September 19, 1900, were translated by the present editor from Francis Bull's article, "Hildur Andersen og Henrik Ibsen," *Edda*, LVII (1957), pp. 47–54.

All the other letters and speeches were translated by John Nilsen Laurvik and Mary Morison in *Letters of Henrik Ibsen* (New York, 1905) (published in England as the *Correspondence of Henrik Ibsen*, London, 1905), and by Arne Kildal in *Speeches and New Letters* (Boston, 1910; London, 1911). These translations were revised by the present editor and checked against the text of the letters as given in the Norwegian Centennial Edition.

CONTENTS

CONTENTS

CHRONOLOGY

1828   March 20. Henrik Ibsen is born in Skien, Norway, a town of two thousand inhabitants about sixty miles southwest of Oslo. Henrik is the second child born to Knud and Marichen Ibsen. The older child, born in 1826, dies less than a month after Henrik is born. Four more children are born between 1830 and 1835.

1832   or 1833. The Ibsen family moves to a more expensive property in Skien, the Hundevad estate.

1834   Knud Ibsen finds himself in increasing financial difficulties, and in 1836 is declared bankrupt.

1835   The family moves from Skien to Venstøp, a small town a short distance away in the parish of Gjerpen.

1843   October 1. Ibsen is confirmed in the Gjerpen church. The family moves back to Skien and lives in a house bought by Knud Ibsen's half brother. Immediately after Christmas, Henrik leaves Skien for Grimstad.

1844   January 3. Ibsen arrives in Grimstad and begins his apprenticeship as an apothecary.

1846   Ibsen becomes the father of a son by a housemaid who is ten years his senior. For the next fifteen years Ibsen has to contribute to the support of the child.

1847   His earliest extant poem, "Resignation," probably dates from this year.

1848   Studies Latin in order to prepare for university examinations.

1848–49   Winter. Writes his first play, *Catiline*.

1849   September 28. "In the Autumn," Ibsen's first poem to be published, appears in *Christiania-Posten*.

1850   April 12. *Catiline* published in an edition of 250 copies, of which all but fifty are later disposed of as waste paper. The cost of printing is paid for by Ole Schulerud. This is the first play to be published in Norway since Wergeland's *The Venetian* in 1843.

    April 13. Leaves Grimstad for Christiania [Oslo] and

probably pays a short visit to his family in Skien. This is the last time he sees his parents.

April 29. Arrives in Christiania to cram for the university entrance examinations. Takes the examinations in the autumn, failing in Greek and mathematics, and passing the others.

Writes a one-act play, *The Warrior's Barrow* (*Kjæmpehøjen*) and nearly completes two acts of a romantic comedy, *The Ptarmigan in Justedal* (*Rypen i Justedal*). On September 26 at the Christiania Theater, *The Warrior's Barrow* becomes the first play by Ibsen to be staged. *The Ptarmigan in Justedal* is later reworked as *Olaf Liljekrans*.

1851   Engages in various journalistic activities. Edits a student paper. Contributes articles to *The Worker's Union Paper*, edited by Theodore Abildgaard. Serves as one of three contributing editors of a short-lived satirical journal, known at first as *The Man* and later as *Andhrimner*. Writes *Norma, or A Politician's Love*, a political squib, based on Bellini's opera and published in *Andhrimner*.

November. Ibsen is engaged as playwright in residence at the newly organized National Theater in Bergen.

1852   April to September. Studies the theater in Copenhagen and Dresden.

1853   January 2. Ibsen's *Midsummer Eve* (*Sancthansnatten*) is performed at Bergen.

1854   January 2. *The Warrior's Barrow* performed at Bergen. To fulfil his obligation to provide the theater with a new play each year Ibsen had completely rewritten the work.

1855   January 2. *Lady Inger of Østraat* performed at Bergen.

1856   January 2. *The Feast at Solhaug* performed at Bergen. Ibsen's first success in the theater. Performed at the Christiania Theater, March 13. Published March 19.

1857   January 2. *Olaf Liljekrans* performed at Bergen.

September 3. Assumes his duties as artistic director of the Norwegian Theater in Christiania.

1858   June 18. Marries Suzannah Thoresen.

November 24. Produces *The Vikings at Helgeland* at the Norwegian Theater in Christiania.

1859   Writes the poems "On the Heights" ("Paa Vidderne") and "In the Picture Gallery."

December 23. Son Sigurd is born, the only child of the marriage.

1861   Writes poem "Terje Vigen."

1862   May. Awarded a grant from the University of Christiania to compile folk songs and tales. Travels extensively in Norway.

Summer. The Norwegian Theater is forced to close.

December. *Love's Comedy* published.

1863   January 1. Becomes literary adviser to the Christiania Theater.

May 23. Receives another grant from the university to collect folk songs in the country. Stays in Christiania.

September 12. Awarded a travel grant by the government.

October. *The Pretenders* published.

1864   January 17. *The Pretenders* performed at the Christiania Theater.

April 5. Leaves Christiania for Copenhagen and Rome.

1864   April–May. Travels to Italy, staying over at Copenhagen, Berlin, and Vienna.

1865   November 14. Receives publishing contract from Frederik Hegel, head of the Gyldendal publishing firm in Copenhagen.

1866   March 15. *Brand* published.

April 30. Is voted a travel grant of 100 specie-dollars ($100) by the Royal Norwegian Science Association.

May 12. Is voted an annual stipend of 400 specie-dollars by the Storting (the Norwegian parliament).

June 28. Another travel grant of 350 specie-dollars is awarded to him by the Storting.

1867   November 14. *Peer Gynt* published.

1868   October 1–2. Moves to Dresden.

1869   June 3. Ibsen's mother dies.

July 3. Receives a grant from the Norwegian government to study in Sweden.

July. Goes to Stockholm as delegate to the Nordic orthographic conference. Receives the Vasa Order from King Charles XV.

September 30. *The League of Youth* published. Performed October 18 at the Christiania Theater.

October–November. Attends the opening of the Suez Canal as the representative of Norway.

1870   July 19. The Franco-Prussian War is declared. Ibsen stays in Copenhagen from July to October.

1871   May 3. Publishes his *Poems*.

Works on *Emperor and Galilean*.

January 24. The Dannebrog Order conferred on Ibsen.

1872   Works on *Emperor and Galilean*.

1873   June–July. Serves as judge at the International Art Exhibit in Vienna.

July. Made a Knight of St. Olaf at the coronation of King Oscar II of Sweden and Norway.

October 16. *Emperor and Galilean* published.

November 24. *Love's Comedy* performed at the Christiania Theater.

1874   July–September. Spends two and a half months in Norway. In August he attends an international conference of archaeologists in Stockholm.

September 10. Honored by Norwegian students in a torchlight procession.

1875   April. Moves to Munich for the benefit of the education of his son, Sigurd.

May 1. Settles in his apartment in Munich.

1876   February 24. *Peer Gynt* performed with music by Edvard Grieg at the Christiania Theater.

April 10. *The Vikings at Helgeland* performed at the Court Theater in Munich, the first of Ibsen's plays to be produced outside Scandinavia.

June. Is guest of honor at the court of the Duke of Saxe-Meiningen, who decorates him with the Ernestine Order.

1877   Ibsen's father dies.

September 6. Honorary doctoral degree conferred on Ibsen at the University of Uppsala, Sweden.

October 11. *The Pillars of Society* published.

November. *The Pillars of Society* performed in the Danish provinces and at the Royal Theater in Copenhagen.

1878 Autumn. Moves to Rome, returning to Munich a year later.

1879 December 4. *A Doll's House* published.

December 21. Première of *A Doll's House* at the Danish Royal Theater in Copenhagen.

1880 Autumn. Moves to Rome when his son finishes his education in Munich.

1881 December. *Ghosts* is published.

1882 May. World première of *Ghosts* takes place in Chicago.

July. University of Rome confers degree of Doctor of Law on Sigurd Ibsen.

November 28. *An Enemy of the People* published.

1883 Revises *The Feast at Solhaug.*

January 13. *An Enemy of the People* performed at the Christiania Theater.

August 28. First European performance of *Ghosts* produced by August Lindberg in Helsingborg, Sweden.

1884 Sigurd Ibsen takes a position in the consulate in Christiania.

November 11. *The Wild Duck* published.

1885 Sigurd enters the Swedish-Norwegian diplomatic service as attaché at the Swedish Department of Foreign Affairs.

January. First performances of *The Wild Duck*, in Bergen, Christiania, and Stockholm.

March 24. The New Theater in Stockholm stages *Brand.*

June–September. Ibsen visits Norway.

June 14. Delivers speech to the workers in Trondhjem.

October. Moves from Rome to Munich.

1886 November 23. *Rosmersholm* published.

December 22. Ibsen is the guest of Duke Georg II of Meiningen for a production of *Ghosts* by the Meiningen Players.

1887 January 17. First performance of *Rosmersholm* staged by the Bergen theater.

July–mid-October. Visits Denmark and Sweden.

December. Ibsen's publisher, Frederik Hegel, dies.

1888   November 28. *The Lady from the Sea* published.

1889   February 12. *The Lady from the Sea* performed by the Christiania Theater and the Court Theater in Weimar simultaneously.

March 3–15. Ibsen is feted in Berlin and Weimar.

Summer. Meets Helene Raff and Emilie Bardach while vacationing in Gossensass in the Tyrol.

1890   Sigurd Ibsen leaves the diplomatic service.

December 16. *Hedda Gabler* published.

1891   January 31. Première of *Hedda Gabler* at the Munich Residenz-Theater.

April. Ibsen feted in Vienna and Budapest.

July. Leaves Munich to settle in Norway.

July 16. Arrives in Christiania. Goes on a tour of the North Cape.

August 17. Returns to Christiania and settles in his apartment on Victoria Terrace.

August. Meets the young pianist Hildur Andersen.

1892   October 11. Sigurd Ibsen marries Bjørnson's daughter Bergliot.

December 12. *The Master Builder* published in Scandinavia. Published in London, December 6.

1893   January 19. Première of *The Master Builder* in Trondhjem.

July 11. Ibsen becomes a grandfather.

1894   December 11. *Little Eyolf* published.

1895   January 12. *Little Eyolf* performed for the first time at the Deutsches Theater in Berlin.

1895   July. Moves to 1 Arbin Street.

1896   December 15. *John Gabriel Borkman* published.

1897   January 10. Première of *John Gabriel Borkman* in Helsinki, closely followed by performances in Germany and Norway.

April 29. The University of Christiania refuses to offer a professorship to Sigurd Ibsen.

1898   March. First volumes of the collected edition of his works published in Denmark and Germany.

March 20–April 16. Seventieth-birthday celebrations. Ibsen honored in Christiania, Copenhagen, and Stockholm; receives the Grand Cross of the Dannebrog Order in Denmark, the Order of the North Star in Sweden.

1899　July 14. Sigurd Ibsen appointed head of the Norwegian Foreign Office.

September. Attends the opening of the new National Theater in Christiania, the first modern theater in Norway.

December 19. *When We Dead Awaken* published in London; published in Scandinavia and Germany, December 22.

1900　January 26. First full production of *When We Dead Awaken* given by the Stuttgart Court Theater; play also staged in Copenhagen (January 28), Helsinki (January 29), Christiania (February 6), and Stockholm (February 14).

1900　March. Ibsen ill with erysipelas.

Summer. Spends the summer at a sea resort undergoing a cure for his illness.

1901　Suffers his first stroke in Christiania.

1903　Suffers another stroke that leaves him unable to write or walk.

1906　May 23. Dies in Christiania.

IBSEN

Letters and Speeches

∗ APPRENTICESHIP IN NORWAY
1828–1864

Memories of Childhood

Skien, 1828–c.1838

Between *A Doll's House* and *Ghosts*, Ibsen toyed with the idea of writing his autobiography, and the following reminiscences date from that time. Written in January, 1881, they were first published in 1888 in Henrik Jaeger's biography of the playwright.

A few years ago when the streets in my native town of Skien were named [1872]—or perhaps simply rechristened —I was honored by having one of the streets named after me. At least the reports said so, and I have heard the same thing from reliable travelers. According to their accounts, this street runs from the market place down to the harbor or the Mud Flats.

Assuming the reports are accurate, I cannot imagine why this street should have come to bear my name, since I was neither born on it nor did I ever live there.

On the contrary, I was born in a house on the market place—the Stockmann house, as it was called. This house faced the front of the church, with its high flight of steps and imposing tower. To the right of the church stood the town pillory and to the left the town hall with the jail and "the madhouse." The Latin school and the common school occupied the fourth side of the square. The church stood by itself in the middle.

This prospect constituted my first view of the world— nothing but buildings; nothing green; no country land-

scapes. But the air above this four-sided enclosure of wood
and stone was filled all day long with the subdued roar
of Long Falls, Cloister Falls, and all the many other rapids
and waterfalls. And the roar was pierced from morning till
night with a sound like that of shrieking and moaning
women. This was the sound of the hundreds of saws in the
mills up at the waterfalls. When I first read about the
guillotine, I could not help but think of these saws.

The church was naturally the most magnificent building
in town. At the end of the last century when a fire broke
out on Christmas Eve through the carelessness of a servant
girl and burned much of the town, the old church burned
too. As might have been expected, the girl was executed.
But the town, rebuilt with broad and straight streets running up and down its hills and through its valleys, gained
a new church, of which the townspeople boasted with a
certain pride that it was built with yellow Dutch bricks,
designed by an architect from Copenhagen, and was, furthermore, almost exactly like the church at Kongsberg. At
that time I was not able to appreciate these fine features.
What impressed me most deeply was a white, stout, thick-
limbed angel, which on weekdays hung high up under the
vaulted roof, holding a bowl in its hands, but which on
Sundays, when a child was to be baptized, was lowered
gently into our midst.

But even more fascinating to my mind than the white
angel was the black poodle that lived at the top of the
tower, where the watchman called out the hours of the
night. It had glowing red eyes, but scarcely anyone ever
saw it. As a matter of fact, as far as I know, it was seen
just once. That was on a New Year's night, and the watchman had just called "one o'clock" from the window in the
front of the tower. Suddenly the black poodle came up the
tower steps behind him, stood there, and stared at him
with those glowing red eyes. That was all. The watchman
fell head first out the window and landed in the city
square, where his corpse was seen in the morning by all
those pious folk on their way to the early morning service.
After that no watchman ever called "one o'clock" from
that window of the Skien church tower.

Of course this incident occurred long before my time,
and I have since heard of similar happenings in various
other Norwegian churches in the olden days. But this par-

ticular tower window has always meant something special to me, for it was from it that I received the first impression that has remained in my memory. One day my nurse carried me up into the tower and let me look out through the open window, holding me from behind with her strong and reliable arms. I remember vividly how strange it seemed to be looking at the tops of hats. I looked down into our own house, saw the window frames and curtains, saw my mother standing in one of the windows. I could even see over the roof of the house into the yard at the back where our brown horse stood tied at the stable, whisking its tail. I remember that on the wall of the stable there hung a bright tin pail. Then suddenly there was a commotion and a crowd began to gather and an arm waved from the street door of our house; and the nurse hastily pulled me in and hurried down the stairs with me. I do not remember the rest of it. But I was often told afterward how my mother had caught sight of me up in the tower, how she had screamed and fainted—as was customary in those days—and, when I was once again in her arms, how she had cried and kissed and hugged me. While I was growing up, I never crossed the square without looking up at that tower window. I felt somehow that it belonged to me and the church poodle.

I can recall only one other memory from those first years of my life. Among my christening gifts I had received a big silver coin with a man's head stamped on it. The man had a high forehead, a big hooked nose, and a protruding lower lip; and his throat and neck were bare, which I thought very strange. The nursemaid informed me that the man on the coin was "King Frederick Rex." One day I decided to roll the coin on the floor, with the unhappy result that the coin fell down through a crack. I believe my parents interpreted this as an evil omen, since the coin was a christening gift. The floor was torn up and the coin was thoroughly searched for and dug for, but King Frederick Rex never again saw the light of day. I do not deny that I felt like the worst sort of criminal for a long time after. And whenever Peter the Dutchman, the town policeman, came out of the town hall and headed for our door, I ran as fast as I could into the nursery and hid myself under the bed.

We did not live for very long in the house by the city

square. My father bought a larger house, which we moved into when I must have been about four. This new home of mine was on a corner, a little farther uptown, just at the bottom of Hundevad Hill. It was named after an old German-speaking doctor, whose imposing wife rode in what was virtually a glass coach and which was transformed into a sleigh in the wintertime. There were many big rooms both upstairs and down in this new house, and we lived a very sociable life there. But we boys did not stay indoors very much. The square where the two biggest schools were located was the meeting place and the battleground for all the boys in town. The Latin school was presided over by Rector Ørn, an old, distinguished, and lovable man. The principal of the common school was Iver Flasrud, another imposing gentleman, who held the post of village barber as well. The boys from these two schools fought many a hot battle in the area around the church; but since I did not go to either of these schools, I was usually a mere spectator. Moreover, as a child I was not at all given to fighting. There lay a much greater attraction for me in the pillory I have mentioned and in the town hall with all the dark mysteries I assumed it concealed. The pillory was a reddish-brown post about the height of a man. On the top was a big round knob that had originally been painted black. It now resembled a kind and friendly human face, tilted at a slight angle. From the front of the post hung an iron chain, and from this an open shackle, which looked to me like two small arms, ready and eager to reach out and grab me by the neck. The pillory had not been used for many years, but all the same I remember very well that it stood there all the time I lived in Skien. It may stand there still for all I know.

Then there was the town hall. It had high steps like the church. Underneath were dungeons with barred windows looking out on the market place. Through those bars I have seen many bleak and gloomy faces. The room farthest down in the cellar was called "the madhouse" and was said to have been used at one time—although it seems almost unbelievable to me now—for confining the insane. This room had a barred window like the others, but inside the grating the whole of the little window opening was filled by a heavy iron plate, perforated with small round holes, so that it looked like a colander. It was also said that this cell once held a notorious criminal named Brendeis who had been branded for life. And I believe it had also held a convict serving a life sentence, who escaped and was captured again and thoroughly flogged up in the Li market place. Eyewitnesses said that the prisoner danced when he was led to the square to be whipped, but that he had to be dragged in a cart back to his cell.

In my boyhood, Skien was an exceptionally lively and sociable town, quite different from what it was to become. Many highly cultured, prominent, and respected families lived in the town and on the great farms nearby. These families were all interrelated to one degree or another, and there was a steady succession of balls, parties, and musicales throughout the winter and summer. There were also many travelers who stayed with friends and relatives since there were no hotels to speak of. We almost always had strangers staying in our roomy house. Especially at Christmastime and during the fairs the house was filled with people, and open house was the rule from morning till evening. The Skien fair which took place in February was an especially happy time for us boys. Half a year before it opened we began to save our pennies so that we might see the jugglers, the tightrope walkers, the horse riders, and buy honey cakes in the fair booths. I do not know how much the fair helped business; I remember it as a great festival that lasted for a whole week.

Norwegian Independence Day, the seventeenth of May, was not made much of in those days in Skien. A few young men might shoot off some blanks up on Blege Hill or set off some fireworks, but that was it. I suspect that this reserve in our usually demonstrative and festive people was due to consideration for a certain highly esteemed gentleman who had a country seat in that area and whom, for various reasons, the townspeople did not want to offend or upset in any way.

But that only made things all the merrier on Midsummer Eve. This was not celebrated by the whole town together. The boys and the grownups divided into five, six, or more parties, each of which went to work to gather material for its own bonfire. Beginning as early as Whitsuntide we would get together and go around to the docks and the shops to beg for old tar barrels. Out of this there had arisen in the distant past a very peculiar custom. Whatever was not freely given to us was stolen by us, but the owner or the police would never think of complaining of this sort of lawlessness. In that way a group could gradually collect a whole pile of barrels. We had the same time-honored right to old barges. If we found one pulled up on the shore and if we could succeed in dragging it away and keeping it concealed, it became ours by right of possession, or at least our claims were not contested. On the day before Midsummer Eve the barge was carried in triumph through the streets to the place of the bonfire. And on top of the barge a fiddler played away. I often watched those processions and I even took part in one.

To Poul Lieungh

Grimstad, May 20, 1844

In 1844 the fifteen-year-old Ibsen left his home in Skien to begin his apprenticeship in Reimann's apothecary in the small town of Grimstad, about sixty miles southwest along the coast from Skien. The following letter is the earliest extant letter from Ibsen and is addressed to a childhood friend.

Dear Poul, You really must forgive me for not answering your letter sooner, but I have been kept so busy I have not had a chance to write before now, and because of lack of time I cannot write a long letter. Hedevall has probably already left by this time, and he will certainly be pleased to hear that at least I am quite contented and have never regretted that I came here, as Reimann is very good to me and does everything possible to get me interested in pharmaceutics, since I had no especially strong desire at first. His wife, on the other hand, I don't think so much of, and we are often mad at each other, because it's impossible to please her. Reimann is also postmaster, so you can have my brother Johan put your letters in with the ones he writes, since in that way you won't have to pay the postage on them. Grimstad and especially the surrounding country is really quite beautiful; and the ladies, although not as flirtatious as in Skien, are quite acceptable; and you can be sure I do everything possible to win their favor, which isn't too difficult. Since the steamship docks at Grimstad twice a week, I hope to take a trip to Skien, provided nothing unforeseen arises to prevent it. I have several questions to ask you which you can answer in the next mail. First and most important, you must tell me how J. J. took the news of the death of her loved one; and let me also know who the lucky fellow is who has taken his place—because I know her too well to believe that she is still mourning him. Then you must tell me if Carl Aamodt is still trying his hand at poetry, and if he is, you must, finally, tell him not to forget to send me a poem so I may see whether he has made any progress. Although I have more to say, I have to stop now because of time, but rest assured I shall write a longer letter next time. Please send the book *William Tell* that Hedevall borrowed back up here, because it does not belong to me. Best wishes, and say hello to all our good friends from your friend,

Henrik J. Ibsen

Please don't let anyone see this, as it is written in the greatest haste.

To Hanna Stenersen

Grimstad, October 6, 1845

Hanna Stenersen was Ibsen's cousin.

Dear Hanna! Forgive me for not answering your letter but it has been absolutely impossible. All summer long I have been made happy by the prospect of coming home for your confirmation. But that cannot be, since there is too much to do right now, and Reimann is not especially eager to do things himself. Therefore, I cannot offer you in person my best wishes and congratulations on this day, which you, like most other young girls, must look forward to so eagerly, since it is so delightful to be grown up—at least so it seems here.

The day before yesterday an important event broke the usual monotony of life here—one of the respectable trades-men of the town got married. It was a gala occasion for Mme. Reimann, although she wasn't exactly a participant —you know how interested women always are in wed-dings—and so of course is Mme. R. She described at great length everything that had been said, done, and eaten;

and it's a genuine delight to hear her relate something because one gets to know a lot more than if one had been there to see it for oneself. Besides that, I don't know what to tell you, except for the extremely sad news that on the fifth day of this month there occurred the death of—Reimann's favorite cat, after having given birth a few hours previously to two thriving kittens, who, though still too young to appreciate their loss fully, join with Reimann in mourning the loss of a loving mother and a dear friend. The dear departed one, whose good mind as well as several fine physical features set her apart from most of her species, was also a good mouser, who caught rats and mice as easily as Mme. Reimann gives a box on the ear.

This will have to do for this time, since you know I simply cannot write long letters, and besides I still have to write home tonight.

Write me as soon as you have time.

Affectionately,
H. J. Ibsen

Preface to the Second Edition [1875] of *Catiline*

Grimstad, 1848–50

Grimstad was not a very happy place for Ibsen. While serving as an apprentice in the apothecary's shop, he wrote his first poems—the earliest extant, "Resignation," dates from about 1847; got involved with an older woman who bore him an illegitimate child, to whose support Ibsen had to contribute a total of 105 specie-dollars (about 105 U.S. dollars) during the next fifteen years; studied Latin to prepare for the University of Christiania entrance examinations; and wrote his first play.

Catiline, the play with which I began my career as an author, was written in the winter of 1848–49, that is, when I was in my twenty-first year.

I found myself at that time in Grimstad, forced to earn my own living and to earn money to pay for lessons that would enable me to pass the university entrance examinations. Those were exciting and stormy times. The February Revolution of 1848, the revolutions in Hungary and else-

where, the Prussian-Danish war over Schleswig and Holstein—all this had a powerful and formative effect on my
development, however incomplete it remained for a long
time thereafter. I wrote resounding poems of encouragement to the Magyars, urging them for the sake of humanity and freedom to fight on in their rightful war against
the "tyrants." I wrote a long series of sonnets to King
Oscar [of Sweden and Norway] containing, as far as I
remember, a plea that he set aside all petty considerations
and without delay, at the head of his army, go to help
his brothers on the frontiers of Schleswig. Since I now
doubt that my winged words could have helped the cause
of either the Magyars or the Scandinavians to any notice-
able degree, I consider it fortunate that they were confined
to the semiprivacy of circulating in manuscript only. However, on certain inspiring or intemperate occasions I was
unable to prevent myself from giving utterance to heated
and impassioned words in the spirit of the poems, with
dubious effect on both those who were my friends and
those who were not—the former, thinking I had real talent
for being unintentionally funny, greeted them with laugh-
ter, while the latter found it altogether remarkable that a
young person in my inferior position could have the nerve
to discuss matters on which they themselves did not dare
to entertain any opinions. Truth compels me to add that
my behavior on many occasions did not do very much to
justify any possible hope on the part of the community
that the bourgeois virtues might grow and flourish in me,
especially since my epigrams and caricatures had gotten
me into trouble with many people who deserved better
treatment from me and whose friendship I really valued.
The upshot of all this was that while the big outside world
was caught in the storm of great events, I found myself on
a war footing with the little community where I felt I was
being suppressed by my situation and by circumstances
in general.

That was the situation when, in preparation for the
university examinations, I read Sallust's *Catiline* and
Cicero's speeches against Catiline. I gobbled up these
writings, and within a few months my play was finished.
As you will see when you read it, I did not at that time
share the view of the two Roman authors in regard to
Catiline's character and conduct, and I am still inclined to

believe that there must have been something distinctly great and significant about a man whom Cicero, that indefatigable spokesman of the majority, was careful not to tackle until circumstances had so changed that there was no longer any danger in attacking him. It should also be borne in mind that there are few personages in history whose posthumous reputation has been so completely in the hands of their enemies as Catiline's has been.

My play was written at night. My hours for study I virtually had to steal from my master, a kind and good-natured man but completely engrossed in his business, and from those stolen hours I had to steal again a few moments for my writing. There was not much else I could do but take advantage of the night. I think this is the unconscious reason why nearly all of the action in the play occurs at night.

Naturally, the fact that I occupied myself with something so incomprehensible as writing plays had to be kept a secret from the community; but since it is impossible for a twenty-year-old poet not to share his secrets with someone, I confided in two friends of my own age.

We three placed great hopes in *Catiline* when it was finished. First of all, it was to be fair-copied in order to be submitted under a pseudonymn to the theater in Christiania,* and after that it was to be printed. One of the two loyal and faithful friends took upon himself the task of furnishing a beautiful, clear copy of my rough, uncorrected draft, a task which he carried out so conscientiously that he did not omit a single one of the innumerable dashes I had jotted down whenever in the heat of writing I could not immediately think of the right word. The other of my friends, whom I shall mention here by name since he is no longer among the living, Ole C. Schulerud, at that time a student and later a lawyer, took the copy with him to Christiania. I can still recall one of his letters in which he informs me that *Catiline* had been submitted to the theater, and that there could be no doubt that it would soon be produced, seeing that the directors of the theater were men of discrimination and taste; just as there could be no doubt, of course, that all of ·the bookshops in the city would gladly pay a handsome royalty for the privilege

* Now called Oslo.

of selling the first edition. It was only a question of finding the bookshop that would make the highest offer.

After a long and tense period of waiting, however, a few difficulties began to manifest themselves. My friend received the script back from the theater with a rejection as polite as it was firm. He then peddled the manuscript from bookshop to bookshop, but they all responded in the same fashion as the theater. The highest bidder turned out to want a certain amount to print the play—and there was no question of royalties.

But none of this defeated my friend's hopes of ultimate victory. On the contrary, he wrote to me that it was best this way. I would be my own publisher; he would advance me the necessary money; and we would split the profits, in as much as he would take care of all the business details—except for the proofreading, which he thought would be superfluous in view of the beautiful and clear copy we had for the compositor. In a subsequent letter he said that in view of these great prospects for the future he was thinking of giving up his studies in order to devote himself completely to the publication of my works. I could easily turn out two or three plays a year, it seemed to him, and, according to his calculations, the profits within a short time would enable us to take that trip through Europe and the Orient we had so often planned or talked about.

For the time being, my travels took me no farther than Christiania. I arrived there early in the spring of 1850, and shortly before that *Catiline* had made its appearance in the bookshops. The play created a stir among the university students, but critics dwelt on the faulty verse and also found that it was an immature work. A more appreciative opinion came from only one quarter, and this came from a man whose appreciation I have always held dear and to whom I now express my renewed gratitude. Not very many copies of the small edition were sold. My friend had a considerable number in his care, and I remember one evening, when the expenses of our joint housekeeping seemed insurmountable, that these bundles of printed matter were converted to waste paper and luckily sold to a junk dealer. During the next few days we lacked none of the necessities of life.

While I was in my homeland last summer, and especially after my return here, shifting scenes from my career
as an author emerged before my eyes more clearly and
sharply than ever before. Among other things, I took another look at *Catiline*. I had forgotten most of the details
of the work, but as I read through it again, I found that
it contained a great deal that I would acknowledge as
mine, especially if it is regarded as my first work. Much
that my later work concerns itself with—the conflict between one's aims and one's abilities, between what man
proposes and what is actually possible, constituting at
once both the tragedy and comedy of mankind and of the
individual—is already vaguely intimated in this work. I
therefore thought it might be a good idea to prepare a new
edition by way of a jubilee publication, and my publisher
quickly approved the idea with his usual readiness and
willingness.

But it clearly would not do to print the original edition
without changes, because that old edition is, as I pointed
out, no more than a copy of my unfinished and uncorrected manuscript or of my very first rough draft. Reading
it through, I could see quite clearly what had originally
been vaguely present in my mind, and I also saw that
practically nowhere did the work express satisfactorily
what I had wanted to say.

I therefore decided to rework this poem of my youth as
I would have then had I had the time and had circumstances been more propitious. But as far as the thoughts
and ideas and the development of the whole work is concerned, I have done nothing to change them. The work
remains as it was originally, except that now it appears in
its finished and complete form.

Having said all this, I hope *Catiline* will be welcomed
by my friends in Scandinavia and elsewhere. I hope that
they will accept it as a greeting from me at the completion
of an era that has been full of changes and contrasts.
Much that I dreamed of twenty-five years ago has come
true, even if not always in the way I had hoped or as soon
as I had hoped. However, I now believe that it was all
for the best. I do not wish that anything from that period
should have gone untested and unexperienced, and when
I look back upon my experiences as a whole, I do so with

a sense of gratitude for all that happened and to all who
were involved.

Henrik Ibsen

Dresden, February 1, 1875

To Ole Schulerud

Grimstad, October 15, 1849

In September, 1849, Schulerud, the good and loyal friend
who had faith in Ibsen's literary abilities, tried to place
Ibsen's first play *Catiline* with the theater and the publishing
houses in Christiania. Disappointed in not hearing from him,
Ibsen dispatched an angry letter, now lost. Schulerud's reply must
have been the letter alluded to in the preface to
Catiline.

My dear Friend, Your last letter has given me pleasure
in more ways than one. In the first place, it leads me to
expect a speedy accomplishment of our undertaking; in
the second, it proves, by your description of my letter to
you as the result of a hasty impulse, that you are my true
friend. Your lenient judgment makes me hope that you
have put yourself in my place and seen the whole affair
from my point of view. I hope you have realized the disappointment I felt every mail day and have understood
that it put me into an exceedingly unpleasant humor. I
could not guess the reason for your silence, and the uncertainty only gave rise to a thousand doubts, all the more
painful because I could not in my heart acknowledge that
any one of them had any basis in fact.

Your letter has explained everything that seemed doubtful in your conduct, and I should ill deserve your friendship if I did not, with the utmost readiness, retract everything in my letter that could be construed as a reflection
on your honesty. I therefore beg you again to ignore the
whole matter as something that can have no effect on our
future friendly relations, and I hope to receive in your next
letter an assurance that you do ignore it. . . .

Schulerud eventually paid for the cost of printing *Catiline*
out of his own pocket, and it became the first play to be pub-

lished in Norway since Wergeland's *The Venetians* in 1843. Only forty-five copies were sold in the bookshops; the rest of the 250 copies were apparently sold as waste paper, as Ibsen states in the preface to the second edition of the play.

To Jens Braage Halvorsen

1840's–1850's

Halvorsen was the editor of a Norwegian biographical dictionary. This letter was written on June 18, 1889.

. . . 1. As a boy I attended drawing school at Skien for a year and learned a little pencil drawing. At the same time, or a little later, I had some instruction in oil painting from a young landscape painter, Mandt, from Telemark, who sometimes stayed at Skien. At Bergen I did some water-color painting under the direction of Magnus Bagge. But in 1860 I began to be much occupied with preparations for writing *Love's Comedy* and *The Pretenders*. After that I shelved forever all my aspirations as a painter.

2. As for the Workingmen's Movement, strictly speaking, I had nothing to do with it. I was a friend of Abildgaard's, and through him became acquainted with Marcus Thrane. I knew a good deal about their plans, and when they were arrested I feared that I might be called as a witness. But, fortunately, my letters to Abildgaard, and possibly also some manuscripts, were among the papers burned. . . .

Abildgaard was arrested on July 7, 1851, as one of the leaders of the workers' union, kept in prison for a few years, and finally sentenced in 1855 to four years of hard labor. Thanks to the quick-thinking manager of the workers' newspaper, Ibsen escaped possible implication in the affair. When the police arrived at the newspaper office, the manager threw most of the incriminating papers on the floor. The police raided the files and ignored the scrap on the floor. Almost certainly some of Ibsen's articles and letters to Abildgaard were trampled on by the officers of the law.

Preface to the Second Edition [1883]
of *The Feast at Solhaug*

Bergen, 1854–55

Ibsen's first success in the theater came with the production of *The Feast at Solhaug* on January 2, 1856. The play was performed six times in Bergen—an unusual number of performances in a town of that size. On March 13 it was performed in Christiania and on November 4, 1857, in Stockholm. It was published March 19, 1856. The public appreciated it more than the critics, who charged that it was a thoroughly unoriginal work, an imitation of Henrik Hertz's *Svend Dyring's House*. In 1883, in the preface to a new edition of the play, Ibsen sought to refute these charges.

I wrote *The Feast at Solhaug* in Bergen in the summer of 1855. . . .

The play was acted for the first time on January 2, 1856, at a gala performance on the anniversary of the establishment of the Norwegian National Theater.

As I was stage manager of the Bergen theater at that time, it was I myself who conducted the rehearsals of my play. It was acted with enthusiasm and in a dedicated spirit, and received by the audience in the same way. The "Bergen emotionalism," which is said to have decided the latest elections in those parts, ran high that evening in the crowded theater. The performance ended with repeated calls for the author and the actors. Later in the evening I was serenaded by the orchestra, accompanied by a large part of the audience. I almost think I was carried away to the extent of making some kind of a speech from my window; at any rate, I know that I was very happy.

A couple of months later *The Feast at Solhaug* was played in Christiania. There, too, it was warmly received, and the day after the first performance [Bjørnstjerne] Bjørnson wrote a friendly, youthfully ardent article on it in *Morgenbladet*. It was not a notice or criticism proper, but rather a free, fanciful improvisation on the play and the performance.

Then came the real criticism, written by the real critics. How did a man in the Christiania of those days—by which I mean the years from 1850 to about 1860—become a real literary critic and, in particular, a real drama critic?

As a rule the process was as follows. After some preparatory exercises in the columns of the *Samfundsblad,* and after having frequently listened in on the discussions that went on in Treschow's café or at "Ingebret's" after the play, the future critic betook himself to Johan Dahl's bookshop and ordered from Copenhagen a copy of J. L. Heiberg's *Prose Works,* among which was to be found—so he had heard it said—an essay entitled "On the Vaudeville." * This essay was in due course read, ruminated on, and possibly to a certain extent understood. From Heiberg's writings the young man learned, moreover, of a controversy which that author had carried on in his day with Professor Oehlenschläger and with the Sorø poet Hauch. And he was simultaneously made aware that J. I. Baggesen (the author of *Letters from the Dead*) had at a still earlier period made a similar attack on the great author [Oehlenschläger] who wrote both *Axel and Valborg* and *Hakon Jarl.*

A quantity of other information useful to a critic was to be extracted from these writings. One learned, for instance, that taste obliged a good critic to be scandalized by a hiatus. If the young critical Jeronimuses of Christiania encountered such a monstrosity in any poem, they were as certain as their prototype in Holberg to shout, "Good gracious! The world will not last till Easter!"

The origin of another idiosyncrasy of the criticism then prevalent in the Norwegian capital was long a puzzle to me. Every time a new author published a book or had a little play acted, our critics were in the habit of flying into an ungovernable passion and behaving as if the publication of the book or the performance of the play were a mortal insult to themselves and the newspapers for which they wrote. As I said, I puzzled for a long time over this peculiarity. At last I got to the bottom of the matter. While reading the Danish *Maanedskrift for Literatur* [*Monthly Journal of Literature*], I was struck by the fact that old Councilor of State [Christian] Molbech was also invariably seized with a fit of rage when a young

* Johan Ludvig Heiberg's "On the Vaudeville as a Dramatic Form and on Its Significance to the Danish Stage, A Dramaturgical Investigation." This long essay first appeared in December, 1826.

author published a book or had a play acted in Copenhagen.

In this way, or in a way closely resembling it, had that tribunal qualified itself which now in the daily press summoned *The Feast at Solhaug* to the bar of criticism in Christiania. It was principally composed of young men who, as regards criticism, lived on loans. Their critical thoughts had long ago been thought and expressed by others; their opinions had long before been formulated elsewhere. Their aesthetic principles were borrowed; their critical method was borrowed; the polemical tactics they employed were borrowed from beginning to end. Even their very frame of mind was borrowed. Everything was borrowed, everything! The one original thing about them was that they invariably made a wrong and unseasonable application of their borrowings.

It can surprise no one, then, that this body of critics who supported themselves by borrowing should have presupposed a similar action on my part as an author. Two, possibly more than two, of the newspapers promptly discovered that I had borrowed this, that, and the other thing from Henrik Hertz's play *Svend Dyring's House*.

This is a baseless and indefensible assertion, evidently to be ascribed to the fact that the meter of the ancient ballads is employed in both plays. But my tone is quite different from Hertz's; the language of my play has a different ring. A light summer breeze plays over the rhythm of my verse; over that of Hertz's brood the storms of autumn.

Nor, as regards the characters, the action, and the contents, is there any other or any greater resemblance between them than that which is a natural consequence of the derivation of the subject matter of both plays from the narrow circle of ideas in which the ancient ballads move.

It might be maintained with quite as much reason, or even more, that Hertz in his *Svend Dyring's House* had borrowed, and to a not inconsiderable extent, from Heinrich von Kleist's *Käthchen von Heilbronn*, a play written at the beginning of this century. Käthchen's relation to Count Wetter von Strahl is in all essentials the same as Ragnhild's to the knight Stig Hvide. Like Ragnhild, Käthchen is compelled by a mysterious, inexplicable power to follow the man she loves wherever he goes, to steal

secretly after him, to lay herself down to sleep near him, to
come back to him as by some innate compulsion, however
often she may be driven away. And other instances of
supernatural interference are to be met with both in
Kleist's play and in Hertz's.

But does anyone doubt that it would be possible with
a little good, or a little ill, will to discover among still older
dramatic literature a play from which it could be maintained that Kleist had borrowed here and there in his
Käthchen von Heilbronn? I, for my part, do not doubt it.
But such suggestions of indebtedness are futile. What
makes a work of art the spiritual property of its creator
is the fact that he has imprinted on it the stamp of his
own personality. Therefore I hold that, in spite of the
above-mentioned points of resemblance, *Svend Dyring's
House* is as incontestably and entirely an original work
by Henrik Hertz as *Käthchen von Heilbronn* is an original
work by Heinrich von Kleist.

I advance the same claim on my own behalf as regards
The Feast at Solhaug, and I trust that for the future each
of the three Henriks will be able to keep in its entirety
what rightfully belongs to him.

Writing of *The Feast at Solhaug* in connection with
Svend Dyring's House, Georg Brandes expresses the opinion not that the former play is founded upon an idea
borrowed from the latter but that it has been written under
the influence exercised by the older author upon the
younger. Brandes invariably criticizes my work in such a
friendly spirit that I have every reason to be obliged to
him for this suggestion as I am for so much else.

Nevertheless I must maintain that in this instance he
too is mistaken. I have never specially admired Henrik
Hertz as a dramatist. Hence it is impossible for me to
believe that he should, unknown to myself, have been able
to exercise any influence on my dramatic production.

As regards this point and the matter in general, I might
confine myself to referring those interested to the writings
of Dr. Valfrid Vasenius, lecturer on aesthetics at the University of Helsinki. In his doctoral dissertation *Henrik
Ibsens dramatiska diktning i dess första skede* (1879), as
well as in his *Henrik Ibsen, ett skaldeporträtt* (343 pages,
Joseph Seligmann & Co., Stockholm, 1882), Vasenius states
and supports his views on the subject of the play in ques-

tion, supplementing them in the latter work by what I told him, very briefly, when we met in Munich three years ago.

But to prevent any misconception, I myself will now give a short account of the origin of *The Feast at Solhaug*.

I began this preface with the statement that *The Feast at Solhaug* was written in the summer of 1855.

In 1854 I had written *Lady Inger of Østraat*. This task had obliged me to devote much attention to the literature and history of Norway during the Middle Ages, especially the latter part of that period. I did my utmost to familiarize myself with the manners and customs, with the emotions, thoughts, and language of the men of those days.

The period, however, is not one which the student is tempted to linger over, nor does it present much material suitable for dramatic treatment.

Consequently I soon deserted it for the saga period. But the sagas of the kings, and in general the more strictly historical traditions of that far-off age, did not attract me greatly; at that time I was unable to put the quarrels between kings and chieftains, parties and clans, to any dramatic purpose. This was to happen later.

In the Icelandic "family" sagas, on the other hand, I found in abundance what I required in the shape of human garb for the moods, conceptions, and thoughts which at that time occupied me, or were, at least, more or less distinctly present in my mind. With these Old Norse contributions to the personal history of our saga period I had had no previous acquaintance; I had hardly so much as heard them named. But now N. M. Petersen's excellent translation—excellent, at least, as far as the style is concerned—fell into my hands. In the pages of these family chronicles, with their variety of scenes and of relations between man and man, between woman and woman, in short, between human being and human being, I encountered a personal, eventful, truly vital life; and as the result of my intercourse with all these distinctly individual men and women, there presented themselves to my mind's eye the first rough, indistinct outlines of *The Vikings at Helgeland*.

How far the details of that drama then took shape, I am no longer able to say. But I remember perfectly that the two figures of which I first caught sight were the two

women who in course of time became Hjørdis and Dagny.
There was to be a great banquet in the play, with passion-
rousing, fateful quarrels during its course. Of other characters and passions, and situations produced by these, I
meant to include whatever seemed to me most typical of
the life which the sagas reveal. In short, it was my intention to reproduce dramatically exactly what the saga of the
Volsungs gives in epic form.

I made no complete, connected plan at that time; but it
was evident to me that such a drama was to be my first
undertaking.

Various obstacles intervened. Most of them were of a
personal nature, and these were probably the most decisive; but it undoubtedly had its significance that I happened just at this time to make a careful study of Land-
stad's collection of Norwegian ballads, published two years
previously. My mood of the moment was more in harmony
with the literary romanticism of the Middle Ages than
with the deeds of the sagas, with poetical than with prose
composition, with the word melody of the ballad than with
the characterization of the saga.

Thus it happened that the fermenting, formless design
for the tragedy *The Vikings at Helgeland* transformed itself temporarily into the lyric drama *The Feast at Solhaug*.

The two female characters, the foster sisters Hjørdis and
Dagny of the projected tragedy, became the sisters Margit
and Signe of the completed lyric drama. The derivation
of the latter pair from the two women of the saga at once
becomes apparent when attention is drawn to it. The
relationship is unmistakable. The tragic hero—so far
only vaguely outlined—Sigurd, the far-traveled Viking,
the welcome guest at the courts of kings, became the
knight and minstrel Gudmund Alfson, who has likewise
been long absent in foreign lands and has lived in the
King's household. His attitude toward the two sisters was
changed to bring it into accordance with the change in
time and circumstances; but the position of both sisters to
him remained practically the same as that in the projected and afterward completed tragedy. The fateful
banquet, the presentation of which had seemed to me of
the first importance in my original plan, became in the
drama the scene upon which its personages made their
appearance; it became the background against which the

action stood out, and communicated to the picture as a whole the general tone at which I aimed. The ending of the play was undoubtedly softened and subdued into harmony with its character as drama, not tragedy; but orthodox aestheticians may still perhaps find it disputable whether, in this ending, a touch of pure tragedy has not been left behind to testify to the origin of the drama.

Upon this subject, however, I shall not enter further at present. My object has simply been to maintain and prove that the play under consideration, like all my other dramatic works, is an inevitable outcome of the tenor of my life at a certain period. It had its origin within, and was not the result of any outward impression or influence.

This, and no other, is the true account of the genesis of *The Feast at Solhaug*.

Henrik Ibsen

Rome, April, 1883

To Suzannah Thoresen

Bergen, January, 1856

On January 7, a few days after the successful première of *The Feast at Solhaug*, Ibsen was invited to the house of Magdalene Thoresen, who had written three plays that had been performed at the Bergen theater; and here for the first time Ibsen met Suzannah Thoresen, Magdalene's nineteen-year-old stepdaughter, whom he saw frequently during the following months. He married her June 18, 1858.

To My Only One:

The ballroom glitters resplendent,
    Already the dance moves fast;
Ladies in rainbow clusters,
    Airily decked, go past.
High overhead the music
    Scatters its witchcraft fine;
Each dancer's in festal humor,
    Each lamp hath a festal shine.

Hark to the ballroom courtships,
    Whisperings soft and low—

All that the moment prompts of all
　　Dreamt or heard long ago.
And the ladies smile demurely
　　As memory's album receives
Speeches, fiery and tender,
　　Nor speaker nor hearer believes.

Throughout the crowded ballroom
　　There's naught but gladness and mirth;
Not one of them all that hath felt it—
　　The weary burden of the earth;
Not one of them all that hath felt it—
　　Not one that could ever guess
How, under the veil of rejoicing,
　　Lurks the horror of emptiness.

Ah yes! there is one, one only,
　　Among so many but one.
Her eyes have a secret sadness;
　　I read in them sorrow begun—
I read in them dreaming fancies
　　That rise and sink without cease—
A heart that longs and throbs upward,
　　And finds in this world no peace.

Dared I but rede thee, thou riddle
　　Of youth and deep dreamings wrought;
Dared I but choose thee boldly
　　To be the bridge of my thought;
Dared I but plunge my spirit
　　Deep in thy spirit's tide,
Dared I but gaze on the visions
　　In thy innocent soul that hide;

Ah, then what fair songs upspringing
　　Should soar from my breast on high;
Ah, then how free I'd go sailing
　　Like a bird toward the coasts of the sky!
Ah, then should my scattered visions
　　To one single harmony throng;
For all of life's fairest visions
　　Would mirror themselves in my song.

> Dared I but rede thee, thou riddle
>   Of youth and deep dreamings wrought;
> Dared I but choose thee boldly
>   To be the bridge of my thought.

Henrik Ibsen

To Paul Botten-Hansen

Bergen, April 17, 1857

Botten-Hansen met Ibsen when they were both students in Christiania. He was one of the first to offer encouragement to the aspiring playwright. At the time of this letter he was editor of *Illustreret Nyhedsblad*.

. . . I have often thought of writing to you, but have always put it off. And I once thought of sending you some of my travel sketches, but nothing came of that either. But this summer, however, I am planning some long trips, and I may be able to send you something you can use. I know of nothing interesting in my own affairs to tell you, except that last year I became engaged to a daughter of Mr. Thoresen, a pastor in this town. Her stepmother is the author of *A Witness* and several other plays which you reviewed in *Illustreret Nyhedsblad* at the time of their publication.

My sincere thanks for your review of *The Feast at Solhaug*. I sent my new play, *Olaf Liljekrans*, to the Christiania Theater several months ago, but Borgaard [the director] is not one to hurt himself by hurrying. He has refused to add my best play, *Lady Inger of Østraat*, to the repertory until I have made several changes, which I won't consent to make. I sent it to the publisher Christian Tønsberg about the beginning of January, but he does not see how he can publish it at present. Since it is highly important for me that this, my best work, be brought out, I put the matter in your hands and beg of you to do what you can for me. The play is at Tønsberg's. Read it through and find me a publisher! I don't care about the conditions—I'm willing to forgo royalties if only you can get it printed—if you will use your good offices for me, I'm sure you will succeed. It has occurred to me that the play might be published for the benefit of the building fund of the Students' Union. If that could be managed, I would like to introduce it with a prologue dedicated to Young Scandinavia. Dear friend, please do what you can for me! I give you full liberty to do as you please with *Lady Inger*. Keep at the publishers until they give in!! . . .

To the Director of the National Theater in Bergen

Bergen, July 23, 1857

From 1851 to 1857 Ibsen was employed at the National Theater in Bergen as playwright and stage manager. The National Theater had been organized in 1850 with the aim of providing Norway with its first truly national theater. The Christiania Theater in the capital was essentially Danish: Danish actors speaking stage Danish in plays of Danish, German, and French origin. As playwright in residence, Ibsen was to supply the Bergen theater with a new play each year. In February, 1852, the theater gave Ibsen a travel grant to study theatrical techniques. He spent most of his time at the Royal Theater in Copenhagen and at the Court Theater in Dresden. Upon his return to Bergen in September, he assumed the duties of stage manager and director. Following the German pattern, the directorial responsibilities were divided between a *Dramaturg*—who would be in charge of the readings and would instruct the actors in diction, characterization, and acquaint them with the general tone of the work—and a stage manager—who would be in charge of "blocking," gestures, movement, costumes and sets, and would have virtually nothing to say about the interpretation of the work. For most plays, Ibsen was the stage manager while Herman Laading was entrusted with the more important function of the *Dramaturg*. Ibsen probably grew increasingly dissatisfied with his position at Bergen. He seemed to be making little progress as a playwright, and as stage manager he had nothing to say about the choice of plays and could do little to improve the acting, which continued to consist of declamations in Danish.

In 1857, shortly after he had renewed his contract with the Bergen theater, Ibsen received an offer from the Norwegian Theater in Christiania. This theater had been founded in 1852 with the same purpose as the National Theater in Bergen: to create a genuinely Norwegian stage. But by 1857 the theater was in serious economic difficulties, and Ibsen was offered the position of head of the theater in charge of productions, at twice his Bergen salary, to save the theater from collapse. The offer was too good to refuse, and Ibsen asked to be released from his contract with the Bergen theater. On August 4, 1857, the board of directors officially agreed to release him.

. . . I need not call your attention to the advantages I would gain from living in the capital. They outweigh all other considerations, and however reluctant I may be to leave Bergen and the Bergen theater, I nevertheless feel that it would be inexcusable of me to reject the opportunity offered by this position that pays reasonably well. I mention the salary and the other advantages, but you must not think I am self-seeking and ungrateful. I shall never forget what I owe to the Bergen theater. But I also have a duty to myself, and the conditions at the Bergen theater have for a long time now oppressed and inhibited me. Every path in which I might have accomplished something has been closed to me. My hands have always been tied, and every day I have been weighed down by the thought that I have had to work without seeing anything result from my work. . . .

To Carl Johan Anker

Christiania, January 30, 1858

Ibsen had gone on a long hiking trip with Anker in 1856.

Dear Friend, What must you think of my having delayed so long in sending a few words in answer to your three friendly letters? For I really have received them all, and as yet have not answered one of them. What do you think of me? I am certain I am less guilty than I seem. At all events, my long silence is not the result of indifference, but rather of an egoistic feeling that one often succumbs to because one does not choose to resist it.

Dear Anker, perhaps you do not understand me. But the fact is that I have thought of you so much every day that anything more seemed superfluous.

Believe me, I often live over again the days of our

short acquaintance. The trip to Hardanger is a bright memory for me, one of those delightful episodes in a man's life from which he draws spiritual nourishment for long, long afterward.

I have often wondered what opinion you really formed of me at that time, wondered if you did not find me hedged about with a sort of repelling coldness that made me rather unapproachable. And yet it was infinitely easier for me to attach myself to you than to anyone else, because you had a youthful soul, a joy in life, and a noble and chivalrous way of looking at things, that did me good. Don't ever lose any of that! I assure you it is not pleasant to see the world as if it were always October. And yet there was, ridiculously enough, a time when I wished for nothing better. I had a burning desire for—I almost prayed for—a great sorrow that might round out my existence, give my life meaning. It was foolish of me, and I have fought my way out of that phase—and yet, the memory of it will always be with me.

A thousand thanks for all your trouble with my play. I shall soon send you a new one, *The Vikings at Helgeland,* which is to be produced here shortly, and perhaps in Copenhagen as well. . . .

Dear Anker, do not retaliate against me, but write me as soon as you can. My conscience bothers me because of my long silence; a few friendly words would ease it.

Sincerely,
Henr. Ibsen

The Vikings at Helgeland was at first accepted for production at the Christiania Theater but shelved in March, 1858, on the grounds that, for the time being, the theater could not afford to pay royalties on new plays. Ibsen immediately started a pen-and-ink war in the Christiania papers by declaring that since the directors of the theater had not even inquired if he would be willing to be paid later, their real reason for not producing the play was that they had no desire to promote and encourage native Norwegian drama. On November 24, 1858, Ibsen produced the play at the Norwegian Theater in Christiania. It was finally staged at the Christiania Theater in 1861.

To the Norwegian Government

Christiania, August 6, 1860

To the King: Henrik Johan Ibsen most humbly petitions that he be granted a sum of 400 specie-dollars [roughly equivalent to United States dollars] out of the fund voted for artists' and scientists' travel abroad, in order that he may spend six months in visiting London, Paris, the larger German cities, Copenhagen, and Stockholm, with the special purpose of studying dramatic art and literature.

During ten years of literary activity, and also while preparing for the same, I have devoted most of my time to the study of dramatic art and literature, the principles, systems, and history of which have been my chief concern. I venture to believe that the reviews of my dramatic works which have been published during this period by both Norwegian and foreign critics contain sufficient evidence that my studies have not been unfruitful; and I trust that the favor with which the public has received my plays, some of which have been produced in Sweden and Denmark as well as in Norway, may be taken as evidence of ability in my chosen calling.

Toward the end of the year 1851 I was appointed stage manager of the theater at Bergen, then newly established. In the beginning of 1852 a grant awarded me by this theater enabled me to devote five months to visiting Copenhagen, Hamburg, Berlin, and Dresden, chiefly with the object of acquainting myself with the technique of dramatic art, the principles of its practice in different places and in its various forms, together with everything pertaining to the management of the theaters.

I held my appointment at the Bergen theater until the summer of 1857, when I accepted that of artistic director of the Norwegian Theater here, a position which I still hold.

Of late years the opinion has become more and more prevalent that the development of art and poetry in their various forms cannot but concern the state, which has, therefore, with ever-increasing readiness, assisted our painters, sculptors, and musicians. Two of our poets, for example, have benefited by a not inconsiderable travel

grant. The reason for the drama having hitherto received
no state aid is not due to any repudiation on the part of
the state of the claims of this art. On the contrary, by
giving its support to poetry, sculpture, painting, and
music, the state has distinctly implied its recognition of
the drama, which is by its very nature a unification of all
these other arts. Moreover, the experience of all other
countries has sufficiently established the fact that the drama
in every age in which it has been cultivated has, more
than any other art, shown itself to be an important element in the education of the people—a fact that is obviously explained by the more intimate and direct relation
this art bears to reality; that is, it is more easily understood
by, and more widely accessible to, the people as a whole.

The reason that state aid has been withheld from the
theater in this country must, if one is to judge from the
utterances of the authorities on the subject, be due to a
disapproval of the form which applications for help have
taken—disapproval, namely, of requests for direct contributions to the working expenses of individual theaters,
to building funds, and the like. It has been felt that a
theater ought to be self-supporting, provided it does not
lack capable artistic management and a national repertory.

Endorsing this view of the matter, I, as playwright and
manager of one of the theaters of the capital, present my
petition.

Permit me to point out that, if the state has, as above
indicated, tacitly acknowledged the right of dramatic art
to existence, it ought also to be concerned to know that the
institutions of scenic art are being managed with the greatest possible ability and insight, especially at a time like
the present. The national drama is in process of development in this country, and the direction that it takes now
and in the near future must vitally influence the forms
it will assume at a more established stage.

Having ten years behind me of activity as a playwright,
and nine of practical work in theatrical management; and
having gained experience on an earlier journey taken with
the same object; and having made many acquaintances
partly on that journey and partly in the course of business;
I believe that I may be regarded as possessing the main
qualifications for undertaking another journey to good
advantage. I therefore hereby petition for a travel grant

of 400 specie-dollars to enable me to spend six months in visiting London, Paris, Copenhagen, Stockholm, and the large German cities, in order to increase my knowledge and understanding of dramatic literature and art.

Your most humble servant,

Henr. Ibsen

Bjørnstjerne Bjørnson and A. O. Vinje also petitioned the government for stipends at this time. Both their requests were granted; Ibsen's was rejected.

Preface to the Second Edition [1867]
of *Love's Comedy*

Christiania, 1862–63

Ibsen felt very despondent during 1860 and the first part of 1861. Not only had his petition for a government grant been rejected but he had been unable to complete a play since he wrote *The Vikings at Helgeland* in 1857. Furthermore, his management of the Norwegian Theater was under attack and he had to defend his policies by writing articles in the newspapers. The writing of the poem "Terje Vigen" in 1861 signals an improvement of his spiritual condition. After the Norwegian Theater finally closed its doors in the summer of 1862, Ibsen returned to a subject that had occupied him as early as 1858 and in a burst of creative energy wrote *Love's Comedy*, a play in verse.

[*Love's Comedy*] was written in the summer of 1862, and the first edition appeared in the winter of the same year.

But I made the mistake of publishing the book in Norway. Both the time and the place were unhappy choices. The play provoked a storm of resentment, more violent and more widespread than most books can claim in a country where the vast majority usually regards literary matters as being scarcely any concern of theirs.

I must say the reception did not surprise me. That "healthy realistic attitude" which we Norwegians may justifiably attribute to ourselves—at least as far as the realism is concerned, if not the healthiness—leads us naturally to see in the conditions that prevail the conditions that should rightfully prevail, and to think that in solving a problem we have understood it. This mental posture provides a feeling of inner satisfaction, though not very much clarity.

When to the best of my ability I cracked the whip over love and marriage, it was only to be expected that the majority would sound off on behalf of love and marriage. Most of our readers and critics have never acquired the intellectual discipline and training that is necessary to see through delusions. However, I have no intention of giving them a course in this. A preface is no primer. . . .

Rome, January, 1867

To the Norwegian Government

Christiania, March 10, 1863

To the King!

Henrik Ibsen most humbly petitions that a proposal with the royal signature be laid before the Storting [Parliament] now assembled, to the effect that the petitioner be granted a yearly salary of 400 specie-dollars from the treasury, to enable him to continue his literary activity.

As justifications for my humble applications, permit me to submit a short sketch of my life and literary activities. I was born at Skien on the twentieth of March, 1828, and, my parents being without means, I had to support myself from the age of fourteen. I obtained a situation first as apprentice and later as assistant in the apothecary's shop at Grimstad, where I remained until the end of 1849, employing all the time left me from my duties to prepare myself for the matriculation examination of the University of Christiania, which I passed in the summer of 1850. By that time, besides a few minor poems published in the *Christiania-Posten*, I had written and published *Catiline*, a three-act drama in verse, which was very favorably noticed by the reviewers, especially in [Christian] Lange's *Tidsskrift for Videnskab og Literatur*. My next work of any length was *The Warrior's Barrow*, a dramatic poem in one act, which was produced in the Christiania Theater in September of 1850, and which was also favorably received by the critics. Toward the close of 1851 I was engaged by the Norwegian [National] Theater, established in Bergen the year before, first as playwright and then also as manager. During the summer of 1852 I went, at the theater's expense, to Copenhagen and several of the larger German cities, to study art and literature. One product of this journey was a new three-act play entitled *Midsummer Eve,* produced later [1853] but still unpublished. In 1854 I wrote *Lady Inger of Østraat,* a historical drama in three acts, which has been played often in various theaters and has been published in Christiania. *The Feast at Solhaug,* a drama in three acts, written in 1855, has also been produced with much success in all the theaters of this country, at Copenhagen, and in the Royal Theater of Stockholm, where it was chosen as the festival play for the celebrations on the fourth of November, 1857. *The Vikings at Helgeland,* a play in four acts, appeared in 1858, and received much and remarkably favorable notice from the reviewers in Denmark and Sweden, as well as in this country; this play, too, has been acted in all our theaters. This year I have published a three-act play in rhymed verse entitled *Love's Comedy.* Moreover, I have in the course of these years of literary activity written a number of minor poems, of which a complete edition is now in preparation.

I resigned my appointment at the Bergen theater in 1857, and at once accepted that of artistic director of the Norwegian Theater here in Christiania, a post which I held until last summer, when the theater went bankrupt and was forced to close. Since the first of January of the present year, I have held a temporary appointment as literary adviser to the Christiania Theater. In 1858 I married a daughter of the late Dean Thoresen of Bergen, and I have one child by this marriage. My salary at the Bergen theater was only 300 specie-dollars [$300] per annum, and I had to leave the town in debt. My appointment at the Norwegian Theater in Christiania brought me an average of 600 specie-dollars per annum, but the failure of that theater meant a loss to me of over 150 specie-dollars, as well as the loss of steady employment. At the Christiania Theater my nominal salary is 25 specie-dollars monthly; but the payment of the full amount is contingent upon the theater's making larger profits than it has done this year. It is impossible in this country to live exclusively or even principally on one's writings. My best paid work, *The Vikings at Helgeland,* which occupied my whole time for nearly a year, brought me in all 227 specie-dollars. Because of these conditions, I have contracted debts amounting to nearly 500 specie-dollars and, being unable to see any prospect of improving my position in this country, I have been obliged to make preparations for emigrating to Denmark this spring.

To leave my native land and give up what I have hitherto regarded, and still regard, as my real lifework, is, however, an unspeakably painful step for me to take; and to avoid it, if possible, I now try the last means in my power. I humbly petition that a proposal signed by the King be laid before the Storting now in session, to the effect that a yearly allowance of 400 specie-dollars be granted me out of the treasury to enable me to continue my work in the service of literature, work which I have reason to believe the public does not wish to see interrupted.

Your humble servant,
Henrik Ibsen

On February 24, 1863, the government had proposed to award Bjørnstjerne Bjørnson an annual pension of 400 specie-dollars, but it refused to take any action on Ibsen's petition. One of the professors at the University of Christiania declared that "the person who had written *Love's Comedy* deserved a stick rather than a stipend." On May 27 Ibsen addressed another petition to the government, reminding it that of all the Norwegian writers who sought to live by their writing alone, he was the only one who had not received any government support.

To Randolph Nilsen

Christiania, June 25, 1863

While waiting for a response to this last petition, Ibsen attended a patriotic song festival in Bergen. Randolph Nilsen, a shipowner, was Ibsen's host, and during the festival Ibsen met many of the town's prominent citizens at the Nilsen home.

My dear Friend, At this very hour a week ago we were bidding each other farewell. The festive mood, thank God, remains with me, and I hope it will long continue to do so. My hearty thanks to you and your dear wife for your inexpressibly great kindness and friendliness to me. The festival itself, and the many lovable, unforgettable people I met at it, acted upon me like an inspiring church service, and I hope and believe that the feeling produced will not be merely a passing one. They were all so good to me in Bergen. It is not so here, where there are many who seek every opportunity to pain and wound me. The powerfully uplifting impression, the feeling of being ennobled in every thought, was shared, I believe, by all the guests at our festival of song; indeed only a very hard and wicked soul could resist such an influence. Herein, perhaps, lies the greatest power for good in such a meeting. . . .

Bjørnson also participated in this song festival and, like Ibsen, wrote poems for the occasion. There can be no doubt that, along with the festival mood, the meeting with the enormously successful Bjørnson inspired Ibsen to write *The Pretenders*. The play was written very quickly in the summer of 1863, while Ibsen was living on the second of two small grants awarded him by the university to collect Norwegian folk songs and folk tales. In September, about the very time the manuscript of the play was sent to the printers, Ibsen was informed that he had finally been granted a government stipend of 400 specie-dollars [$400] to study art and literature abroad. The years of his greatest hardship were over; he had passed through the first stage of his struggle for recognition.

To Clemens Petersen

Christiania, August 10, 1863

Clemens Petersen, the leading Danish literary critic, had written a lengthy review of Ibsen's works, mainly on *Love's Comedy*.

Mr. Clemens Petersen: I can never get on with letter writing, mostly because I apprehend that my authorship in this line may, with good reason, be characterized in the same fashion as you—rather harshly, it would seem to me—characterize my prose in general. Nevertheless I must write you a few lines to thank you, sincerely and cordially, for your review of my book. I thank you both for that in which I agree with you (which is not exclusively those parts of your criticism complimentary to me) and for that about which, when I am sometime fortunate enough to meet you personally, I shall at least try to argue with you. I thank you especially because I see that you do not have so much against me, after all, as I had instinctively imagined up to now. This has to me an importance it would be difficult to convince you of, who do not know to how terrible a degree I feel intellectually alone up here. My "friends'" view of me does not, by the way, do me any harm; I see myself in all respects more clearly than all my friends do—and this certainly not to my advantage. I am now working on a historical play in five acts [*The Pretenders*], but in prose; I cannot write it in verse. You do me some little injustice when you hint that I have tried to imitate Bjørnson's manner; *Lady Inger of Østraat* and *The Vikings at Helgeland* were written before Bjørnson had yet written a line. (N.B. It is possible that *Between the Battles* existed at the time when I wrote *The Vikings,* but it did not and could not have come to my attention.) As to *Love's Comedy,* I can assure you that if ever it was necessary for an author to rid himself of a sentiment and a subject it was so with me when I began that work. I shall follow your kind advice to send *Lady Inger* to the Royal Theater; I only wish that I might handle the matter in the right way and that it might succeed. I have felt a strong desire to send you these few grateful lines, for I have a deep, personal feeling that you have done me a good service by not putting my book aside in silence.

Faithfully yours,
Henrik Ibsen

✳ EXILE IN ROME
1864–1868

To Bjørnstjerne Bjørnson

Rome, September 16, 1864

From 1862 to 1865 the Christiania Theater was being reorganized. Seeing that the theater was in trouble, Bjørnson in 1864 offered his services as managing director, on condition that he be given rather sweeping powers. While he was negotiating with the board of the theater, they offered the position to Ibsen, who had served as literary adviser to the theater from January, 1863, until the spring of 1864, when he left Christiania on the travel grant the government had awarded him. This grant had had to be supplemented with private contributions, raised in part by the good and indefatigable Bjørnson.

Dear Bjørnson, Dietrichson [a Norwegian critic living in Italy] has shown me your letter. It seemed extraordinary to me that, at the time you wrote it, toward the end of August, you did not know of my reply to the offer made to me by the management of the Christiania Theater. But that you should for a single moment have wondered what answer I would give is more than extraordinary. I did indeed receive the kind of advice you inferred; and had I suspected the possibility of your being in doubt as to my position throughout the whole course of the recent transaction, I should have acquainted you at the time with the nature of my answer to the theater management. I can well imagine that such uncertainty on your part can hardly have furthered the progress of the negotiations. But, as I have said, its possibility never occurred to me.

In the middle of July (dated the sixteenth), Richard Petersen [head of the theater] wrote, informing me that negotiations with you had failed, and offering me, on behalf of the theater, the position of artistic director— or rather, to be quite correct, he represented to me that since you *would not* accept the appointment, I *must*. Some clippings from *Morgenbladet* enclosed in the letter showed me the outward aspect of the affair at the moment. As I was staying at Genzano then, the letter was long in reaching me. But the moment I received it, I replied without hesitation. I declined the offer—declined it absolutely —without reservation, and without suggesting any possibility that altered circumstances might induce me to change my mind. Never, either then or since, has it occurred to me for a moment that any answer could have been given but an absolute refusal.

So you see, dear Bjørnson, that you have done me an injustice by harboring the suspicions indicated in your letter to Dietrichson. However, I must admit that I can understand how they arose; and I do not lay the blame so much upon you as upon myself. I know it to be a defect in me that I am incapable of entering into close and intimate relations with people who demand that one should yield oneself up entirely and unreservedly. I have something of the same feeling as the Skald in *The Pretenders*: I can never bear to strip myself completely. I am conscious in personal intercourse of only being able to give incorrect expression to what lies deepest in me and constitutes my real self; therefore, I prefer to lock it up. That is why we have sometimes stood, as it were, observing one another from a distance. But you yourself must have understood this, or at least something of the kind. Otherwise, you could not have preserved in your heart such a warm feeling of friendship for me. I cannot explain your having been kept so long in ignorance of my answer; or rather, I prefer not to try to explain it to myself. No more on that subject.

Accept my thanks for all the beauty I have imbibed on my journey. It has done me good, I can assure you. My mind has been flooded with new impressions, especially here in Rome. But I have not yet come to an understanding with ancient art; I cannot make out its relation to our own times. I miss the sense of illusion, and, above all, a feeling of personal and individual expression, both in the work itself and on the part of the artist. And though I have tried not to, I still see only the conventions of the time in what others maintain are enduring laws. It seems to me that the sculptures of antiquity, like our heroic ballads, were the product of their age rather than of this or that artist. That is why I think a great many of our modern sculptors make a vital mistake in continuing to compose heroic ballads in clay and marble nowadays. I understand Michelangelo and Bernini and his school better. Those fellows had the courage to do something crazy once in a while. The architecture has impressed me more. But neither antique architecture nor its descendants appeal to me so much as the Gothic. To me the cathedral of Milan is the most overpowering creation I can imagine in the domain of architecture. The man capable of conceiving such a work might also, in his leisure hours, conceive of making a moon and throwing it out into space. I am sure you disapprove of many of the ideas that I have jotted down here. But I believe they are in harmony with my general outlook, and that my understanding of art will develop along these lines.

Here in Rome there is blessed peace for writing. I am working at a long poem [the epic *Brand*], and I have also in preparation a tragedy, *Julianus Apostata*, a work which fills me with irrepressible joy. I am sure it will be a success. I hope to have both works finished in the spring or at any rate in the course of the summer. My wife and little boy are to join me here in the autumn. I hope that you will approve of this arrangement. Leaving more directly personal motives out of the question, I shall only remark that it will be cheaper for us to live together than for me, as hitherto, to maintain a separate household in Copenhagen. Besides, Dietrichson is leaving Rome in the beginning of next year, and I am to take his appointment [as librarian of the Scandinavian Society], which will give me a free house and its appurtenances, and also a small salary. Four hundred specie-dollars [$400] will cover my expenses in Rome for a year. My brother-in-law in Christiania will provide my wife's traveling expenses out of what remains of my travel grant. We expect them to be moderate, as she is coming with a lady from Copenhagen who has been here before and is experienced in traveling economically.

By the beginning of October I shall be in need of money; I can tell by your letter that that will not surprise you. Will you kindly manage to have some sent to me by that time?

I congratulate you on the addition to your family, which was a surprise to me, and please give my kindest regards to your wife. And please remember me very kindly to Dunker [an official of the theater]. I should be glad if you would show him this letter, since most of what I have said to you I should also wish to say to him. And I suppose the same possibilities that suggested themselves to you with regard to my behavior in the theater affair also occurred to him. Every time he sends me money he writes a few friendly words. I shall always remember with gratitude his tactfulness and consideration, which has never permitted him, in spite of the fact that I owe him so much, to hint by so much as a word that he regards me as his investment while I am abroad, or to give me definite instructions of any kind. My debt to you both is a double one; your help has been great, and it has been given with delicacy and tact.

You are mistaken in inferring from my letter from Copenhagen that I do not desire to keep up a correspondence. I know I am poor at writing letters, and that is why I often am afraid of sitting down to write one. But I thirst for even the most meager note from home. . . .

The political situation at home has grieved me very much and embittered many a pleasant moment for me. So it was all nothing but lies and dreams! I know that these will have a profound influence on me, at any rate. We may now consign our ancient history to oblivion. The Norwegians of the present age have clearly no more relation to those of the past than the Greek pirates of today have to the race that sailed to Troy and were helped by the gods. I see by your letter that you do not despair. Ah, well, I hope that you are right and will not be disappointed. Farewell!

Yours,

Henrik Ibsen

The last paragraph of this letter and much of the following correspondence must be read against the background of the Prussian-Danish war of 1864 over the duchies of Schleswig and Holstein. Denmark was overwhelmed by the Prussian forces when neither Sweden nor Norway came to the aid of their sister state as they had indicated they would do.

To Bjørnstjerne Bjørnson

Rome, January 28, 1865

Dear Bjørnson, Let me tell you I am very worried and troubled. About the middle of last month I wrote acknowledging and thanking you for the check for 100 specie-dollars [$100] enclosed in your letter of the fourth of October. At the same time I took advantage of the kind suggestion you made in that letter that I should let you know when I needed more money, and informed you that I would be penniless toward the end of the month. In fact, my money gave out before that; for my monthly outlay comes to 40 scudi [$40], and I had been obliged to borrow to cover my expenses from the first of October until the arrival of the remittance on the sixteenth of October.

To this last letter of mine I have received no answer; and although I can imagine many reasons for delay on your part, such as your having been away from Christiania, or your having had difficulty in procuring the money, etc., etc., I am inclined to believe that my letter did not reach you. In spite of my being kept in such suspense, I am really glad if this is the case; I must confess (supposing that you have not read it) that the letter was written in an unamiable, bitter, and possibly too hopeless spirit, insofar as it concerned the affairs and the outlook of our country. I have regretted pouring out all that bitterness to you, instead of giving you glowing descriptions of all the splendor here. Without your help I would not be in a position now to be ennobled and uplifted by them. But I cannot keep myself from dwelling with sadness on the situation at home, nor was I able to do so during my whole journey. If I had stayed longer in Berlin, where I saw the triumphal entrance in April, with the howling rabble tumbling about among the trophies from Dybbøl, riding on the gun carriages and spitting into the mouths of the cannon—the cannon that received no help and yet went on shooting until they burst—I think I should have gone out of my mind.

When you write, be sure to tell me what you think of the condition of our affairs? What direction are they likely to take? And what do you believe our leaders can accomplish with the present generation? It would be a comfort to hear from you, for I know that you have hope and confidence. But on what do you base your confidence? The complete ruin of our nation often seems inconceivable to me, too. A political state may be annihilated, but not a nation. Poland is not really a nation; it is a state. The aristocracy have their interests, the citizens theirs, and the peasants theirs—all independent of, or even antagonistic to, each other. And Poland has no literature, art, or science with any special mission for the world's advancement. If Poland is made Russian, the Polish people will cease to exist. But we Scandinavians, even if we were deprived of our apparent independence, even if our countries were conquered and our states disintegrated, would still survive as a nation. The Jews were both a state and a nation; the Jewish state was destroyed, but the nation still lives. Thus, what is best in us will, I believe, live on —provided our national spirit is strong enough to thrive on misfortune. But that is the great and decisive question. Oh, for faith and confidence! But a truce to politics for today.

I am becoming more and more aware of classical sculpture, just as you predicted in your letter. The awareness comes in flashes, but each flash reveals whole new areas. Do you remember "The Tragic Muse" that stands in the room outside the Rotunda in the Vatican? No statue that I have yet seen in Italy has taught me so much. I would say that it has revealed the essence of Greek tragedy to me. That indescribably sublime, calm joy in the expression of the face, that laurel-crowned head with something supernaturally exuberant and bacchantic about it, those eyes that look both inward and yet through and far beyond the outward object they are fixed on—that is Greek tragedy. The statue of Demosthenes in the Lateran, the faun in the Villa Borghese, and the faun (Praxiteles')

in the Vatican (Bracchio Nuovo) have also given me a
deep insight into Greek life and character, and have,
moreover, helped me to understand what the imperishable
element in beauty really is. Would that I could bring this
understanding to bear upon my work. I had not seen
Michelangelo's "Moses" in San Pietro in Vincoli when I
last wrote to you, but I had read about it, and conceived
in my mind a vision that the real thing did not quite
come up to. However, I have only seen it once.

How glorious nature is down here! There is an indescribable harmony both of form and color. I often lie
for half a day among the tombs on the Via Latina, or on
the old Appian Way, certain that this idleness is not a
waste of time. The Baths of Caracalla is another place
that has a special attraction for me.

There is still something left of my travel grant, and
perhaps also a little of what was due me by the theater.
I have thought of spending this on a trip through the
Sabine Hills. . . .

I intend soon to make an application to the Norwegian
Science Association in Trondhjem, and I hope that you will
interest yourself in the matter. I have been living on
borrowed money since before Christmas, and must continue to do so until I receive a letter from you. A large
part of what I receive this time will have been spent in
advance. If you can possibly send me a larger amount than
last time, it would be a great help. But do what you can
or think best. My deep thanks for all that you have done
for me and for your last kind letter. You may be quite
certain that I shall wholeheartedly join forces with you in
everything when I get home. For I shall be going home,
although I believe I said the contrary in the letter which
I now wish and hope you may not have read.

My Zouave [Ibsen's son, to whom Bjørnson had given a
Zouave costume] asks to be remembered to you and sends
you many thanks. Our very kindest remembrances to your
wife. We are very happy and comfortable, and when the
little suspense I am in now is over, I shall take to my work
with renewed energy. It is work that gives me great
pleasure, although I expect it will be a rather somber work.

I congratulate you upon your play *Mary Stuart*. Along
with all the Scandinavians here, I rejoice greatly over the
reception it has had. I do not know how we are to get

hold of it here. The Norwegian papers are a month old when they reach us from the Scandinavian Society in Hamburg. I still do not know if you have accepted the directorship of the theater. The management of the theater was guilty of a falsehood when it asserted in its annual report that it had entered into negotiations with me. They received my refusal long before the report was issued. Remember me most cordially and gratefully to Dunker.

Yours,

Henrik Ibsen

Speech at the Unveiling of the Memorial Statue on P. A. Munch's Grave in Rome

Rome, June 12, 1865

Peter Andreas Munch (1810–63) was an important figure in the Norwegian nationalistic movement of the nineteenth century. His chief work was *Det norske Folks Historie* (*The History of the Norwegian People,* 8 vols., 1851–63), which asserted that the Norwegians were the original founders of Scandinavia.

. . . Whatever Munch had to say was his conviction at the moment he said it. Of that I am convinced, and that ought to soften your feelings toward him. For once— I say this to you Swedes and Danes and Norwegians—for once let truth become a power in our community of nations. We have seen what empty phrases lead to. So far in our national negotiations we have parleyed like diplomats, we have exchanged polite notes, we have been as delicate as perfume. It was not until the serious part of the affair was to begin that we fully realized what the whole business amounted to—an airy fragrance, neither more nor less.

People in Norway were wont to say that Munch was inconsistent, and people abroad echoed this. But it all depends on the point of view. A statesman or, in general, a man, who has a great, definite, and absolutely imperative task to perform may declare that no storm shall drive him from his path—and if the man is as strong as his words, no storm will drive him from his path.

But the scientific investigator neither can nor should

make such a declaration. The road is not staked out for
him. He must clear his way through thickets and mire;
must double back time and again and start from a new
point in order to reach his goal, a goal that he cannot
arbitrarily fix in advance but that he must discover through
his laborious investigations. In this respect, Munch has
been inconsistent; and here on his grave it must be
declared to his credit and honor that he was inconsistent.

I think, therefore, I may say, after all, that we are all
assembled here in common love and respect for the
memory of the deceased.

The stone that is erected here was not the gift of his
country. It comes from a small circle of friends. But I hope
that the state will follow their example. I hope that in our
native country the government will erect a visible memorial, just as worthy of him in its way as the one that marks
his grave here.

I know there are many people who think that the state
did exceedingly much for Munch and his scientific work
during his lifetime. But that is a misunderstanding, and
I must utter a protest. The state did its duty, nothing
more. The misunderstanding arises from the fact that in
similar cases the state does much less than its duty. The
result is a lowering of the standard of what can rightfully
be demanded from the state.

As long as the state authorities only regard themselves
as called upon to tend to the *happiness and welfare of the
community* and do not consider the *development of the
nation's life* as of equal importance, they can fulfill only
one half of the task before them, and the less important
half at that. States like ours cannot defend themselves by
their material prosperity. But states like ours can do so if
they fulfill themselves in the service of culture, science,
art, and literature, and if they earn for themselves a right
to exist, a right that history shows violence and force from
without have always been careful not to attack.

In our native lands the individual has, as far as his
ability goes, both the support and the good will of the
people for any work that aims to elevate the plane of our
inner national life. From my own experience I can gratefully acknowledge this, and I think that several of my
countrymen here could do the same. But in our countries
the state as such still sees in free science, in art, and in

literature only the decorations, not the pillars and beams of the edifice. I think it is about time that this humiliating state of affairs came to an end. The man who does the intellectual work in a nation has a right to carry his head high. He has a right to protest when he sees that he is offered for his labors only a part of the surplus left over after the material needs of the nation have been satisfied, and only, of course, when there is a surplus.

Things cannot go on like this. I hope that the serious and sad events of recent years [the Prussian-Danish war of 1864] have opened our eyes to the fact that it is not the strength of the state but the spiritual strength of the *nation* that can save us—if indeed there is any possibility of salvation—and in this lies a hint for every state that wants to preserve its existence and that has no superior might to depend on.

Therefore I hope that as one of the many things which may testify to a more enlightened program for the future, the state authorities will erect a memorial to Munch in his home country, a memorial worthy of his country, of himself, and of his work.

To Bjørnstjerne Bjørnson

Ariccia, near Rome
September 12, 1865

My dear Bjørnson, Your letter and check from Hegel came very opportunely. Thank you, my dear, good friend, for both! But, kind and loving as your letter was—nay, for that very reason—I have read it with self-reproach, because it reveals how anxious and worried you have been on my account. I am very grateful. All that I owe you comes down to one thing, the most important thing that has ever happened to me—namely, my having met and really gotten to know you—this I shall never be able to repay except by a devotion that neither my friends nor your enemies will be able to alter. I know that you understand me; you know that I am not referring to Bjørnson, the subscription-collector. Well—more of this when we meet. I can talk to you frankly now; I never could do so before.

Things are going well with me now; and they have been doing so the whole time, except on the one or two occasions when I have been at my wits' end, not only in regard to money, but in regard to my work [on *Brand*] also. I could make no progress on it. Then one day I strolled into St. Peter's—I had gone to Rome on an errand—and there I suddenly saw strongly and clearly the form for what I had to say.

I threw to the winds all that I had been unavailingly torturing myself with for a whole year [the epic version of *Brand*] and in the middle of July began something new, which progressed as nothing has ever progressed with me before. I mean new in the sense that I only began to write it then, but the subject and the mood have been weighing on me like a nightmare ever since the many lamentable political occurrences at home first made me examine myself and the condition of our national life, and think about things that before had not concerned me very deeply. It is a dramatic poem, modern in subject, serious in tone, five acts in rhymed verse (not a second *Love's Comedy*). The fourth act is now nearly finished, and the fifth I feel I can write in a week. I work both in the morning and the afternoon, which I have never been able to do before. It is delightfully peaceful here; no acquaintances; I read nothing but the Bible—it has vigor and power.

If I were asked at this moment what has been the chief result of my stay abroad, I would say that it lies in my having purged myself of that aesthetic point of view—existing in isolation and demanding that there be no other concerns in life—which formerly exercised a great power over me. Aestheticism of this kind seems to me now as great a curse to poetry as theology is to religion. You have never been troubled with it. You have never gone about looking at things through the hollow of your hand [as an artist might do to get the right perspective, an allusion to Ibsen's poem "On the Heights" ("Paa Vidderne"), in which he most strongly expressed the purely aesthetic attitude].

Is it not an inexpressibly great gift to be able to write? But it brings with it great responsibility; and I am now sufficiently serious to realize this and to be very severe with myself. An aesthete in Copenhagen once said to me: "Christ is really the most interesting phenomenon in the world's history." The aesthete enjoyed him as the glutton does the sight of an oyster. I have always been too strong to become a creature of that type. But I wonder what the intellectual asses might have made of me if they had had me all to themselves. It was you, dear Bjørnson, who prevented them from having their way with me. You are clear-sighted enough, regarding both yourself and me, to see that my need corresponds to what you have given and intended to give. I seem to have no end of things to say to you. They come rushing into my mind in a disorderly manner, and if I were to write them all down, there would be more than any amount of postage could cover—so let me come at once to business.

You say that the Storting *must* grant my petition. Do you really believe it will? I have an impression that my new work will not dispose the members more charitably toward me. But hang me if I can or will, on that account, suppress a single line, no matter what these "pocket-edition" souls think of it. Let me rather be a beggar all my life! If I cannot be myself in what I write, then everything is nothing but lies and humbug; and of that our country has enough without giving special grants to get more. I will make the attempt, however. What is the best plan? May I send the petition through you? There is time enough yet, I suppose, but I will not delay too long.

The Trondhjem people [of the Royal Norwegian Science Association] are surely making a lame excuse in asserting that my petition arrived too late. It is dated the twenty-sixth of March. If school superintendent Müller [who reviewed *Catiline* rather unfavorably] is on the board of management, I have reason to believe that I have an enemy there. Thank you for not letting the matter drop, and also for applying in my behalf for the appointment at the university library. I do not know what appointment it is; but that is of no consequence.

The Ancker Scholarship funds are not likely, in present circumstances, to be given to "Scandinavians," either Norwegians or Danes, but if you will apply, I shall be grateful for your good offices in this matter also.*

Will you kindly forward the enclosed letter to Attorney Sverdrup [see below]? Before my departure he asked me to let him know if I needed money at any time during

---

* Bjørnson was later informed the scholarship was available only to Danes.

my absence. So far I have not made use of his offer. But
my debt to Bravo [the Norwegian consul in Rome]
weighs upon me; and I cannot send the manuscript before
the whole is finished, unless I make a copy for my own use
during the writing of the rest, and that would delay me.*
I do not believe the theater could produce the play—even
if I were running the theater myself, I should have to vote
against it. But if you can make use of my new play, that
is quite another matter. It is undoubtedly dramatic; but
how far it is presentable in other respects is something
you must decide for yourself. . . .

To Johan Sverdrup

Ariccia, September 12, 1865

Sverdrup was the leader of the Liberal Party in Norway.

Dear Mr. Sverdrup: A short time before my departure
from Christiania, about a year and a half ago, you volun-
teered the suggestion that if I should find myself financially
embarrassed while living abroad I should turn to you,
who with the assistance of your friends would come to
my aid. The time for me to turn to you has now arrived.
My friend Bjørnson, who has worked tirelessly to help me,
has exhausted all the possible sources of assistance that
he has been able to discover; and I can draw no further
advances from the Gyldendal Publishing Company in
Copenhagen on the new work I have sold them. I am
therefore taking advantage of your invitation, and I hasten
to inform you that at the moment I am greatly in need of
assistance. Bjørnson can explain the situation further.

In another connection, I shall shortly be in need of your
great influence, but since that matter does not have the
same urgency for me as does the matter which I have felt

* Frederik Hegel, who had agreed to publish *Brand,* paid for each
section of the manuscript upon delivery. Author's royalties were based
on the size of the book as well as the size of the printing. In the case
of *Brand,* for instance, Ibsen was paid 30 Danish rix-dollars (probably
$15) per octavo signature for an initial printing of 1,250 copies. Since
Brand came to 270 pages in print, Ibsen must have received about $255
from the first printing. One can infer from Ibsen's letters that he continued to receive royalties at the same rate on his other works, at least
through the 1870's.

compelled to write you about now, I shall postpone any discussion of it until a more crucial time. Meanwhile, I shall be waiting expectantly to hear through Bjørnson what you have been able to do by way of fulfilling your kind and generous promise to me.

Faithfully yours,
Henr. Ibsen

To Frederik Hegel

Rome, November 15, 1865

On November 14 Ibsen received a formal contract from Frederik Hegel, head of Gyldendal, the largest publishing house in Denmark and Norway. Hegel was Bjørnson's publisher, and it was Bjørnson who, once again, had come to Ibsen's help by strongly recommending the relatively unknown playwright to Hegel's attention.

Dear Councilor Hegel: I am pleased to send herewith the last eighty-four pages of the manuscript [of *Brand*]. I received your very good letter yesterday, and I wish to express my sincere gratitude for the terms and conditions you offer. I think it highly desirable that the work be published by Christmas; and if time does not permit the galleys to be sent down here, I shall have to rely on fortune and the accuracy of Copenhagen's far-famed proofreaders. . . .

To Magdalene Thoresen

Rome, December 3, 1865

My dear Mother-in-law, For a long time now I have intended to write to you. There was a time I could not bring myself to it. I was never able to be myself with you, neither face to face nor in my letters. My innermost thoughts and feelings always sounded false when I expressed them, and realizing this, I kept them to myself. But going abroad changes a man, and in my case the change has been for the better.

I am not going to tell you about my experiences and

the sights I have seen. I could not even start to tell you everything. Besides all that is not what counts. What is truly significant and important is that I have got far enough away from home to see the meanness and deliberate hypocrisy of our so-called public life, and to realize the hollowness in all those phrasemakers who are glib enough in talking about "our great cause" but who have neither the will nor the ability nor the sense of commitment to perform a great deed. How often do we not hear the good people of Norway talking with smug self-satisfaction about Norwegian discretion, which is actually nothing more than a lukewarmness of spirit that makes those inoffensive souls incapable of committing a folly in the grand style. But they are well drilled, that cannot be denied. The uniformity is, in its way, exemplary. Everyone keeps in line and stays in step. But it is very different here, I can tell you! Anyone from up there who has managed to retain a certain amount of human feeling becomes keenly conscious down here that there is something more worth having than a clever head, and that is a whole soul. I know of mothers away up in the Piedmont, in Genoa, Novara, Alessandria, who took their boys of fourteen from school to let them go with Garibaldi on his daring expedition to Palermo. Nor was it a case of saving their country then, but simply of realizing an idea. How many of the members of our Storting do you suppose will do the same when the Russians enter Finnmark? With us any deed that asks more of us than getting through the day is "impossible."

My journey down here was by no means a pleasure trip, I assure you. I was in Berlin when the triumphal entry took place. I saw the rabble spit into the mouths of the cannon from Dybbøl, and to me it seemed an omen that history will one day spit in the face of Sweden and Norway because of their behavior then. Here in Rome I found the Scandinavians lost in a spiritual mire. What will you think when I tell you that even the Danes sat among the Germans in the chapel of the Prussian Embassy on Sundays while the war was going on, listening devoutly to the Prussian clergyman praying for the success of Prussian arms in their just war against the enemy? But I assure you I have stormed and raged and put things into a little better order. Down here I am afraid of nothing. At home I was afraid, when I stood in that clammy crowd and sensed their evil smiles behind my back. Why do you want to go to Norway? [Magdalene Thoresen had moved to Copenhagen after the death of her husband in 1858 only a few days before Ibsen's marriage to her stepdaughter.] In Denmark there is so much that is good and beautiful even now. My little boy shall never with my consent belong to a people whose aim it is to become Englishmen instead of human beings. It often seems hopeless to work at a time like the present. Unless the spiritual life of the people has an endless future before it, it does not matter whether the time granted is one year or a hundred years. This is what I think of my native Norway and Sweden: we have not the strength of will to make the sacrifice when the time comes. We have nothing to rally around—no great sorrow, such as Denmark has. Our people lack sufficient depth of soul to be able to feel sorrow. Our countrymen regard the downfall of the *state* as the worst thing that could happen. But the downfall of a *state* cannot be reason for sorrow; and they do not understand what the downfall of a nation means. Denmark will not perish as a nation; for as long as a people can feel sorrow, so long will that people live. I do not understand anyone saying that Denmark is the worst off of the Nordic countries. I tell you it is not true. . . .

To Clemens Petersen

Rome, December 4, 1865

Dear Mr. Petersen: At Christmas there will appear a dramatic poem by me which I most urgently ask you to interest yourself in as far as your conscience will permit. The mean and hopeless spirit that prevails in my home country has forced me to examine myself and current conditions; the sentiment and the subject matter of the poem have developed from this. You once wrote of me that the versified form imbued with symbolic meaning was my natural mode of expression. I have often thought about that remark. I agree with you, and it is in accordance with that thought that the poem has shaped itself. But I have not been able to avoid hitting hard. I ask you, if you can, not to examine this aspect of the work under a magnifying glass. Your review will be a decisive factor in my countrymen's reception of the poem and of those truths that I have not been able to withhold; but of course I should like to avoid martyrdom as long as possible.

The journalistic scribblers who practice criticism in Norway will not understand it. I therefore urgently ask that you give me your support, as promptly and as strongly as you possibly can, on all those points where you find either the subject matter or I myself deserve it. Should you have anything to communicate to me that does not find a place in your review—which I await with assurance and eagerness—I would thank you most warmly for a few lines. I am unbearably oppressed by the feeling that I stand all alone.

Yours truly,
Henrik Ibsen

To Bjørnstjerne Bjørnson

Rome, March 4, 1866

Dear Bjørnson, Yesterday I received from Norway a reminder so harsh and so wounding to my pride that I can only believe that it is due to some misunderstanding. Tell me, did you receive a letter from me about the middle of December, which was sent from here enclosed in a communication from Ravnkilde to F. Baetzman? In it I wrote that, having just heard from you regarding the payment of my debt to Bravo, I had taken the liberty to oblige Ravnkilde by drawing a draft on you to the amount of 25 specie-dollars, which amount I received from him and paid to Bravo. I asked, moreover, that if, contrary to the expectation you had expressed, such a sum should not yet have been paid to you on my account, you would kindly advance the amount yourself, notify me of it, and accept from me a counterdraft on Hegel, from whom I have not received anything except what you sent me this autumn. My dear Bjørnson, if what I have done has offended you, do not leave me tortured by doubts and all sorts of painful conjectures. Write to me and tell me frankly how my letter can have had such an effect. Compared with all you have so generously and magnanimously done for me at home, what I asked of you this time was surely no more than a drop in the sea.

Yesterday Ravnkilde received an extremely scornful, insolent, and, to a certain extent, inexplicable letter from Baetzman, who returned the draft, making use of the expression, "He won't get away with that!"—words such as would be used if one saw through some scheme and caught the swindler in the act. I will not allow such words to be written about me. If anyone were to say them to my face, I would kill him on the spot. Dear Bjørnson, if you know, tell me frankly what reason Baetzman can have had for writing as he did. I made a mistake, perhaps, in not at once sending the counterdraft on Hegel. I am enclosing it here; and now you must help me to get the matter cleared up, for I cannot bear to be dishonored in Ravnkilde's estimation. Dear friend, it is of course quite within the realm of possibility that you may someday have to break with me. But it is inconceivable that the breach should come about through an affair like this is. You are noble-minded. This makes it all the more inexplicable that you have not sent a few lines in answer to the many questions that I asked in my letter. Please write to me and put an end to my doubts.

Because of your silence on the subject, I have not sent in any application to the Storting or the government. I knew it would only have meant pointless humiliation. However, if you think it might do any good I will apply for a second travel grant. Tell me at the same time if the application sent to Trondhjem would need to be renewed.

My new book [Brand] should appear any day now. You say Hegel is a fine and good man, and Mrs. Thoresen says the same thing. But to me his goodness is of the Ditmar Meidellian* sort. He is respectful, cautious, and afraid of offending anyone. I have had a thousand little difficulties with him, and I gave in on all of them in order to get my book published by Christmastime, but it still did not appear then. Among other things, he said, long after the book was on the press, that you had described the action of the poem as taking place in old Viking times. Is there some misunderstanding here? I recall distinctly that I once wrote

---

* Ditmar Meidell was editor of *Krydseren* from 1849 and later of *Aftenbladet*; both were opposition papers.

you that the subject matter was taken from contemporary life, but that the work was no *Love's Comedy*. You can well understand that during all this I have neither asked for nor received any advances on royalties from him; and as to my present situation—worn out with the anxiety and suspense of waiting—looking forward to the appearance of the book and to the possibility of its producing strife and attacks of all sorts—unable in such circumstances to begin a new work [*Peer Gynt*] that lies already fully developed in my mind—about all this I will say no more.

Dear Bjørnson, it seems to me as if I were separated from both God and men by an infinitely great void. Last summer when I was writing my drama [*Brand*], I was indescribably happy, even in the midst of all my pain and misery. I felt the exultation of a Crusader; I would have had the courage to face anything on earth. But there is nothing so enervating and exhausting as waiting hopelessly. I suppose this is only a transitional phase. Eventually, I shall—I will score a victory. If the powers that be have been so unkind as to place me in this world and make me what I am, they must expect the consequences. Enough of this.

Though I am late in sending my wishes for a happy and prosperous year for you and yours and for success in all you undertake, I still send them to you. We in Rome have already received from you the best New Year's greeting you could have sent, your play *The Newly Married Couple*. It was read at Andreas Munch's [Norwegian poet] to a group of Scandinavians, all of whom send you their enthusiastic thanks. Yes, that is how the modern drama must take shape with us. Is it not strange —up there in the north the day is dawning, the sun is shining, the birds are singing, and the people are being offered the most powerful and beautiful means by which to raise themselves, means offered to no other people of our time. But they do not take advantage of them. I have a terrible foreboding that our nation is not faced with a limitless future, but with a definite end. When I read the news from home, when I think of all that respectable, all that estimable narrow-mindedness and materialism, I feel like an insane man hopelessly staring at one single spot of deepest blackness. . . .

You will receive my book as soon as it is published.

And you will be doing me more than a favor if you will let me know fully and frankly what you think of it. . . .

I will send in a report of my activities while abroad, with a petition for another travel grant, if you think it will do any good. Please assist and advise me in this matter. Be kind enough to give the enclosed letter to Dunker. The matter of the enclosed counterdraft concerns my honor. For God's sake, settle it, and then write one of your kind letters to put an end to my anxiety. You are my one and only trusted friend. You do not know what it means to have only one.

I have written to Clemens Petersen asking him to do as much for my book as his conscience will allow. I do not look for any instructive criticism from the Norwegian reviewers. I am certain to be attacked. Things will just have to take their course. I have right on my side, and nothing they can say will make me yield. Remember me most kindly to your wife, and write soon to

Your devoted,

Henrik Ibsen

P.S. My dear Bjørnson! This time I take advantage of your suggestion that I should not prepay the postage on my letters. I do it unwillingly, but I have no choice.

H. I.

To Frederik Hegel

Rome, March 16, 1866

Frederik Hegel was to publish all of Ibsen's works from *Brand* on. Ibsen signed a contract with him in 1865, and *Brand* was published March 15, 1866, in a first printing of 1,250 copies. Three more printings were called for in the same year.

. . . I hope that in the future I shall continue to enjoy the honor and pleasure of being associated with your company, just as it is my intention to be as closely associated with Denmark as possible. Norway and Sweden have a terrible debt of blood to wash away, and I feel that it is my task in life to use the gifts God has given me to awaken my countrymen from their torpor and to force them to see where the great questions are leading us. . . .

To John Grieg

Rome, March 22, 1866

John Grieg, the brother of the composer Edvard Grieg, was interested in translating *The Pretenders* into German.

. . . Of course I would be glad to have my work translated. If it proves capable of influencing and elevating anyone outside of our own country, it would please me very much. In our own country poetry must, unfortunately, strike into another path now. At present there is really no call or need to reawaken our historical memories. What has occurred in the last two or three years in our country— or rather what has not occurred—sufficiently demonstrates that there is no more connection between the Norwegians of today and those of the great days of old than there is between the Greek pirates of modern times and those ancient Greeks who had courage and faith and strength of will—and therefore the gods too—on their side. Well, things may brighten again, but for the present our fatherland stands in need of something else.

I am convinced that you will be successful with your adaptation, and that it will be a success, in the best sense of the word, with the public for which it is intended. I have been looking through the play again and find that there is a good deal in it that should awaken some response in Germany. It is strange how history repeats itself in different forms, like variations on a musical theme. In Germany at the present time they are fighting the same battle over the question of unity or separation, and the same passions and interests are at work. In a way the Germans have both their Bishop Nicholas and their Earl Skule, and Haakon is the man for whom they long and in whom they place their hopes— It is quite true that I have a strong dislike, not, as you put it, of Germans, but of Germanism and Germanomania. When we meet, as I hope we someday shall, you will allow me to explain myself further. I do not like to write long letters. I shall only say that in many respects I am fully aware of the beauty and the goodness that exist in such abundance among these, our born enemies—for that is what they are at the moment. But the situation must and will change, for it is unnatural to the last degree. Several years ago [1852] I lived in Dresden for a period of four months, and my recollections of that time are among the pleasantest and brightest that I possess.

As to whether it is best to make the translation in iambic verse, I dare not give an opinion. I trust entirely to your judgment in this as in all else. I quite agree with you that this form of translation necessarily entails a free treatment of details. . . .

To His Majesty Charles XV, King of Sweden and Norway

Rome, April 15, 1866

I, the undersigned Henrik Ibsen, hereby most humbly petition that Your Majesty, acting through the Norwegian government, may be pleased to lay before the present session of the Storting a proposition to the effect that there be granted to me a yearly pension of 400 specie-dollars [$400] to enable me to devote myself exclusively to my calling as a writer. . . .

The first fruits of my [1863 grant] have now been given to the public in the form of a dramatic poem *Brand,* which was published in Copenhagen and which in the few weeks since its publication has attracted attention abroad as well as at home. But I cannot live on expressions of gratitude; and the royalties I have been paid, though most liberal under the circumstances, are likewise insufficient to enable me to reside abroad or, indeed, even to provide for my immediate future.

It is in consequence of advice wired to me by my friends in Christiania that I venture to take the unusual step of addressing Your Majesty directly. . . .

I am not fighting for an existence free from care but for that lifework which I firmly believe God has given me to do—the work that seems to me to be the most necessary and imperative to Norway, the work of arousing the people of our nation and urging them to think great thoughts.

The private proposal that I have been told several members of the Storting intend to present has no chance of success; and time does not permit of an application to the government.

My King is therefore my one last hope.

It remains with Your Majesty to decide whether or not I shall have to keep silence and suffer the bitterest disappointment that can befall a human soul—the disappointment of having to give up one's lifework, of having to surrender when I know that I have been given exactly the intellectual and spiritual weapons required for the struggle. And what makes surrender ten times harder for me is that I have never given in before.

But I am full of hope, for, having indicated to you what my lifework is, I have at the same time shown myself to be a soldier fighting under Your Majesty's spiritual banner. . . .

On May 12 the pension was almost unanimously voted by the Norwegian Storting.

To Georg Brandes

Rome, April 25, 1866

This letter inaugurates what will be to many readers the most vital part of Ibsen's correspondence, his letters to the Danish critic Georg Brandes. Shortly before the time of this letter the young Brandes had begun to quarrel with the supporters of religious orthodoxy in Denmark. Through Brandes' close friend Ludvig David, Ibsen heard about the dispute. On March 25 David committed suicide, and Ibsen wrote a long letter describing to Brandes the circumstances of Ludvig's death. At the end of the letter, he said:

. . . I wish to thank you for the kind words from you that have been conveyed to me. I look forward with pleasure to making your personal acquaintance. If it lies in my choice, my future place of residence will be Copenhagen; I have no desire to go farther north. . . .

My best wishes to you. Fight the courageous fight. In many ways that is what we northerners badly need. . . .

To Michael Birkeland

Rome, May 4, 1866

Birkeland, National Archivist of Norway, was a member of the literary circle Ibsen belonged to in Christiania, and one of the ardent supporters of Ibsen's petition for a writer's pension.

My dear and great friend, . . . I did not expect [*Brand*] to be so well received. Any number of greetings, congratulations, and expressions of gratitude have come to me from Denmark, some of them from such well-known people as Councilors Krieger and David, and Mrs. Heiberg. I have also received invitations and kind offers, all of which I appreciate very much, since Copenhagen may possibly be my home in the future. . . .

Rome is beautiful, wonderful, magical. I have an extraordinary capacity for work, and I feel as strong as a giant killer. I kept struggling with [*Brand*] for a whole year before it took shape clearly. But once I had hold of it, I wrote from morning to night, and finished it in less than three months. It is impossible to write about Rome, especially for anyone who knows it as thoroughly as I do. Taking one district at a time, I have walked with my knapsack on my back through the greater part of the Papal States. The brigands are not so dangerous as we imagine at home.

I am not giving up *Julian*, though I see that Carsten Hauch has treated the same subject [in a dramatic poem *Julian the Apostate*, published in April, 1866].

You write that the classical scholars are cudgeling their brains over *quantum satis*. Confound me, however, if it wasn't good Latin in my day, though, no doubt, "doctor's Latin." Any medical student will tell you that it is a standing formula on prescriptions when the quantity ordered is not a certain quantity by weight, but as much as is necessary, or a sufficient quantity. It is the doctor in [*Brand*] who uses the phrase first; and remembering it, Brand repeats it. I do not now whether *caritas* is a classical expression or not; but it is used in modern ecclesiastical Latin (as distinct from *amor*—earthly love) to express heavenly love, with the idea of mercy included. We have the same in the Italian *carità*.

. . . As regards the inner man, I believe that I am in some ways very much changed. Yet it seems to me that I am more myself now than I have ever been. As regards the outer man, I have grown thin, which I shall prove by a photograph to be sent with Fladager when he goes home this summer. . . .

To Frederik Hegel

Frascati, June 9, 1866

Dear Councilor Hegel, Many thanks for the reviews forwarded to me! I have read Pastor Helveg's with much interest; it corrects several mistakes made by most of the other critics.

My address is still the same. I am living out here in the hills. I never see a newspaper, and know nothing of what is going on in the outside world. But it is wonderfully beautiful here. Best wishes to you.

Yours most sincerely,
Henrik Ibsen

P.S. . . . To return to Helveg's book. I must, for the sake of the record, say that his assumption that I had Søren Kierkegaard in mind when I wrote [*Brand*] is incorrect. But of course, the depiction of a man whose sole aim in life is to realize his ideals will always bear a certain resemblance to Kierkegaard's life.

H. I.

To Paul Botten-Hansen

Frascati, July 22, 1866

. . . My wife wishes to be remembered to you and your wife. We are in excellent health, but have, of course, been obliged to leave Rome during these hot summer months when the poisonous sirocco is blowing over the Campagna. We are staying at Frascati, up in the Alban Hills, where we have rooms in an old palace, Palazzo Gratioso, and live most comfortably and cheaply. Frascati lies below ancient Tusculum, where Cicero, you remember, had a magnificent villa, where he wrote his *Tusculan Disputations*. The ruins of his villa are still there. His small theater, which is presumably what he called his *schola*, where he used to deliver speeches to a select audience, is still virtually undamaged. It is indescribably delightful to sit up here in the evening, two thousand feet over the sea, enjoying the magnificent view of the Mediterranean, the Campagna, and Rome. The mountainous Sabine country, with the Apennines, lies to the east, while to the south rise the Volscian Mountains on the Neapolitan frontier. From the windows of my study I see in the extreme distance Mount Soracte rising, isolated and beautiful, from the level of the immense plain—in short, whichever way you turn you seem to be looking over that battlefield where the spirit of world history arranged her greatest events. . . .

To Frederik Hegel

Frascati, August 22, 1866

Dear Councilor Hegel, I received with pleasure your kind letter of August 5, and I suppose that by this time the third printing [of *Brand*] is already on the market. I want you to know that I am, and ever shall be, fully aware of how much the success of my book owes to your deservedly esteemed name. I only hope that in the future our literary relations may give you a small measure of the satisfaction that they have already given me.

At present I am in doubt as to whether my new work [*Peer Gynt*] will be finished by autumn. But I have a proposal to make, namely, that you should publish *Love's Comedy* for the Christmas season. It came out at New Year's, 1863, as a supplement to *Illustreret Nyhedsblad*—a New Year's gift to its subscribers—and cannot possibly be well known in Denmark. The book may be regarded as a forerunner of *Brand*, and it will find a public in Denmark. Some of the language must be altered; other corrections made; and the new edition should be accompanied by a few prefatory words. I have a copy here that I will send you, revised and corrected, if you, who are in a better position to judge, agree to my proposal. May I hear from you soon in regard to it? . . .

I learn from the Norwegian newspapers that the government has (without any application from me) granted me, in addition to my pension, 350 specie-dollars [\$350] from the fund for artists' and scientists' foreign travel. This makes it possible that I may take a trip to Greece next summer.

I do not remember if I have already asked you to give my kind regards to Brandes, and to thank him for his friendly and warm review. I hear that he also has received a travel grant. It would give me great pleasure if we could meet somewhere here in the South; but he probably has other plans. . . .

Preface to the Second Edition of *Love's Comedy*

(See page 29.)

Rome, January, 1867

To Frederik Hegel

Rome, January 5, 1867

Dear Councilor Hegel, I have the pleasure of sending you herewith the preface for *Love's Comedy* [see page 29]. These few lines have taxed my brain more than the whole poem. I have written and rewritten them times without number, and finally settled on my first draft. If you do not like the preface, you have my permission to dispense with it, but in that case, something to the effect of what it contains ought to be inserted in one of the most widely circulated newspapers to help orient Danish readers. I would prefer to see my own lines appear at the beginning of the book. But I leave the matter to your decision. . . .

I do not know if you read the Norwegian newspapers. If you do, you will have noticed that . . . an entire literature on *Brand* has sprung up in them. The articles in *Morgenbladet* of the first and fourth of December contain, in my opinion, the best Norwegian criticism of the poem that has yet appeared. I do not know who the author is.

And now I must tell you that my new work [*Peer Gynt*] is well under way, and will, if nothing untoward happens, be finished early in the summer. It will be a long dramatic poem, having as its chief figure one of those half-mythical, fanciful characters existing in the annals of the Norwegian peasantry of *modern* times. It will have no resemblance to *Brand*, will contain no direct polemic, etc. I have long had the subject in mind, and now the entire plan is worked out and written down, and I have started the first act. The thing grows as I work at it, and I am certain that you will be satisfied with it. But I must ask you to keep all this a secret for the present. . . .

To Frederik Hegel

Rome, March 8, 1867

The biography referred to in this letter was written by a Danish journalist, Axel Falkmann, who stated that H. Riddervold, head of the Norwegian Ecclesiastical Department had refused to support the application for a state grant made by the author of *Love's Comedy*. There was no truth in this.

. . . I have received the two numbers of *Illustreret Tidende* and am much obliged to you for your trouble. But who is the biographer? None of the Danes here knows him. The tactlessness with which he treats private and irrelevant matters makes me suspect he is a Norwegian; but that is hardly possible. In many respects his criticism is kindly and appreciative. He is, however, guilty of several inaccuracies, as, for instance, in his account of Councilor Riddervold's attitude at the time of the granting of my pension. He is also wrong in saying that I have made a thorough study of Heine. I have only once read through a volume of his travel books and his *Buch der Lieder*. The same applies to Kierkegaard, of whom I have read little and understood less. But it would interest me to know who the man is.

My new dramatic poem has now advanced to the middle of the second act. There will be five acts, and, as far as I am able to judge now, the book will run to about 250 pages. If you want me to, I shall be able to send you the manuscript in July. . . .

To Clemens Petersen

Rome, March 9, 1867

Dear Mr. Petersen: Although I have confined myself— for nearly a year now—to expressing through a third person my gratitude for your review of *Brand* and the advantages thereby secured to me, it is certainly not from a lack of appreciation of your services. But you once took occasion to write a few words about undue intimacy after short and hasty acquaintance, and those words have left me somewhat shy. I feel sure, however, that there has been no such "affectation" in my appeals to you; yet the characteristic, such as you interpret it, is at any rate so truly Norwegian that I can easily see it was a Norwegian who gave you the opportunity for the observation and the remark.

In spite of this, I still venture to send you my thanks for the review—both for the expressed criticism and for the implicit one. The first has been a great personal joy to me and of great help in establishing my position with the public; the latter has certainly not been any joy to me, but has for just that reason been all the more helpful in self-analysis, which cannot be shirked with impunity.

But I have to thank you for more than the reviews of *Brand* and my other works. I want to thank you for every word you have written besides, and I hope that in my new work [*Peer Gynt*] you will acknowledge that I have taken an essential step forward.

I have been told that you once said you did not believe it would be of any use to review my works since I would not follow suggestions for improvement. Certainly I could not follow directions simply upon the strength of mere authority, for then I would not be true to myself; and such a blind acceptance of your suggestions would, I am quite sure, afford you no satisfaction either. But the step forward of which I speak lies precisely in the fact that hereafter it is no longer a question for me of "want to be" but of "must be." You have helped me across that yawning gulf, and therefore I thank you now and shall always thank you.

Hoping that in these lines you will not read anything more or less than our certainly remote acquaintance grants me the privilege of writing, I am

Your ever grateful,
Henrik Ibsen

To Frederik Hegel

Villa Pisani, Casamicciola, Ischia, August 8, 1867

. . . Today I am sending you, through Consul General Danchertsen of Naples, the manuscript of the first three acts of my new work, the title of which is: *Peer Gynt, A Dramatic Poem.* I hope that you will receive it about the same time as this letter. What I have sent you will run in print to about 120 pages, and there is about as much more to come. I hope to send you the fourth act toward the end of this month, and the rest not very long afterward.

I am curious to hear how you like it. I am very hopeful myself. It may interest you to know that Peer Gynt was a real person, who lived in Gudbrandsdal, probably at the end of the last century or the beginning of this. His name is still well known among the peasants there. But of his exploits not much more is known than is to be found in Asbjørnsen's *Book of Norwegian Folk Tales,* in the section "Mountain Scenes." So I have not had very much to work with, but on the other hand I have had so much more freedom to invent. I would like very much to know what Clemens Petersen thinks of it.

Assuming you are satisfied with it, the next question is, Do you wish to bring out the book at Christmas? I would prefer that, but I leave the matter in your hands.

And now, taking advantage of the kind offer you made me some time ago, I should like to ask you for an advance of 200 rix-dollars [probably about $100]. This, together with the small amount due me, you might send in the form of a draft on Paris in a registered letter addressed to: Cavaliere D. Danchertsen, Console-Generale di Danimarca, Vico Calanzione, Pizzofalcone, Napoli. If I could count on finding such a letter at Naples toward the end of the month, I would be exceedingly obliged to you. I am going to Sorrento about that time to put the finishing touches on my work.

We have been living in Ischia since the middle of May. The thermometer has sometimes gone as high 30° Reaumur [100° Fahrenheit] and to keep on working in good spirits in such heat, you have to be strong—which, thank God, I am.

How is *Love's Comedy* selling? I hope it will not prove to be a bad deal for you. I often think about it. . . .

To Jonas Collin

Sorrento, October 21, 1867

Jonas Collin was the son of a Danish family well known for their literary interests.

. . . I see from [the Danish newspaper] *Dagbladet* that a pen-and-ink war has broken out between the philosophers and the theologians. I do not understand the matter well enough to form any opinion on it, but I must confess that there is unusual energy and strength of conviction in Georg Brandes' behavior. I do not know whether you are his friend or his opponent; but it is clear to me that this man will play a prominent part in the intellectual life of Scandinavia. In saying this, I am not, of course, expressing my opinion of his point of view. . . .

To Bjørnstjerne Bjørnson

Rome, December 9, 1867

Peer Gynt was published by Hegel on November 14, 1867, and sold so well that a second printing of 2,000 was called for two weeks later. Bjørnson reviewed it immediately in *Norsk Folkebladet* calling it a magnificent poetic achievement, "a satire on Norwegian selfishness, narrow-mindedness, and smugness, carried out so that I not only laughed aloud time after time but had to pause to say to myself, as I now say publicly, how much I thank the author for giving it to us." And in a letter to Ibsen, Bjørnson wrote, "Nowadays I cannot talk of anything but your poem nor think of anything but you. . . . I love you for your devotion to our great aims. . . . I love you for being strong, I love you for being bold and reckless."

Clemens Petersen, the most influential Danish critic, had a different opinion. Reviewing *Peer Gynt* in *Fædrelandet* (*The Fatherland*) a week after Bjørnson's review, he declared categorically that the work was not "truly poetry" because in adapting reality to art Ibsen had disregarded the demands of both. He went on to say that the poem was filled with intellectual tricks and riddles that could not be understood or unraveled because they really meant nothing. Actually, the poem was no more than a piece of polemic journalism.

The M. J. Monrad who is mentioned in this letter was a Hegelian philosopher who had criticized *Love's Comedy* for furthering religious disbelief and aggravating the skeptical temper of the times, and *Brand* for ignoring the fact that true self-sacrifice lay precisely in that spirit of compromise which the heroic priest of the drama sought to destroy.

Dear Bjørnson, What sort of infernal nonsense is it that comes between us at every turn? It is as if the devil himself were casting his shadow between us. I received your letter. There can be no deceit in anyone who writes what you write. There are things which are impossible to counterfeit. I prepared a reply, written from a full and grateful heart, not expressing my thanks for being praised but for being understood. It is that that makes one grateful beyond words. But now I can't send my letter. I have torn it to pieces. An hour ago I read Mr. Clemens Petersen's review in *Fædrelandet*. Now if I am going to answer your letter, I must begin in another way: I must acknowledge the receipt of your esteemed communication of such and such a date with the accompanying criticism from the previously mentioned paper.

If I were in Copenhagen and had a friend as close to me as Clemens Petersen is to you, I would have beaten the life out of him rather than let him commit such a biased and prejudiced crime against truth and justice. Clemens

Petersen has built his review on a lie—not in what he says but in what he refrains from saying. And he very deliberately refrains from saying a good deal. You are quite at liberty to show him this letter. As surely as I know him to be profoundly and seriously concerned with what really makes life worth living, so surely do I know that his review will someday burn and sear his soul; for one can lie as much by keeping silent as by speaking out. And on Clemens Petersen's shoulders there rests a great responsibility; God has entrusted him with a great task.

Do not think that I am a blind, conceited fool! I assure you that in my quiet moments I sound and probe and dissect the innermost parts of my soul—and where it hurts most, too.

My book *is* poetry. And if it is not, then it shall be. The conception of poetry in our country, in Norway, shall be made to conform to my book. There is nothing fixed and eternal in the world of ideas. The Scandinavians of this century are not Greeks. He says that the Strange Passenger is a symbol of terror and anxiety [*Angst*]. If I were on the verge of being executed, and if all it would take to save my life would be an explanation like that, it still would not occur to me. I never thought of such a thing. I stuck in the scene as a mere caprice. And as for Peer Gynt, is he not a completely rounded human being with an individual personality? *I* know that he is. And what about his mother, is she not? There are many things one can learn from Clemens Petersen, and I have learned much from him. But there is something that it might do him good to learn, and which I, even though I cannot teach it to him, have the advantage of him—and that is what you in your letter call "loyalty." That is precisely the right word! Not loyalty to a friend, or a program, or anything like that, but to something infinitely higher.

However, I am glad of the injustice that has been done me. There is a divine dispensation in it; for I can feel my strength growing as my anger increases. If it is to be war, then let it be war! If I am no poet, then I have nothing to lose. I shall try my luck as a photographer. One by one I shall come to grips with my contemporaries in the North, as I have already come to grips with the Norwegian nationalist language reformers [in the character of Huha in

Peer Gynt]. I shall not spare the child in the mother's womb, nor respect the thought or feeling that lies behind the word of any living soul who merits my attention.

Dear Bjørnson, you are a good, warmhearted soul. You have let me share more of your noble and fine nature than I can ever repay you. But there is something in your nature that may easily cause your good fortune—precisely that—to become a curse to you. I have a right to tell you this, for I know that underneath the crust of my foolishness and swinishness, I have always taken life very seriously. Do you know that I have entirely separated myself forever from my own parents, from my whole family, because being only half understood was unendurable to me?

This letter is somewhat incoherent. Adding it up, it comes to this: I will not be an antiquarian nor a geographer; I will not cultivate my talent for the furtherance of Monrad's philosophy; in short, I will not follow good advice. But one thing I will do, even though the powers without and the powers within drive me to pull the roof down upon my head—I will always, *so help me God,* be your faithful and sincerely devoted servant.

Henrik Ibsen

December 10

I have slept upon the above lines, and have now reread them in cold blood. They are the expression of yesterday's mood, but I shall still send them.

Let me tell you, calmly and deliberately, what will come of Mr. Clemens Petersen's article.

I have no intention of yielding, and Mr. Clemens Petersen cannot oust me; it is too late for that. He may possibly oblige me to withdraw from Denmark, but in that case I intend to change more than my publisher. Do not underestimate my friends and my adherents in Norway. The party whose newspaper has opened its pages to calumnies about me will see that I do not stand alone. When things go beyond a certain point, I feel no respect for others; and if I am only careful to do what I am quite capable of, namely, combining this relentlessness of mind with deliberateness in the choice of means, my enemies shall be made to feel that if I am not a builder, I am at least capable of destroying.

But this concerns only the future. Now let me tell you something about the present.

I am carrying on no correspondence with anyone at home. Nevertheless I can give you a bit of news from there. Do you know what they are saying now in Norway wherever Carl Ploug's paper [*Fædrelandet*] is read? They are saying: "It is evident from Clemens Petersen's review that Bjørnson is in Copenhagen."

If you have reviewed *Peer Gynt* in *Norsk Folkebladet*, they will be saying: "A diplomatic maneuver but not clever enough." Some will say it in all good faith; others out of vindictiveness and resentment. The critics will divide into parties for or against. You will see.

They will call Clemens Petersen's review a return for favors received. A man unknown to me wrote some articles in *Morgenbladet* lately, in which he unmercifully disparaged Mr. Petersen's literary work, while I was favorably mentioned. These associations and combinations will be recalled. I know how these fellows reason.

Dear Bjørnson, do let us try to stick together. Our friends have often enough made life miserable for us and our struggle more onerous than it should be.

You can see from the very fact that I write all this to you that I harbor no suspicion of you in this matter. I have never taken and never will take sides with my adherents when they are opposed to you. When I am opposed to your friends, that is another matter.

Mr. Petersen's article—to return to that again—will not do me any harm. The absentee has always a great advantage in the very fact of his being absent. But to write the article in such a style was imprudent. In his review of *Brand* he treated me with respect, and the public will not find anything in the intervening year that renders me deserving of contempt. The public will not permit Mr. Petersen to dismiss me as summarily as he has attempted to do. He ought to leave such attempts to those of his colleagues who live *by* their work as a critic. Until now I believed that Mr. Petersen lived *for* his.

All I reproach you with is inaction. It was not kind of you to allow, through negligence, this attempt to sell my literary reputation to the highest bidder in my absence.*

* Ibsen is alluding to an auction of his belongings that took place in 1866 in order to satisfy his creditors. Ibsen knew nothing about it until it was all over.

There! I have written myself into a good temper again. Now you go ahead and pour abuse on my head—preferably in a long, long letter, if you find it necessary.

Please accept a warm greeting from us all. Do not show your wife this letter; but give her our best wishes for Christmas and New Year, and, most particularly, for the approaching third happy event.

Yours,
Henrik Ibsen

To Bjørnstjerne Bjørnson

Rome, December 28, 1867

Dear Bjørnson, Nothing in the whole wide world could have been more welcome than the greeting which your letter, received on Christmas morning, brought me.

Thinking of that cargo of nonsense which I shipped to you in my last epistle left me without a moment of peace. The worst that a man can do to himself is to do injustice to others. Thank you, noble-minded man that you are, for taking the matter as you have. I could see nothing before me but trouble and bitterness for a long time to come, but now, looking back, I see it as only natural that you should take it just as you did. I read your letter over and over again every day to free myself from the tormenting thought that I have hurt you.

Do not understand what I said in my former letter to mean that my conception of what is essential in poetry is entirely different from Clemens Petersen's. On the contrary, I understand and am pretty much in accord with him. But I contend that I have fulfilled the requirements. He says no.

He writes of our overreflective age which sees the witches in *Macbeth* as symbolizing something that takes place in Macbeth himself; yet in the very same article he himself makes a distracted passenger on board a ship symbolize *Angst!* Why, proceeding in this manner, I will undertake to turn your works and those of every other poet into allegories from beginning to end. Take [Goethe's] *Götz von Berlichingen.* Let Götz himself represent the idea of liberty fermenting in the nation; let the Emperor repre-

sent the idea of the state, etc., etc.; and what do you
arrive at? Why, that is not poetry!

As for my "paroxysms," do not worry about them. There
is nothing unhealthy in them in any respect. I shall very
probably take your advice and write a comedy for the
stage; the idea had been occupying my mind. It is possible that we shall go to northern Italy for the summer, but
I do not know where we shall spend next winter. I only
know that it will not be in Norway. Were I to go home
now, one of two things would happen: within a month
I would make an enemy of everyone there; or else I would
worm my way back into favor again, using all sorts of dis-
guises, and thus become a lie both to myself and others.

Dear Bjørnson, are you really going back to work in the
theater again? There is undoubtedly need for you there,
but there is a much greater need for you to continue your
writing. If your taking up theatrical work meant merely
wasting time, meant merely that all the visions, moods, and
imaginings of the poet were put aside for the time being
to make their appearance later, it would not matter so
much. But such is not the case. Other ideas may come, but
the ones in between die unborn. For a poet, working in a
theater is equivalent to repeated, daily abortions. This is a
crime according to the civil laws; I do not know if God
is more lenient. Think it over, dear Bjørnson! The gift of
writing is not a privilege, it is a responsibility. Go abroad,
carissimo! Both because distance gives one perspective,
and because it is good to be out of the sight of one's
public. I am certain that the good people of Weimar were
Goethe's worst public. . . .

My sincere conviction obliges me to disagree entirely
with you on the subject of "decorations." We live under a
monarchy and not under a republic. For my part, I am not
partial to a republic. "The resemblance to Consul Bravo"
already exists. We accept a salary from the state just as he
does. We accept money from the government in the form
of grants; royalty gives us decorations because it respects
the popular feeling and acknowledges its existence. Why
reject the one when both are expressions for the same
thing? Let us examine ourselves carefully! Do we intend
to be ascetics from now on? Do we intend to decline every
kindly meant festivity offered us, every toast, etc.? If not,
then of what avail is the rejection of this one particular

thing? Orla Lehmann has declaimed against decorations and titles; but, do you honestly know a vainer man than he? August Blanche has spoken sarcastically about such matters; but does he not permit himself to be starred and beribboned all over by popular favor in the Opera Restaurant and other places? For my part, I feel that by declining I should be deceiving myself and others. If I had had any real desire for such finery, I should certainly have refrained from playing the part of "state satirist." But if the finery comes my way—why make a fuss about it!

I will soon write you another long letter; this one is by no means what it should be. As to my "friends of *Morgenbladet*," do not worry about them—they will never be able to hurt me. I know no more who these friends are than I know the critics in the South Sea Islands. I have no correspondence with Norway except an exchange of a letter with my brother-in-law every three months.

And now I wish you a happy New Year! Write when you can—and may I hear from you that all is well! Remember us all to your wife and the little boys.

Your devoted,

Henrik Ibsen

To Frederik Hegel

Rome, February 24, 1868

. . . What is the news concerning *Peer Gynt*? As far as I can judge from the newspaper reviews, it has been very well received in Sweden; but are the sales correspondingly good?

I hear that the book stirred up a storm in Norway. This does not trouble me in the least. But both there and in Denmark they have discovered much more satire in it than I intended. Why can they not read the work as a poem? That is what I wrote. The satirical passages are fairly isolated. If the Norwegians of today recognize themselves in Peer Gynt, as it seems they do, that is their own affair. . . .

My next work will probably be a play for the theater, and I hope it will not be long before I begin to work at it seriously. . . .

Yes, I have had thoughts of making a collection of my scattered and unpublished poems. But it cannot be done down here, for they must be hunted up in a variety of newspapers, etc. I shall have to go north again sometime, and then I shall probably pay a visit to Christiania, on which occasion the undertaking might be set agoing. Thank you for having broached the subject. With a hearty, though somewhat late, New Year's greeting, and with thanks, no less warm, for the past year, I am

Yours most respectfully and sincerely,

Henrik Ibsen

P.S. In addition to all you have done for me, may I ask one more favor of you? Would you purchase and add to my account a geography book, a universal history, a history of Scandinavia, a book of natural history, an arithmetic, and the first books used in religious instruction— all suitable for a child of eight, who, however, is not entirely a beginner. My little boy has read a great deal, especially general and Bible history, but hitherto quite unsystematically, and he must not go on in this way. If it is not too expensive, please send them in the mail, but if that is not practicable, then perhaps some traveler coming this way will find room for them in his trunk. I hope you are not annoyed by this request; it is a matter of importance to me.

Yours,

H. I.

To Magdalene Thoresen

Rome, March 31, 1868

My dear Mother-in-law, Will you accept a few lines from a correspondent as negligent as I am? I feel there is no end of the things I have to say to you, but in writing them down they never come to anything. I trust that in talking together they would. I am sure that they would, although I am well aware that only when I am alone with my thoughts am I truly myself.

I can hardly imagine how it will be possible to live out of Italy—and in Christiania of all places! But it will have

to be done. I feel, however, that one must isolate oneself
up there—at least I must, if I do not want to make an
enemy of every other person. I can put up with everything
else, but not this flirting with the Swedes. Because of the
very foundation of their civilization, the Swedes are our
spiritual enemies. And yet some people treat the whole
matter as if it were a little quarrel that could be patched
up by mutual complaisance or something of the kind! It is
lucky for the fellows who feel this way that our press is in
such a condition that no decent person would have anything to do with it without first putting his gloves on. And
with them on, it is difficult to write polemics. And whom
would one have on one's side? No one. One would stand
alone. It is clear enough to me that for anyone in our
country with a heart and soul there is nothing to do but
withdraw like a wounded deer into a thicket to die in
solitude and silence. The best thing that could befall our
country would be a great national disaster. If we could not
endure that, we would have no right to exist. I have been
a witness here to sacrifices, which enables me to make
comparisons—and the comparison does no credit to our
country. . . .

✳ EXILE IN DRESDEN
1868–1875

To Frederik Hegel

Dresden, October 31, 1868

Brand and *Peer Gynt* made Ibsen famous throughout Scandinavia, and early in 1868, growing more and more concerned about his son Sigurd's education, he thought about returning to live in Norway. However, after spending the summer in Berchtesgaden, Bavaria, Ibsen and his family moved to Dresden in the first days of October.

At Berchtesgaden Ibsen had begun to work on *The League of Youth*, perhaps taking a hint from Bjørnson, who had remarked after reading *Peer Gynt* that Ibsen's forte was satiric comedy, even farce. But unlike *Peer Gynt*, the new play was to be tailored for the theater and was also to be "completely realistic." Working within these strictures, Ibsen found *The League of Youth* much more difficult to write than his vast poetic dramas.

. . . My new work is making rapid progress. I have been wrestling with it all summer without writing anything down. Now the whole outline is finished and on paper. The first act is completed, the second will be in the course of a week, and by the end of the year I hope to have the whole play ready. It will be in prose and in every way suitable for the stage. The title is *The League of Youth, or The Almighty & Co.*, a comedy in five acts. It deals with forces and frictions in modern life, and though the action takes place in Norway, it can be just as well adapted for Denmark. I am in a peaceful and happy frame of mind, and write accordingly; this time that dear and excellent man, G. Brandes, shall have no cause to complain of illicit intercourse with the Muses. By the bye, would you be kind enough to send me a copy of Brandes' *Aesthetic Studies*, charging it to my account? Before we left Rome I heard that he was writing an essay on comedy, a subject on which, as far as theory is concerned, I must confess that I have no very distinct ideas, and which I would be very glad to have elucidated for me—particularly by Brandes. . . .

Do you not know any Danes who intend to winter in Dresden? I am longing greatly for the society of Scandinavians. Possibly there are some here already, but I have not met any and the consul knows of none.

Dresden is a very pleasant and very cheap place to live. But as we have made preparations for remaining here six months, various payments have had to be made in advance, and I have consequently run short of money. I therefore take advantage of your kind offer made some time ago, and ask you to be good enough to send me 200 rix-dollars [about $100]. Now, please do not be alarmed and, remembering the handsome amounts which I have already drawn on you this summer, jump to the conclusion that I have become a *Verschwender* here in Germany. The case is rather the reverse. I have been so fortunate this year as to be able to save my Norwegian pension, and I am unwilling to draw any of it from the Christiania Credit Office, in which it is deposited.

I thank you very much for sending a copy of the fifth printing of *Brand*, and I hope the sale will be brisk. What I have written regarding the title of my new play is strictly between ourselves. Of course, it is no secret that I am engaged on a new work. . . .

The weather is raw and stormy, but good when regarded as working weather; and we are comfortably situated in every respect. I go a great deal to the theater. It is one of the best in Germany, but in matters of taste and art it ranks far, far below Copenhagen's. The same applies to German theaters generally. . . .*

---

* H. C. Andersen expressed the same opinion of German theaters in 1842 in his book of travel sketches, *En Digters Bazar* (*A Poet's Bazaar*, Boston, n.d., pp. 332–4.)

To Frederik Hegel

Dresden, December 22, 1868

. . . Georg Brandes' *Aesthetic Studies* has been an absolute gold mine to me, especially in regard to the study of the comic spirit. Brandes has a remarkable talent for seeing clearly and deeply and for thinking logically and consistently, and I might add that, if it were possible, his ability to make thoughts clear to the reader and, above all, to express ideas so that they stay in one's memory is even greater. . . .

To Frederik Hegel

Dresden, March 14, 1869

. . . Brandes is indeed quite harsh in his criticism of [Bjørnson's] *The Newly Married Couple,* but I certainly cannot say that he is unfair.

Cannot Bjørnson's Danish friends persuade him to leave Norway? He will ruin himself if he stays there any longer. The fact that he stirs up hatred and anger against himself is not so terrible; but his enemies take advantage of the great number of opportunities offered to make him look ridiculous, and this is what is really bad. Now and then I think of writing to him, but I am afraid it would not do much good.

A German, Mr. Siebold, writes to me that he has translated *Brand* and is arranging for its publication here. Do you know him? I must confess that I have no confidence in the undertaking. However, I do desire to have my works circulated in Germany. It ought to be from Leipzig, I imagine. To whom should I apply there? Of course, this is not a matter of immediate importance. . . .

To Frederik Hegel

Dresden, April 7, 1869

. . . I shall write you later about a possible German translation of my work. I have never expected to make any money from it.

That is a terrible story about Clemens Petersen! What is behind it all? And where has he disappeared to? I have always harbored strong suspicions about his character, but that something like this—! . . .*

Bjørnson's becoming editor of *For Ide og Virkelighed* [*For Idea and Reality*] is another stupid act on his part. I don't understand how he can want to occupy the seat that is still warm from his predecessor. . . .

To P. F. Siebold

Dresden, May 9, 1869

Siebold was a German traveling salesman and a student of Scandinavian literature. He had translated *Brand* but was having difficulty finding a publisher.

Dear Mr. Siebold, I have to ask your pardon for a great deal. First, I must ask you to pardon the state in which I return your manuscript; in destroying some of my useless rough drafts I unfortunately happened to tear your preface in two and only discovered afterward what had happened. My delay in answering your greatly esteemed letters is due to the fact that I have been waiting for answers to certain inquiries I have had made in Leipzig. According to information that I have now received, Dr. Helms is no longer connected with the Scandinavian bookstore there. Literary friends have advised me to handle the matter in the following way. You are connected with the Leipzig *Illustrierte Zeitung;* if it were possible for you to get a biography of me printed there, I could furnish the necessary portrait. Councilor Hegel would furnish you with the

* The Danish critic Petersen departed hastily for America in March, 1869. He had been accused of molesting small girls.

needed material. Such a biography ought only to contain favorable matter; the German critics will surely find enough that is objectionable later on. I should particularly like you to mention, in case you think it helpful, what I had to struggle against in the early days, and that you would also emphasize the fact that the Cabinet and Storting, acknowledging the position I hold in Norwegian literature, several years ago unanimously granted me a pension for life, besides providing ample traveling stipends, etc. My dear Mr. Siebold, you must not understand me as wishing this in any way to partake of humbug; that is against my nature. But people assure me those things are necessary. If my name were in that way introduced into Germany, it would be far easier to get your translation published. If you would later on send it to me I would take it to Leipzig, have the translation reviewed in some of the periodicals, talk with those concerned, and not give up until the book is published. The preface might then be made considerably shorter by referring to the biography. If you favor this plan, write to me. Henceforth I shall have time at my disposal and will do everything possible to advance an enterprise that is so much to my own interest. I have a belief that *The Pretenders* might also be suitable for translation, and could be performed in German theaters. The subject of the play is remarkably well suited to later German conditions: the unification of parts of the country under one head, etc. And were I first known there, I have no doubt but that I could induce the present theater manager of Leipzig, Heinrich Laube, to make a beginning. These last plans, however, are for the future. At present I await your answer regarding the biography, and hope that you will have the same pleasant memories of me as I shall always continue to have of you.

Respectfully yours,

Henrik Ibsen

To Lorentz Dietrichson

Dresden, May 28, 1869

Dietrichson and Ibsen had met in Rome in 1864 (see letter to Bjørnson, September 16, 1864), and except for one serious quarrel in 1885, they remained good friends for life.

Hey, Carissimo! I hope that in spite of your professor-ship and all other dignities I may be allowed to use our old Roman salutation.

So you are a professor now! Dear friend, accept my most sincere congratulations. I take it for granted that it is not simply an honorary title but that a considerable income goes along with it. And your also being Curator of the National Museum must mean that you are comfortably settled in Stockholm for a long time to come. Please give me all the details.

There were two reasons for my not answering your kind letter of last autumn. The first was that I had second thoughts in regard to *The Pretenders*; the second, simply that I am a perfect wretch when it comes to writing letters. During the winter I wrote a new dramatic work, a comedy in five acts entitled *The League of Youth,* which is now in the press, and which I wanted to offer to the theater before *The Pretenders.* I shall send it to you in about a month, trusting that you will do the best you can for it.

I don't suppose I was mistaken in recognizing your friendly pen in Swedish reviews of *Brand* and *Peer Gynt.* For them, as well as for much else, I hope to be able to thank you personally in the not too distant future.

I have a special reason for doing my bounden duty in writing to you today. I wish to draw on our friendship for a favor.

Let me explain. A German literary man, P. F. Siebold of Cassel, has translated *Brand* and the book is to be published at Leipzig in the autumn. But he, or his publisher, or both of them, think that the public ought to be pre-pared for it. They therefore intend as soon as possible to publish my portrait in a German magazine, most likely the *Illustrierte Zeitung,* along with a short biography contain-ing information as to my position in Scandinavian litera-ture, my personal circumstances, etc. They have applied to me for such information. But I do not care to give it myself, and Herr Siebold is of course not sufficiently ac-quainted with the facts of the case. You can understand that the matter is one of considerable interest to me. Therefore I turn to you as my old friend. String some facts together that will suit the Germans, and write as favorably as your conscience will permit. Forget about the sufferings of the starving poet—no one is interested in that nowadays. Say rather that I have received grants from the government and the Storting; that I am traveling; that I am presently living *in dem grossen Vaterland*," etc.

I hope I am not asking too much of you. Will you help me? If you do write, write briefly and concisely, and send your article either to me or to: Herr P. F. Siebold in Cassel. That is all the address necessary. He will translate it into German. I know no one better fitted than you whom I could ask; otherwise I would not trouble you. Write me whatever you decide. From the eighth of June my address will be: Königsbrückerstrasse, No. 33, 1 Etage.

It would take too much time to give you an account of my travels since we last saw each other. I am living a comfortable and carefree life, and expect to tackle *Julian* in the autumn. Please remember us very kindly to Mrs. Dietrichson and your little daughter. I plan on going to Stockholm next year; but more of this another time. . . .

When is the next volume of your history of Norwegian literature to appear? I cannot sufficiently thank you for the volume already in print. It has given us great pleasure; and I may honestly say that it is the only book, except Holberg's *Comedies*, which I never tire of reading. My wife knows it almost by heart. With this, dear friend, I shall take leave of you for today. I know that you will do your best to help me in the above-mentioned matter. Remember me to all our mutual friends.

Yours sincerely,
Henrik Ibsen

To Lorentz Dietrichson

Dresden, June 19, 1869

Carissimo! My warmest thanks for your kind letter, and also, in advance, for your biographical labors.

I enclose the requested portrait of my ugly visage. I wonder if you, who knew me in my bearded period, will recognize me. They tell me that it is a good likeness, and I am inclined to think so.

I hope that you have by this time received a copy of *The League of Youth*. I place it entirely in your hands to do with as best you can. I cannot expect to receive pay-

ment for it; fortunately that is not what is most important
to me.

As you will see, the play is a simple comedy and nothing more. In Norway they will perhaps say that I have
portrayed actual persons and conditions. However, that is
not so. I have, of course, used models, which are just as
necessary for the writer of comedies as for the painter and
sculptor.

It seems to me that what the play says fits Sweden too—
that is to say, the Sweden of real life. Whether it fits the
stage in that country is something you will have to decide.
At any rate, it is easy to put on, requires no expensive set,
requires nothing in fact but a payment to the translator—
so, dear old friend, do your utmost to have it produced.

If you succeed, I shall probably pay a visit to Stockholm; but more of that in good time. Let me hear from
you as soon as possible. Give me your opinion of the play.
It will not be published until autumn.

A hearty greeting from us to you all! Good-by for now.
People who have as much to tell each other as we have
cannot write long letters; it must all wait until we meet.

> Your devoted friend,
> Henrik Ibsen . . .

To Georg Brandes

Dresden, June 26, 1869

Perhaps more than anyone else in Scandinavia, Brandes represented the break with the old school of literature and philosophy; and the battle lines between the two generations
of critics and writers were laid down according to the posi-
tions adopted by Brandes. Apart from some pieces in the
newspapers, Brandes' first salvo was fired in the autumn of
1866 in an essay *Dualism in Our Latest Philosophy*, in which
he supported positivism against the religious orthodoxy of
Rasmus Nielsen, who sought to save the Christian faith by
relegating science and theology to separate compartments.
The David-and-Goliath spectacle of a twenty-four-year-old
enfant terrible taking on the dean of Danish philosophers and
accusing him of being a dangerous reactionary, whose attempts to hold up progress would be in vain, stirred up a
controversy that attracted attention throughout Scandinavia.

Among others, Bjørnson, whose religious crisis still lay ten years in the future, entered the lists with an unsigned article in *Fædrelandet* indignantly protesting against Brandes' attack on orthodoxy.

As is apparent from his letters of April 25, 1866, and October 21, 1867, Ibsen followed the dispute very closely. In December, 1867, Bjørnson pleaded with Ibsen to stop being "difficult" and to align himself with Rasmus Nielsen. Ibsen's letters to Brandes from 1869 on make it clear that the playwright was drawn to the critic, not only because of Brandes' critical acumen and intellectual courage, but because both had made the same enemies. The fact that Brandes had reviewed *Brand* favorably as soon as it appeared, and that in 1867 he had written a long essay for the *Dansk Maanedskrift* —reprinted in Brandes' *Aesthetic Studies*—which was the first to call attention to Ibsen's potential greatness, could only strengthen Ibsen's attachment to him. Although he was fourteen years Ibsen's junior, the playwright listened to him as he listened to no other critic. Both Clemens Petersen and Georg Brandes disapproved of *Peer Gynt* on formal grounds, but whereas Ibsen was furious with the former (see letter to Bjørnson, December 9, 1867), he was patient and persuasive with the latter. For the first time in his life, Ibsen, whose writings before 1866 reveal a heartaching sense of isolation, had found a true comrade in arms.

Dear Mr. Brandes, It has been a great relief to receive your friendly words, for I had good reason to fear that you thought me very ungrateful—not writing you so much as a word after you had done more than anyone else to throw light on my work. But indeed I am not ungrateful. For most assuredly the important thing is not to be blindly admired but to be understood.

The reason I did not write was that my answer grew in my mind into a whole article on aesthetics. And when I found that I had to begin it by answering the question, What is poetry?, you must admit that the letter threatened to become rather lengthy, and that the subject might better be discussed in a personal conversation.

Brand has been misconstrued, at least as far as my intention was concerned (to which you may reply that the critic is not concerned with the artist's intention). The misunderstanding has evidently arisen from the fact that Brand is a priest and that the problem is presented as a religious problem. But both these circumstances are quite unimportant. I could just as easily have constructed the same syllogism about a sculptor or a politician as about a priest. I could have found an equally satisfactory expression for the feelings that impelled me to create if, instead of Brand, I had written of Galileo, say (making him of course hold his ground and not admit that the earth stands still). Indeed, who knows—had I been born a hundred years later I might with equal enthusiasm have written about you and your battle with Rasmus Nielsen's philosophy of compromise. On the whole there is a great deal more disguised objectivity in *Brand* than anyone has so far perceived; and of this, qua poet, I am quite proud.

In my new comedy [*The League of Youth*] you will find I have stayed on the level of ordinary, everyday life—no strong emotions, no deep feelings, and, above all, no thoughts isolated from the main subject. Your just condemnation of the unmotivated and unprepared-for "remarks by the author" in *The Pretenders* has had its effect. Your article—and here I am going to express the warmest thanks I can possibly give you—has been to me what Mons Wingaard's Chronicles were to Jacob von Thyboe: "I have read it sixteen times and sixteen times more, and hope to make use of it in sundry wars" [Holberg's *Jacob von Thyboe, or The Braggart Soldier*, Act II, scene 1].

I am very anxious to hear what you have to say about my new work. It is written in prose, which gives it a strong realistic coloring. I have paid particular attention to form, and among other things I have accomplished the feat of doing without a single monologue, in fact without a single "aside." All this of course proves nothing, and therefore I earnestly beseech you, if you have a free moment, to do me the kindness of reading it and of letting me hear your verdict. Whatever you think, you will do me a real favor here in my loneliness by expressing your opinion. The book will not be published until autumn, and that is a long time to wait. . . .

I regret on my own account that in all probability we shall not meet during your intended tour. But I am heartily glad for you, since it means that you are going to the South. It is an inexpressibly happy experience to go there for the first time.

Accept my hearty thanks for your letter, and for everything else.

Yours most sincerely,
Henrik Ibsen . . .

To Georg Brandes

Dresden, July 15, 1869

Bjørnson, who had been very hostile toward Brandes at first, now desired a rapprochement and invited Brandes to accompany him on a trip to Nordland during which they might discuss possible collaborative efforts. Brandes categorically rejected the invitation.

Dear Mr. Brandes, What you tell me about Bjørnson does not surprise me. There exist only two kinds of people for him: those he can take advantage of and those who might be an embarrassment to him. Moreover, B.'s cleverness as a psychologist when dealing with his own fictional characters is only equaled by his inability to figure out real people.

I am beginning to suspect that perhaps I ought not to have asked you to read my new comedy. Thinking it over, I see that what really interests you in literature are the tragedies and comedies that take place in the inner life of the individual, and that you care little or nothing about actually existing outward conditions—political or any other. If that is the case, you may ask in regard to my play: "What's Hecuba to me?" But this time I did not wish to convey anything but what the work contains, and it must be judged accordingly. Moreover, you yourself are not entirely without responsibility in this matter, since you in a sense steered me in this direction by a remark made in your aesthetic studies. More about this when I get a chance to speak to you.

You are wrong in thinking that I said you do not like strong emotions or deep feelings. I said nothing of the kind. I was only trying to warn you against expecting what you would not find.

I cannot agree with you regarding the parts of *Peer Gynt* referred to. Of course I bow before the laws of beauty; but I have no regard for its conventions. You mention Michelangelo. In my opinion no one has sinned more against the established conventions of beauty than he. Nevertheless, everything which he has created is beautiful because it is full of character. Raphael's art has never really moved me. His people belong to a period before the fall of man. Besides, the Latin's aesthetic principles are quite different from ours: he wants absolute formal beauty, while to us conventional ugliness may be beautiful by virtue of its inherent truth. But there is no use in quarreling in pen and ink—we must meet.

I must stick to what I said about *Brand.* You surely cannot blame me because the book may have given pietism some support. You might just as well reproach Luther with having introduced philistinism into the world. It was certainly not his intention to do so, and he must be held blameless.

But no matter how we disagree, I thank you for your letter; and I thank you a thousand times for your friendship. It is a great blessing to have found a man of genuine and undivided character.

On Thursday I leave for Stockholm* while my family remains here. When I rejoin them in the autumn, I shall probably travel by way of Copenhagen, so as to talk with you—not only about literary matters, on which we disagree, but also about more human problems, on which I believe we are in much closer agreement.

Yours most sincerely,
Henrik Ibsen . . .

To Hedvig Stousland

Stockholm, September 26, 1869

Hedvig Stousland, Ibsen's sister, belonged to a strict religious sect.

Dear Hedvig, Months have passed since I received your kind letter—and only now do I answer it. But there is so much that stands between us, and between me and my old home. Please understand me and do not think it is indifference which has kept me silent all these long years,

* Ibsen had been invited to the Nordic orthographic conference. While there, he received the Vasa Order from Charles XV.

and even this summer [Ibsen's mother died on June 3]. I cannot write letters; I must be near a person and give myself wholly and entirely. But you, on the other hand, you can write. Do so! Write often! I will answer with at least a loving greeting, with a message I trust will not grieve you.

I look into myself; there is where I fight my battles, now conquering, now suffering defeat. But I cannot write about all this in a letter. Make no attempts at converting me. I will be honest; what is to come, will come.

So our dear old mother is dead. Thank you for having so lovingly carried out by yourself the duties which the rest of us should have shared. You are certainly the best one!

I travel a great deal about the world. Who knows but that I may come to Norway next summer. Then I shall see the old home to which I still cling with so many roots. Give Father my love; explain to him about me—what you understand so well; perhaps he does not.

I have been here in Stockholm since the middle of July. Now I am going by way of Dresden and Paris to Egypt, where, as you now have possibly learned from the newspapers, I am to be a guest of the Khedive. By the middle of December I expect to be back in Dresden, where my wife is and where my little boy goes to school. I have only the one boy.

Enclosed I send you my photograph. If you have any of yourself and your family, send them to us in return. I wish you knew my wife; she is the perfect wife for me. She asks to be remembered to you. Our address in Dresden is Königsbrückerstrasse, No. 33.

This letter is short, and I have avoided what you perhaps wished most that I should write about. It cannot be otherwise at present. But do not think that I lack that warmth of heart which is the first requisite for a true and thriving spiritual life. . . .

To Frederik Hegel

Dresden, December 14, 1869

The League of Youth was published on September 30, 1869, in a printing of 2,000 copies; a second printing appeared on

November 4. When it was staged in Christiania in October, supporters of the Liberal Party interrupted the performance with whistles and catcalls, and a month later Bjørnson, one of the leaders of the party, expressed in a poem in honor of the liberal politician Johan Sverdrup his indignation at the comedy, which he described as an attempted "assassination in the grove of the Muses."

. . . I am very happy with the reception given *The League of Youth*. I was prepared for the opposition to it, and I would have been disapointed if it had not arisen. But what I was not prepared for was that Bjørnson, from what I have heard, should feel that he personally was attacked in the play. Does he really feel this way? He must certainly see that not he but his corrupt and "lie-ridden" political clique served as my models. Anyway, I shall write to him today or tomorrow, and I hope that the affair, in spite of all our differences, will end in a reconciliation. That a second printing has already been published goes beyond anything I expected. Now I am only anxious to see how the play will go in Copenhagen. . . .

To Rudolf Schmidt

Dresden, December 27, 1869

Rudolf Schmidt was one of the editors of a new magazine, *For Ide og Virkelighed* (*For Idea and Reality*), for which Rasmus Nielsen, Clemens Petersen, and Bjørnson were contributing editors and sponsors. The magazine was little more than an organ for promoting the dualistic philosophy of Nielsen and his numerous followers. (See notes to letter to Brandes, June 26, 1869.) When asked to contribute to the magazine, Ibsen replied negatively in a letter of January 26, 1869: "I cannot bring myself to collaborate with men of whom I have the impression, based on experience, that at the first opportunity they will use their newspapers and pens against me. . . . I find Bjørnstjerne Bjørnson named as probable co-editor. . . . This in itself would be decisive for me, even if other motives were not abundantly present."

Dear Mr. Schmidt: If, as you say, you have written two letters which I have not answered, then it can only be that those letters dealt with your editorial affairs, and on that subject, which does not concern me in the slightest, I have nothing to say.

It is a matter of indifference to me whether you, my dear sir, interpret Mr. Lie's scribblings from "a social-political point of view" or not. I have found two other points of view in them: affectation and hack journalism.

That Mr. Bjørnson's bad conscience makes him regard as his enemy the man whom he has infamously slandered in the presence of a number of people, while at the same time, perhaps on the very same day, he has written him a long letter filled with ingratiating declarations of friendship—all of which can be documented and corroborated by witnesses—I find quite natural.

And when I consider that gang of cheap and common people Bjørnson has unfortunately got himself involved with—if such people were to put a foot in my house, I would have to air out the place—it seems every bit as natural that he should consider me just as base as that man who sets the tone for the behavior of the whole crowd.

But it does not follow that I feel any obligation to utter a protest and to expose whatever such people may have cooked up.

However, should I feel the need to take such a step, I can assure you that my desire to keep myself out of bad company would force me to choose a publication that does not list Mr. Lie among its collaborators. The fact that he has been hailed at Tromsø as an epic writer does not raise him the slightest in my estimation.

Respectfully,
Henrik Ibsen

Jonas Lie became a close friend of Bjørnson's when they were both students at Christiania. Lie practiced law for a number of years, but when he lost his entire fortune in 1868, he tried to support himself and his family by writing political pieces for various papers. He also turned to writing fiction, and in 1869 Bjørnson in a speech at Tromsø declared Lie would be a great author, a prediction which Lie was to fulfill during the following years.

To Jonas Collin

Dresden, January 4, 1870

. . . From what I hear, my new comedy is causing a disturbance at home. They are considering it from the political, instead of from the artistic, point of view. From the attacks on it that have caught my eye, it would appear that phrasemongering, insincerity, and scoundrelism are regarded as national characteristics that must not be meddled with. But all of this does not bother me in the slightest. . . .

To Frederik Hegel

Dresden, January 25, 1870

. . . Mr. R. Schmidt has written to me again, this time asking me to insert in his magazine a public protest against an alleged rumor that I meant Stensgaard [in *The League of Youth*] as a portrait of Bjørnson. However, I sent him such an emphatic answer that I hope I shall be spared any future correspondence with him. . . .

To J. P. Andresen

Dresden, February 10, 1870

Andresen was chairman of the board of governors of the Christiania Theater. Dissatisfaction within the ranks of the theater had been brewing since 1868 when a Dane instead of a Norwegian had been appointed head of the theater in charge of productions (as distinct from purely administrative duties). In January, 1870, the board of governors asked Ibsen if he were interested in taking over the office. But Bjørnson considered himself the most likely candidate, and knowing that he had the support of several of the best actors at the theater, he hoped that the management would feel compelled not only to offer him the position as head of the theater but entrust him with unusually wide powers. The fact that Bjørnson was one of the leading spokesmen of the rising

Liberal Party gave a political cast to the struggle for power within the theater.

Dear Mr. Andresen: I was pleased in more ways than one to receive your kind letter of the twenty-fourth of last month. First of all, I want to thank you for being the first, as far as I know, who has clearly and lucidly expressed my own view of *The League of Youth*. Just as you say, the political matter in the play, as far as one can say there is any, has not been the essential thing to me. I simply needed an intrigue in which the characters could develop, and the most obvious thing was to make use of circumstances and situations that might be said to be typical, at least to a degree, of our communal life. If I have hurt certain individuals, I did so inadvertently; and it would have been a much more serious criticism of the play if one could have said that the characters and the situations in it did not correspond to reality as we know it. As I see it, comedy nowadays must be strongly realistic. At any rate, the writer of comedies must, like any other artist, use models. But there is a big difference between the model and the portrait.

I hope all this will become clear to the public after things have stopped fermenting. But right now things are in an uproar and will probably remain so for some time. And that is exactly why I have strong doubts as to the advisability of my accepting your very flattering offer of a position with the theater. I am regarded by a certain loudmouthed individual as what I least am and least wish to be—a party man. I am hardly mistaken when I foresee that my taking a position with the theater will be looked upon as equivalent to throwing down the gauntlet, which certainly will not remain lying on the ground. An institute devoted to art needs a peaceful atmosphere in order to work effectively, and especially in our straitened circumstances it needs the support of the entire public. A split within the ranks might be stimulating for a while, but it will not be good in the long run. All this you know, of course, better than I do, far from it all as I am; and if I go into all this, it is only to advise you as to the nature of my reservations. May I ask you a direct question? Do you consider Bjørnson as impossible for the post of director of the theater; and is it inconceivable that there might be a reconciliation between him and the present administration? As the sole artistic adviser, Bjørnson is not the most desirable man; but if all the practical details remained in the hands of more skillful and sober-minded persons, he could perhaps fulfill his duties. There is another thing I would very much like to know: how do the theater staff and the actors feel toward Bjørnson? And further: is there any evidence that these two groups wish to see me occupy a position with the theater? I have been involved in theater matters before, and I don't flatter myself that I had the support I needed.

I would have to be clear about all this before I could give any definite answer. And even if the situation seemed quite favorable, I still might have to turn down the offer. Would it therefore not be advisable to look for someone else in the meantime, or else to let things go on as at present for another season? I plan to visit Christiania this summer, and perhaps then we could talk about the matter in more detail. . . .

To Georg Brandes

Dresden, March 6, 1870

Brandes had received his doctoral degree from the University of Copenhagen on February 25 for his dissertation *Contemporary French Aesthetics,* and planned to go on a trip to Italy in the spring.

Dear Mr. Brandes, The reason why I have not got around to your friendly note until today is (along with the fact that it was belated—probably because of ice conditions in the Belt [between Sjælland and Fyn in Denmark]) that I have been asking myself for several days now whether I ought not go to Copenhagen right away.

Upon due consideration, however, I have decided that it would be foolish, since I shall have to go there in the summer anyway. Besides, I suspect that you are so busy preparing for your journey that you have no time for anything else.

I have had no opportunity of seeing the Danish papers

recently. But by now you are certainly Doctor Brandes, aren't you? Accept my heartiest congratulations.

You say that you have no friends at home. That is what I have supposed for a long time. Anyone who stands in a close personal relationship to his lifework, as you do, cannot reasonably expect to keep his "friends." But I believe that it is good for you to go abroad without leaving any friends at home. Friends are an expensive luxury; and when a man's whole capital is invested in a calling and a mission in life, he simply cannot afford to keep them. The expense of keeping friends does not lie in what one does for them, but in what one refrains from doing out of consideration for them. The result is that one's intellectual and spiritual development is stunted. I know this from personal experience, and there are, consequently, many years in my life during which it was not possible for me to be myself.

Enough of that for the present. I often think of you. I have conceived a picture of you as you are now and as you will be in the future. For, little as I know you personally, you are closely associated with what moves my spirit, what it lives on, and makes poetry of.

There are many other things I want to say to you, but they must wait. Thank you for your review of *The League of Youth,* and thank you for your letter! I hope you will thoroughly enjoy all the loveliness that awaits you. Write to me from the land of sunshine.

Dear friend, you must believe me when I tell you this: I do not require the kind of unanimity upon which the preservation of friendship usually depends.

Yours most sincerely,
Henrik Ibsen

To Frederik Hegel

Dresden, May 5, 1870

. . . My reservations about dedicating the book [the second edition of *The Pretenders*] to Bjørnson do not stem from his attitude toward me, although that is anything but friendly. But the fact of the matter is that his behavior as a publicist threatens to do a lot of damage in Norway, and consequently there has been building up against him, especially among the book-buying public, such a strong opposition that a dedication to him at the present time would be a simply inexcusable gesture on my part toward you as publisher. Actually, I would like nothing better than a reconciliation, and it would please me very much if you could find the opportunity to tell him that the rumor he believes and is helping to spread, namely, that I am seeking to take over the position of artistic director at the Christiania Theater, is completely false. The position has been offered to me, but I have taken advantage of the opportunity to work on his behalf, with Mr. Brun remaining as stage director, which I think is most advantageous in all respects. . . .

To J. P. Andresen

Dresden, May 12, 1870

In February several of the leading actors at the Christiania Theater resigned in protest against the failure of the board of governors to appoint Bjørnson as head of the theater.

Dear Mr. Andresen: You can well imagine the interest with which I have been following the events at the theater, and I am therefore especially grateful to you for the survey of the situation that you were so kind as to give me in your letter.

As far as I can judge from a distance, I think the theater is to be congratulated on the present rebellion. The number of those who have resigned is not sufficient to stop work at the theater, and yet large enough to convince the public that they, the public, will be the ones to suffer as long as the agitation continues. If the ill will that is provoked can be made use of in all possible ways, a great deal will be gained.

It is apparent that the rebels have risked their careers only in the certain hope that the management would soon have to give in to their terms. If this hope is defeated, the ranks of the rebels will soon be split. They cannot hope to withstand a long siege, nor is that troupe so constituted that they can form their own repertory company. On the basis of my knowledge of the persons involved, I would say that Isachsen will be the first to creep to the cross, with Gundersen following. But as a precaution against such uprisings in the future, one should make it as hot as possible for them. If at the present moment I had any influence on the affairs of the theater, I would, for the sake of emphasis, urge the staff of the theater to present to the board of governors a statement suggesting that only a part of those who have resigned be allowed to return, and only then on condition that they accept a significantly lower salary and lose their share in the retirement fund that had accumulated up to the time of their return to the ranks. In any case, I can tell you that if I were to take a position with the theater, I would have to be certain that such disturbances would not occur again. It is very likely that if I accepted a position there, the rebels might return, either because they saw in me "a transition to Bjørnson" or because they would expect my sympathies to lie with them, sympathies I no longer share. But if they were disappointed in me for one or both of these reasons, the theater would have to go through the same turmoil next year. These people must be taught that it is easier to resign than to return, and there is no better time to besiege them than the long salary-less summer months.

I quite agree with you that a compromise with Bjørnson is impossible in the present circumstances; nor do I believe that Bjørnson under any circumstances whatsoever should be given absolute authority over the artistic aspects of the theater. He lacks, to a striking degree, any thorough knowledge of literature, and for that reason alone, he will never be able to build up a repertory with purpose and principle behind it. Nor will the stage design and the rehearsal methods gain anything from his employment. But nevertheless he will be able to exert a stimulating influence on the personnel, and, generally speaking, his very presence would be a great advantage to the theater.

Because of a combination of circumstances I left this letter unfinished, and in the meantime the theater problem has been fundamentally changed, due to a tragic event. Yesterday I received the news of Krohn's death.* Presumably that will break up the Bjørnson plot, and the

* By suicide. Georg Krohn, who excelled in character roles, was one of the actors who had resigned.

board of governors will be free to lay down any conditions they please. I hope that advantage will be taken of the opportunity to safeguard the future of the theater.

Because of the changed situation I will keep to myself the thought with which I had intended to end this letter. Of course, I do not regard the negotiations involving me as having in any way committed the theater. If a decent settlement can be arranged that will bring in Bjørnson as reader or chief of the literary staff while Mr. Brun remains on as stage director and stage manager, I should be very pleased.

Only, in that case I would suggest that Bjørnson be sworn to a binding agreement by which he would not be allowed to proscribe me or other Norwegian authors from the repertory. If the board of governors is unwilling to include such a paragraph in the coming peace treaty, would you please inform me in order that I may justifiably direct my proposal to the staff of the theater? I am very eager to know what the immediate future will bring, and I hope for the best. With all my best wishes, to you, I am
                                        Sincerely yours,
                                        Henrik Ibsen

In the autumn the actors who had resigned established a new theater company under Bjørnson's leadership. Isachsen did not return to the Christiania Theater until the fall of 1871. A union of the two companies was effected in 1872.

To Magdalene Thoresen

Dresden, May 29, 1870

Dear Mother-in-law, I do not know what the critics have had to say [about her new play]. If they have been finding fault, then to the devil with them! When reduced to its essentials, most critical faultfinding simply amounts to reproaching the author with being himself—with thinking, feeling, seeing, and creating as himself instead of seeing and creating in the way the critic would have done —if he had been able. The important thing is to fence in what is one's own—to keep it free and clear of everything outside that has no connection with it. And, furthermore, to be extremely careful in discriminating between what one has observed and what one has lived through because only the latter can be the basis of creative work. If one is strict about this, no everyday, commonplace subject is too prosaic to be sublimated into poetry. . . .

I see that we two are completely at variance in our views of the theater question, which doesn't surprise me. I am entirely on the side of the management as opposed to the rebels. I cannot share this sentimental sympathy with all kinds of disloyalty. The management of a theater cannot adopt the point of view of the Bible, according to which the lost sheep is everything and the rest of the flock nothing. Carrying such theories into practice would result in nothing but chaos and wrangling and confusion, as in the days when Lamartine tried to govern France. I myself have been manager of a theater; I know that in ninety-nine cases out of a hundred the actors are indisputably in the wrong, and the management is right. *Vae victis!* they said in ancient times, and the same should be said today. It would be acting most unpardonably toward the institution not to put a check on the spirit of rebellion on such an occasion as the present. An actor stands in a different position from other artists. He is not independent, he is part of a complicated machine in the working of which he is bound by law to take part, and if he has chosen to be an actor he must bear the responsibilities that go with the position. I am not being hardhearted but simply relying on sound experience. . . .

To Laura Petersen Kieler

Dresden, June 11, 1870

Laura Petersen Kieler was author of *Brand's Daughters,* a sequel to *Brand*.

Dear Miss Laura Petersen, Please accept my sincere thanks for the compliment you have paid me by dedicating your book to me. But if I were to express an opinion on the work itself, I would find myself in a difficulty of sorts. You want the book regarded as a religious work, and I am no judge of that kind of literature. What appealed to me and interested me in reading it is the description of character—in combination with your unmis-

takable imaginative gift. Of course I have no idea whether
you regard that as a compliment.

I have the impression that you would probably be
horrified by the idea that you had written "a novel." In
that case, we two do not understand each other: *Brand*
is an artistic work, pure and simple, and not a bit of
anything else. What it may have destroyed or built up is a
matter of absolute indifference to me. It came into existence as the result of something that I had lived through,
not simply observed. It was necessary for me to free myself from something within me that I had done with by
giving it poetic form, and when I had got rid of it, my
poem no longer held any interest for me.

It is not clear to me how you regard this kind of secular
work. I am certain that you have the natural qualifications
to write in this secular domain; but I must remind you
that it is impossible to combine two things that have no
connection with each other. And perhaps you have not
yet clearly understood what art and poetry really are. In
the meantime, do try to believe that they are not basically
evil!

What continued to occupy my mind long after reading
Brand's Daughters was the personality of its authoress—
your inner, psychological relation to your book. It is possible that if one got to the root of this, one would find after
all that the book, despite your protest, came into being as
a poem, an artistic creation, or whatever bad name is
usually given to such a production. Everything that is in
the book, simply for the sake of your religious purpose
could be removed without injuring the organism as a
whole.

Do you intend to pursue the career of an author? For
that something more than talent is required. One must
have something to create from, some life experience. The
author who does not have that does not create; he only
writes books. Now I know very well that a life in solitude
is not a life devoid of experiences. But the human being
is in the spiritual sense a long-sighted creature. We see
most clearly at a distance; details confuse us; we must get
away from what we desire to judge; summer is best
described on a winter day.

I have a thousand things to say; but in a letter one can
only hint at them. It is always risky to give advice; and,

moreover, you have not asked for it. The important thing is to be honest and truthful in dealing with oneself. It is not a question of deciding to do this, that, or the other thing, but of deciding to do what one *must* do because one is oneself. All the rest simply leads to lies.

I intend to visit Norway sooner or later, and perhaps then I shall have an opportunity of seeing you, as my tour will also include the north. You must not believe that I am so unkindly disposed toward my countrymen as many accuse me of being. But, however that may be, I can at least assure you that I am not kinder to myself than to others. With best wishes, I am,

Yours respectfully,
Henrik Ibsen

To Anton Klubien, Danish lawyer

Copenhagen, September 9, 1870

. . . When the play *Salomon de Caus* by my countryman A. Munch was performed in Denmark, he was honored with the Order of Dannebrog; [J. S.] Welhaven received the same honor although he had published only one volume of poetry here in Denmark. In the time of distress I fought with my pen on Denmark's side just as courageously as Welhaven. In the course of six years I have published in Denmark: *Brand* in five printings; a new edition of *Love's Comedy*; *Peer Gynt* in two printings; *The League of Youth* in two printings; and in a few weeks a new Danish edition of *The Pretenders*, which was accepted by the theater on miserable terms, will appear. Don't misunderstand me. Do not suppose I am saying that Denmark is in debt to me. Far from it. If I were a native-born Danish author, it would not mean so much. But when I see how my Norwegian colleagues have been honored in a manner that makes an extraordinary impression on Norwegian public opinion, then it seems to me that justice should be done me. The fact that it has not been done is not due to any ulterior motive; I know of nothing I have done to deserve that. Practically every foreign music virtuoso who has performed here in recent years has been honored with the Order of Dannebrog. And I might as well confess that I am simply greedy for any recognition that Denmark might bestow on me. You cannot imagine what an impression such things make in Norway. But from your experience as a diplomat in Paris, you must know as well as I that one has to drop a hint. And that is exactly *what I am doing now.* You know certain officials who, I believe, are well disposed toward me. Attend to the matter. A recognition of merit from Denmark would provide powerful support for my position in Norway. I know I need not remind you of the necessity for diplomatic discretion. . . .

If I had *Social Ambition* at hand, I could list an enormous number of arguments in addition, but since you know your Holberg by heart, it won't be necessary. . . .

To Peter Hansen

Dresden, October 28, 1870

Hansen had requested biographical details from Ibsen for an anthology of Norwegian poets.

My dear Friend, I had the best of intentions that Sunday afternoon when I received and read your letter. "Within three days he shall have my answer," I told myself—and now nearly three weeks have passed. One thing has been gained by my delay, however. Haste now compels me to be briefer than I at first intended. I believe this is better for you, as it leaves you a freer hand.

Since we parted, I have often regretted that we did not manage to talk over these matters. Writing is so much less convenient. But never mind.

Biographical data that misrepresents me the least can be found in a biography written by P. Botten-Hansen in *Illustreret Nyhedsblad* for 1862, if I remember rightly [July 1863, actually].

But it is really the story of my intellectual development that you want. Well, here it is.

Everything that I have created as a poet has had its origin in a frame of mind and a situation in my life. I never wrote because I had, as they say, "found a good subject."

Now I shall make confession in chronological order.

Catiline was written in a little provincial Philistine town, where it was impossible for me to express all that was fermenting in me, except by playing crazy, riotous pranks that brought down upon me the ill will of all the respectable citizens, who could not enter into the world where I fought my battle alone.

Lady Inger of Østraat is the result of a love affair*— hastily entered into and violently broken off—to which several smaller poems may also be attributed, such as "Markblomster og potteplanter" ["Field Flowers and Potted Plants"], "Fuglevise" ["Bird Song"], etc., which were printed in *Nyhedsblad* (and to which, by the way, I call your attention.) †

The Vikings at Helgeland I wrote while I was engaged to be married. For Hjørdis I used the same model as later for Svanhild in *Love's Comedy*.

Not until I was married did I take life more seriously. The first fruit of this change was a rather long poem, "Paa Vidderne" ["On the Heights"]. The desire for freedom which pervades this poem did not, however, receive its full expression until I wrote *Love's Comedy*.

This work gave rise to a lot of gossip in Norway. People mixed up my personal affairs in the discussion, and my reputation suffered considerably. The only person at that time who approved of the book was my wife. She is a woman of great character, exactly the person I need— illogical, but with a strong poetic instinct, a broad and liberal mind, and an almost violent hatred of all petty considerations. All this my countrymen did not understand, and I did not choose to make them my father-confessors. So they excommunicated me. Everybody was against me.

Exactly at the time when *The Pretenders* appeared, Frederick VII [of Denmark] died, and the [Danish-Prussian] war began. I wrote a poem, "En broder i nød" ["A Brother in Need"]. It had no effect against the Norwegian Americanism that had driven me back at every point. That's when I went into exile!

About the time of my arrival in Copenhagen, the Danes

---

* In 1853 Ibsen had fallen in love with Rikke Holst, only fifteen and a half years old. Her father sent Ibsen packing.—Editor.

† *The Feast at Solhaug* is a study which I have disowned, but it too had its origin in a personal experience.—Ibsen's note.

were defeated at Dybbøl. In Berlin I saw Kaiser Wilhelm's triumphal entry with trophies and war booty. During those days *Brand* began to grow within me like an embryo. When I arrived in Italy, the work of unification there had already been completed by means of a spirit of self-sacrifice that knew no bounds, while in Norway—! Add to this: Rome with its perfect peace and calm, my association with carefree artists, an existence which in its atmosphere can only be compared with Shakespeare's *As You Like It*—and you have the conditions productive of *Brand*. It is a great mistake to suppose that I have depicted the life and career of Søren Kierkegaard. (I have read very little of S. K., and understood even less.) That Brand is a clergyman is really immaterial. The demand of "All or Nothing" is made in all domains of life—in love, in art, etc. Brand is myself in my best moments—and it is equally true that by analyzing myself I brought to light many of both Peer Gynt's and Stensgaard's characteristics.

While I was writing *Brand* I had on my desk a glass with a scorpion in it. Now and then the little creature became ill. Then I would give it a piece of soft fruit. It would attack it furiously and empty its poison into it—after which it was well again.

Does not something of the same kind happen with us poets? The laws of nature also apply to the inner world of our spirit.

After *Brand* came *Peer Gynt*, as though of itself. It was written in southern Italy, on the island of Ischia and at Sorrento.* Being so far away from one's future readers makes one reckless. This poem contains much that is reminiscent of my own youth. For Aase my own mother— with necessary exaggerations—served as model (as she also did for Inga in *The Pretenders*).

Environment has a great influence upon the forms in which the imagination creates. Cannot I, like Christoff in [Holberg's] *Jacob von Tyboe*, point at *Brand* and *Peer Gynt*, and say, "See, the effects of wine"? And is there not something in *The League of Youth* which reminds one of *Knackwurst und Bier*? I do not mean to degrade the latter. I only mean that my point of view has changed

---

* It appears, however, from some extant notes, that the play was at least outlined while Ibsen was still in Rome. (See also letter of January 5, 1867.)

because I am living in a community that is well ordered to the point of boredom. What on earth will happen when I resettle at home! I shall have to find salvation in remoteness of subject. That is when I intend to begin *Emperor Julian*.

I prefer to leave the choice of the poems to you, since I have the greatest confidence in your judgment in this matter as in many others. Most of the small pieces in question are to be found in *Illustreret Nyhedsblad* for the years 1858–64.

Now I have provided you with the required skeleton. It is up to you to put flesh on it and breathe life into it. Use these notes in any way you please. Regard them as a simple musical theme on which you may freely extemporize. I am sure that you will make the best of it. Use whatever instruments you fancy. I know "this fellow plays them *all* well." . . .

To Johan Herman Thoresen

Dresden, November 21, 1870

Dear Brother-in-law, . . . The political sky is now beginning to look threatening in the East also. Where is it all going to end? The feeling here is very pessimistic. Even the surrender of Metz did not arouse the slightest enthusiasm. According to official reports, Dresden has fifteen thousand prisoners to provide for; and the arrival of four thousand more has been announced. Two thousand sick and wounded lie in the hospitals. Great barracks have been built quite near our house for the Imperial Guard, and we see them pass every day, taking the walk prescribed for their health. They show no signs of having suffered any hardships at Metz. They are dressed as if for parade. The sick and wounded Saxons ordered home look as if they had gone through much more. The Frenchmen are very well treated, and bear their captivity with incredible indifference. It strikes me that many of them are happy to have got out of their difficulties so easily. In the alehouses it is the noncommissioned officers who lay down the law, rail against the Kaiser, against the generals, against everything except themselves. The situation in France does not

seem to bother them. All this, however, is perfectly natural
in a revolutionary nation, lacking proper discipline and
order. We Norwegians ought to take a lesson from this;
for it is in the direction of exactly such internal disinte-
gration that fellows like Jaabaek, Johan Sverdrup, etc.
[leaders of the opposition Liberal Party in Norway] are
trying to draw our nation. . . .

To Ohan Demirgian

Dresden, November 23, 1870

Ohan Demirgian, Habib Bey, was Royal Equerry at the
Swedish court, an Armenian who had arrived at the Swedish
court along with the Barbary horses that the Khedive of
Egypt had given to the Swedish king. Demirgian had ar-
ranged that Ibsen be sent an invitation to the opening of the
Suez Canal in 1869.

Dear Mr. Demirgian, Equerry to the King of Sweden:
Having learned a few days ago of your return to Sweden,
I should like to take the liberty of sending you my warmest
and most respectful thanks for the invitation to Egypt,
which through your assistance I had the honor of receiving. . . .

My stay in Egypt was the most interesting and educational period in my life, and I shall never forget the service
you have rendered me; nor shall I ever forget the thanks
I owe to you.

But there is one point on which I need some enlightenment, and no one can give it to me except you.

The situation is this:

While I was in Cairo, I was shown a letter from you
informing me that, as Norway's representative at the opening of the Suez Canal, I should be among those to be
decorated by His Highness the Khedive. Furthermore, this
summer in Copenhagen I was shown several more recent
letters from you to the same person in which you state that
the conferring of the honor had already taken place and
that you would bring the decoration with you to Sweden.

This honor is highly flattering to me, and *it would also
be of the greatest possible advantage in establishing my*

literary position in Norway. It would also help make up for the disregard I have suffered in my country when the Order of St. Olaf was given to several artists, painters, composers, and musicians while I was ignored—in spite of the fact that I loyally stand by the government and support it with my pen and all my abilities.

Since I saw your written word, I did not hesitate to mention the honor to my friends, and you can see how I have now been placed in an embarrassing position, which can only be relieved by your fulfilling your promise, or else by the granting of an equivalent honor. . . .

I have no doubt that in one way or another you will show me the good will of arranging matters so that I will receive some satisfaction. . . .

To Georg Brandes

Dresden, December 20, 1870

Brandes was lying ill with typhoid fever in Rome, which had been conquered by the Italian army in September, 1870, after the withdrawal of the French troops in the Franco-Prussian War. After a plebiscite on October 2, Rome was annexed to Italy.

Dear Georg Brandes, You have been in my thoughts every day lately. I heard of your illness both from Councilor Hegel and from the Norwegian papers, but I did not write to you since I was afraid that you might still be too weak to receive letters. Your kind note received yesterday has, however, quite reassured me. Many thanks for thinking of me!

You ask what you ought to undertake in the future. I can tell you: in the immediate future you must undertake nothing at all. You must give your mind a holiday for an indefinite period. You must lie still and grow strong. You see, these illnesses bring a blessing with them—the condition in which one comes out of them! A glorious time awaits you when you begin to regain your strength. I know this from personal experience. All evil thoughts had left me; I felt like eating only the lightest and most delicate foods—anything coarse, I thought, would taint me. It is an indescribable state of thankfulness and well-being.

And when you have grown strong and fit again, then what will you do? Why, then you will do what you must do. A nature such as yours has no choice.

I am not going to write a long letter; that would not be good for you. And you had better not write to me for some time yet.

I was in Copenhagen last summer. You have many, many friends and adherents there; perhaps more than you realize. If you are away for a while, so much the better; one always gains something by being missed.

They have finally taken Rome away from us human beings and given it to the politicians. Where shall we take refuge now? Rome was the one sanctuary in Europe, the only place that enjoyed true freedom—freedom from the tyranny of political freedom. I do not think I shall visit it again after what has happened. All that was delightful —the unsophisticatedness, the dirt—all that will disappear. For every statesman who crops up there, an artist will be ruined. And the glorious longing for liberty—that is at an end now. Yes—I for one must confess that the only thing I love about liberty is the struggle for it; I care nothing for the possession of it.

One morning some time ago my new work [on Julian the Apostate] became strikingly clear to me; and in my exuberance I dashed off a letter to you. But I never sent it. The mood did not last long, and when it was over, the letter was useless.

Moreover, the historic events of today are claiming a large share of my thoughts. The old illusory France has been smashed to bits, and as soon as the new, *de facto* Prussia is also smashed too, we shall enter the age of the future in one leap. How the old ideas will come tumbling about our ears! And it is high time they did. Up till now we have been living on nothing but crumbs from the revolutionary table of last century, and I think we have been chewing on that stuff long enough. The old terms must be invested with new meaning, and given new explanations. Liberty, equality, and fraternity are no longer what they were in the days of the late-lamented guillotine. This is what the politicians will not understand; and that is why I hate them. They want only their own special revolutions—external revolutions, political revolutions, etc. But that is only dabbling. What is really needed is a revolution of the human spirit. And in this *you* shall be one of those who take the lead. But the first thing to do is to get that fever out of your system.

> Your devoted friend,
> Henrik Ibsen

To Anton Klubien

Dresden, February 13, 1871

Dear Klubien, I received an extremely beautiful document in the mail today, a paper from the Minister of Culture making me a Knight of Dannebrog. The decoration will be forwarded to me by the vice-chancellor in charge of royal decorations.

If only I could adequately thank all those who have aided me in this matter! If things go as I hope, I shall sing their praises at their respective diamond jubilees. But since that lies rather far in the future, I beg you to convey my thanks to them privately. As for your part in all this, I trust you understand how I feel.

But you must also inform me as to what I must do officially. . . . I am unfamiliar with Danish customs in these matters. Give me a few words of advice.

Again, my thanks. The honor bestowed on me is of great importance to me, greater than I can say. . . .

To Frederik Hegel

Dresden, February 16, 1871

. . . I shall never be able to thank sufficiently those men who helped me get this award. Now my countrymen will find my forthcoming volume of poems twice as good as otherwise. . . .

To Georg Brandes

Dresden, February 17, 1871

Brandes had replied to Ibsen's letter of December 20, 1870, with a fervent poem in which he resolved to fight in the spiritual revolution led by Ibsen.

Dear Brandes, I suspected that my long silence would make you angry. But I confidently trust that our relations are such that they will stand the strain. In fact, I have a decided feeling that a brisk correspondence would be much more dangerous to our friendship. Once we have actually met, many things will assume another aspect; much will be cleared up on both sides. Until then I really run the danger of exhibiting myself to you through my casual remarks in quite a wrong light. You philosophers can prove black is white—and I have no desire to allow myself to be reduced, per correspondence, to a stone or a cock—even if it is possible to restore me after an oral explanation to the rank of a human being [a reference to Holberg's *Erasmus Montanus*]. In your previous letter you ironically admire my undisturbed mental equilibrium under the present conditions. There we have the stone! And now in your last friendly(?) note, you make me out a hater of liberty. The cock! The fact is that my mind is relatively calm because I regard France's present misfortune as the greatest good fortune that could befall her. As to liberty, I take it that our disagreement is a disagreement about words. I shall never agree to making liberty synonymous with political liberty. What you call liberty, I call liberties; and what I call the struggle for liberty is nothing but the steady, vital growth and pursuit of the very conception of liberty. He who possesses liberty as something already achieved possesses it dead and soulless; for the essence of the idea of liberty is that it continue to develop steadily as men pursue it and make it part of their being. Anyone who stops in the middle of the struggle and says, "Now I have it," shows that he has lost it. It is exactly this tendency to stop dead when a certain given amount of liberty has been acquired that is characteristic of the political state—and it is this that I said was not good.

Of course it is a benefit to possess the right to vote, the right of self-taxation, etc. But who benefits? The citizen, not the individual. Now, there is absolutely no logical necessity for the individual to be a citizen. On the contrary—the state is the curse of the individual. How did Prussia purchase its strength as a state? By absorbing the spirit of the individual into a political and geographical conception. The waiter makes the best soldier. Now, turn to the Jewish nation, the nobility of the human race. How has it managed to preserve itself—in its isolation, in its poetry—despite all the barbarity of the outside world? Because it had no state to burden it. Had the Jewish people remained in Palestine, it would long since have been ruined in the process of construction, like all the other nations. The state must be abolished! In that revolution I will take part. Undermine the idea of the state; make willingness and spiritual kinship the only essentials for union—and you have the beginning of a liberty that is of some value. Changing one form of government for another is merely a matter of toying with various degrees of the same thing—a little more or a little less. Folly, all of it.

Yes, dear friend, the great thing is not to allow oneself to be frightened by the venerableness of institutions. The state has its roots in time: it will reach its height in time. Greater things than it will fall; all religion will fall. Neither standards of morality nor of art are eternal. What is there that we are really obliged to hold on to? Who will vouch for it that two and two do not make five up on Jupiter? °

I cannot and will not enlarge upon these points in a letter. My best thanks for your poem! It is not the last one you will write. The poet's calling proclaims itself in every line. You overestimate me, but I set that down to our friendship. But thank you, thank you! Keep me ever so in your thoughts. I shall not fail you!

Now get well and strong again. And come to Dresden on two sound legs! That leg business—did you not feel as if there were a nemesis in it? You were once so furious with another philosopher because he stood on *two* legs. Thank God that you did not have to demonstrate the possibility of a philosopher's being able to do with *one*. I take it for granted that all danger is past, otherwise I should most certainly not jest on the subject.

I have as yet received only the First Part of your *Criticisms and Portraits* from Hegel; but even if I had received the whole, I would have confined myself just to thanking you heartily for the book. I am an exceedingly poor critic. Concerning certain works I am unable to ex-

---

° The anonymous author of the story "A Barrister" had endeavored to show how two and two might make five on Jupiter.

press myself; and you already know my opinion of you
as a man of complete and undivided character.

I have been occupied almost night and day since Christmas preparing for the publication of my collected poems.
It has been an accursed business, having to go through
all the stages I had passed through long ago. However,
taken together, they do make something like a whole; and
I am very anxious to hear what you will say about the
book.

The thousand and one things in your letter which might
spur me to write some more, I shall leave untouched for
now. I must first find out if I may expect to see you here
soon. Then we shall discuss both "Bishop Arius and the
Seven Electors" [one of the stock subjects of Gert Westphaler in Holberg's *Gert Westphaler, or The Loquacious
Barber*]. You shall see that it is not for nothing I have
lived two years in the vicinity of Gert Westphaler's native
land.

Sincerest wishes for restored health and all that is good,
from

Yours most sincerely,
Henrik Ibsen

P.S. As soon as I come into possession of a fairly respectable photograph of myself, I will send it to you. Meanwhile accept the enclosed. I hope you will send one in
return.

To Frederik Hegel
Dresden, May 9, 1871

. . . P.S. I must tell you some news I just heard this
minute. All the Swedes and Norwegians who had been
invited by the viceroy of Egypt to the opening of the
Suez Canal have been decorated (with *Turkish* orders since
the viceroy has none of his own to award). As for myself,
I have been awarded the Star of a Commander of the
Medjidie Order, a magnificent trinket, which I received
today along with a huge, unreadable diploma from the
Grand Turk himself!! In Norway they thought I had received the invitation to Egypt because I laid a large part

of the action of *Peer Gynt* in the land of the Nile. If I had now been the only one to be decorated, they would probably have believed that my "Balloon Letter to a Swedish Lady" * had been translated into Egyptian! However, the true reason is that we delivered a great many Swedish and Norwegian decorations to Egyptian dignitaries, and they are now repaying the compliment. Our host the viceroy has in this way once again given evidence of his generosity, since he must have furnished the decorations himself and ordered only the diplomas from Constantinople.

Yours,
H. I.

To Georg Brandes

Dresden, May 18, 1871

After Paris capitulated to the Germans in January, the Radical Republicans and the Socialists, who refused to see Paris surrendered to the Germans, established the Commune in March. Just after the writing of this letter there occurred the events of the "Bloody Week" when the French national troops entered Paris and destroyed the Commune.

Dear Brandes, I hope that you received a greeting from me recently through our old consul; at all events, I sent you one. I heard with great pleasure from Copenhagen that you were out of danger long ago, and are now well again. As for the danger, I never really believed in it. The hero does not die in the first act, and the great World Dramatist needs you for a leading part in the *Haupt- und Staatsaktion*,† which is doubtlessly being prepared for performance before a most highly esteemed public.

Many thanks for the photograph! It has been a great help to me in trying to understand your character, or

* In this poem Ibsen makes use of his trip up the Nile as an occasion for assailing Bismarck's Prussia. It was written in Dresden in December, 1870, when Paris was besieged by the Germans and the Parisians were sending messages by balloon.

† A type of entertainment popular in Germany in the seventeenth and eighteenth centuries, consisting of a chronicle play, improvised farce, and spectacular effects. The chronicle play presented the extravagant and absurd adventures of an emperor or general over a period of many years.

rather to familiarize myself with it. No doubt it is clear enough from your works; but I always like to have a definite picture with which I can connect my thoughts. And therefore I shall not be satisfied until I have met you. I think it will then become apparent that we have more in common than a partiality for velvet coats.

During this rather long interval I could not induce myself to write to you. From your last letter I gathered that you were rather annoyed with me; and as my poems were then about to be published, I did not want to make any advances that might look like an attempt to conciliate you before you had read them. I know well enough that you cannot be corrupted, but tact bade me avoid any appearance of even having imagined such a thing to be possible. Dear friend, I know you will understand this.

I hope Hegel sent you the book of poems long ago. There are both new and old things in it, and much which I regard as of no great importance. Yet it is all part of the story of my development. Let me know your verdict; I attach the greatest importance to it.

And with what are you occuping yourself in beautiful, warm Italy? You will reap one benefit from your illness— a summer spent in Italy. I think of you every day. Now I picture you at Frascati, now at Albano or Ariccia. Am I right? And what new things are being prepared down there for our intellectual future? I am sure that something has ripened during your long illness. One of the blessings of such an illness is that it washes one clean and promotes the growth of so much which otherwise would lie buried and undeveloped. Only once have I been really ill; but for that very reason, perhaps, I have never been really well. *Chi lo sa!*

Is it not shameful of the Commune in Paris to have gone and spoiled my excellent state theory—or rather non-state theory? The idea is now ruined for a long time to come. I cannot even proclaim it in verse with any decency. But there is a sound core in it. I see that very clearly. And someday it will be put into practice, without any caricature.

I have often thought of something you once wrote. You said that I had not adopted the modern scientific point of view. What opportunity have I had of doing so? And yet, is not each generation born with the marks of its age?

Have you never noticed in a collection of portraits of some past century a curious family resemblance between persons of the same period? It is the same in spiritual matters. What we the profane do not possess through knowledge, we possess to a certain degree through intuition or instinct. Anyway, the poet's essential task is not to reflect but to *see*. For me in particular, there would be a danger in too much reflection.

Dear Brandes, it is always a relief to me to talk to you. And a great, great pleasure to hear you talk, even though only on paper. Let me hear you again soon.

Yours most sincerely,
Henrik Ibsen

To Frederik Hegel

Dresden, July 12, 1871

. . . And now the reason for my long silence: I am hard at work on *Emperor Julian*. This book will be my chief work, and it is taking up all my thoughts and all my time. That positive philosophy of life which the critics have demanded of me will finally be given to them. But now I have a great favor to ask of you. In the spring of 1866 Pastor Listov wrote an article on the life of Julian, which ran in three numbers of *Fædrelandet*. If you could lend these three numbers to me, you would be doing me a great service. And one more favor. Does there exist in Danish any other historical treatment of this subject, in which the *facts* are at all thoroughly entered into? If so, please buy it for me and send it at my expense. I have Neander's German work* on the subject. Also D. Strauss's†—but the latter contains only wild interpretations, and I can furnish those myself. Facts are what I need. Please do not be annoyed with me for troubling you with this matter! . . .

---

* August Neander, *Kaiser Julian und sein Zeitalter,* Berlin, 1812.
† David Strauss, *Der Romantiker auf dem Throne der Cäsaren, oder Julian der Abtrünnige,* first printed Mannheim, 1847.

To Georg Brandes

Dresden, September 24, 1871

In July, 1871, Brandes and Ibsen finally met in Dresden. When they greeted each other, Ibsen gave Brandes such a warm hug that Brandes could scarcely breathe; and when they parted, Ibsen said with a smile, "You stir up the Danes, and I'll stir up the Norwegians!"

Dear Brandes, I always read your letters with strangely mixed feelings. They are more like poems than letters. What you write strikes me like a cry of distress from one who has been left the sole survivor in some great lifeless desert. And I cannot but rejoice, and thank you, that you direct this cry to me. But on the other hand, I begin to worry. I ask myself: "What will such a mood lead to?" And I have nothing to comfort myself with but the hope that it is only temporary. You seem to me to be passing through the same crisis that I passed through when I began to write *Brand*. I am convinced that you, too, will find the medicine that will drive the disease out of your system.

Energetic productivity is an excellent remedy. What I recommend for you is a thoroughgoing, full-blooded egoism, which will force you for a time to regard yourself and your work as the only things of consequence in this world, and everything else as simply nonexistent. Now, don't take this as evidence of something brutal in my nature! There is no way in which you can benefit society more than by coining the metal you have in yourself. I have never really had a very great feeling for solidarity. In fact, I have allowed it in my mental cargo only because it is a traditional article of belief. If one had the courage to throw it overboard altogether, one would be getting rid of the ballast that weighs most heavily on the personality. There are actually moments when the whole history of the world reminds one of a sinking ship; the only thing to do is to save oneself.

Nothing will come from special reforms. The whole human race is on the wrong track. That is the trouble. Is there really anything tenable in the present situation—with its unattainable ideals, etc.? All of human history reminds me of a cobbler who doesn't stick to his last but goes on the stage to act. And we have made a fiasco in both the roles of hero and lover. The only part in which we have shown a little talent is that of the naive comic; and with our more highly developed self-consciousness we shall no longer be fitted even for that. I do not believe that things are better in other countries. The masses, both at home and abroad, have absolutely no understanding of higher things.

And so I should raise a banner, should I? My dear friend, I would be putting on the same kind of performance Louis Napoleon did when he landed at Boulogne with an eagle on his head.* Later, when the hour of his destiny struck, he didn't need any eagle. In the course of my work on Julian, I have become a fatalist in a way; yet this play will be a kind of banner. But do not worry—this will not be a tendentious work. I explore the characters, their conflicting plans, the plot, and do not concern myself with the moral of the whole—always assuming, however, that by the moral of the story you do not mean its philosophy. You can take it for granted that the philosophy will burst forth as the final verdict on the struggle and on the victory. But this is too abstract to make much sense. You must look at the work itself.

Your last letter on this subject did not cause me any uneasiness. In the first place, I was prepared for such misgivings on your part; and in the second, I am not handling the subject in the way you assume.

I have received your book [probably *Criticisms and Portraits*], and all I can say is that I return to it again and again. It is incomprehensible to me, my dear, good Brandes, that you of all people can be despondent. Very few have received the call of the spirit as clearly and unmistakably as you have. What is the use of despairing? Have you any right to do so? But don't think I don't understand you perfectly.

. . . And now in conclusion accept my heartfelt thanks

* In 1840 Louis Napoleon, seeking to end his exile and to assume the throne of France, made a foolish and theatrical descent on Boulogne. He was captured, tried, and imprisoned.

for your visit to Dresden. Those were festive hours for me. Best wishes for health, courage, happiness—everything good!

Yours sincerely,
Henrik Ibsen

To P. F. Siebold

Dresden, March 6, 1872

Siebold's translation of *Brand* was finally published in 1872. (See letter to Siebold, May 9, 1869.)

. . . I don't know if you are aware that I have been involved this winter in a pen-and-ink war with the periodical *Im neuen Reich,* which is published in Leipzig under the editorship of Dr. A. Dowe and Gustav Freytag. The occasion for this skirmish was some remarks I made in my poems about Prussian politics. The war has, however, been carried out in a very gentlemanly fashion. The explanation I offered for my stand has been found satisfactory, and the whole affair, which I at first found quite disagreeable, will, my literary friends assure me, only serve to advertise the translations of my works. You are mistaken in thinking that I do not recognize the greatness of a man like Bismarck. But I also see in him an absolute hindrance to good and friendly relations between Germany and Scandinavia. The present tension is unnatural between two so closely related peoples. A closer alliance must be found; the interest of both parties demands it. During my long stay in Germany I have in general changed my opinions about many things. But that is too broad a subject to treat in a letter. . . .

To Frederik Gjertsen

Dresden, March 21, 1872

Gjertsen was principal of a private school in Norway.

Dear Mr. Gjertsen, Some little time ago I was pleasantly surprised to receive directly from you, your translation of

Horace's *Ars Poetica.* The pleasure was a double one. I was delighted to receive tangible evidence of the fitness of our language when properly used to reproduce the substance and form of classic thought. And it gave me no less pleasure to learn that you had preserved a friendly remembrance of me all this time.

It is difficult to translate well. It is not simply a question of rendering the meaning, but also, to a certain extent, of remodeling the expression and the metaphors, of accommodating the outward form to the structure and requirements of the language into which one is translating. For instance, I am very much in doubt as to whether [Christian Knud Frederik] Molbech in his translation of the *Divina Commedia* has done wisely to use only feminine rhymes. If the Italian language had contained masculine rhymes, Dante would naturally have made use of them; and I do not see any sense when translating the work into Danish to burden the translation with a defect from which the Danish language does not suffer. It may be asserted, quite truthfully, that the soft terminal rhymes give a sort of Italian coloring to the Danish version. But this is of consequence only to the few who are acquainted with the original, or, at any rate, know Italian. I believe that a translator should employ the style which the original author would have used if he had written in the language of those who are to read him in translation.

From this point of view it seems to me that you have been extraordinarily successful; and a large measure of the success is due to the judgment you have shown in choosing the meter. The hexameter is unsuited to our Scandinavian languages. Both Meisling and Wilster have, in their otherwise meritorious translations, sufficiently proved this. The meaning is obscured by this foreign meter. The effect it produces on the language acts like a disturbing melody coming between the reader and the sense of what he is reading. The same seems to me to be the case with German poems written in hexameters in the original. In *Hermann und Dorothea,* both the characters and the situations have been conventionalized by the meter to a degree observable nowhere else in Goethe, and incompatible with the demand of our age for realistic representation.

I have often wondered why you have not attempted to translate Byron. Judging by the specimens which you published some time ago in *Nyhedsbladet*, it seems to me that you ought to be the very person to do it. A knowledge of the English language is very general among us, it is true; but chiefly in those classes where one cannot assume any particular interest in poetry. I have not read very much of Byron, but I have a feeling that his works translated into our language would be of great assistance in freeing our aesthetics from many moral prejudices—which would be a great gain. There is a great lack of freedom in our public opinion; the different spiritual spheres are confused with one another. What will not pass muster when tried by our conventional national standard of morality is at once condemned as not fulfilling the requirements of the aesthetic standard either. But a foreign authority carries weight. It is acknowledged here that German literature required Byron's assistance to enable it to reach its present standpoint; and I maintain that *we* need him to free us from ours.

. . . There is a little circle at home which I must always think of in connection with you. Some of its members I knew well, others less intimately. Please remember me to them all. I have not many friends; but I am quite ready to increase their number—it would be running no risk. There is no immediate danger of my having to surrender, out of regard for myself and my own peace of mind, what is my fundamental principle in every field and domain: that the minority is always in the right. Best wishes, and thank you for thinking of me.

Cordially yours,
Henrik Ibsen

To Edmund Gosse

Dresden, April 2, 1872

Gosse's first article on Ibsen—and the first on Ibsen in the English language—was a review of Ibsen's *Poems* in *The Spectator*, March 16, 1872.

Dear Sir, A few days ago I had the great pleasure of receiving your very flattering letter, together with your kind review in *The Spectator*.

My knowledge of the English language is unfortunately

not so thorough that I can venture to write in English. I hope you will forgive me for employing my native tongue to express my most sincere and grateful thanks for the favor which you have shown to my literary labors.

I could not wish a better or more laudatory introduction to a foreign nation than the one you have given me in your excellent review. Nor is there any nation to whose reading public I should feel it a greater honor to be made known than yours. If it can be done with your friendly and capable assistance, I shall be forever indebted to you.

Your esteemed letter does not make it quite clear to me, however, whether you yourself intend to translate my writings or whether you will confine yourself to drawing attention to them in England by means of reviews. If the former is the case, it would naturally be an honor and a pleasure to place my books at your disposal, as I feel certain that I could not place them in better hands. I would be particularly happy to hear your views on this subject.

I very much regret that circumstances do not permit my visiting Scandinavia this summer, and that I shall thereby miss a pleasant and much-desired opportunity of personally expressing my sincere gratitude for the important step that you have already taken toward realizing one of my fondest literary dreams. The English people are very closely related to us Scandinavians, and consequently it has pained me to think that language should form a barrier between my work and the whole of this great kindred world. So you can imagine what pleasure you gave me by holding out the prospect of demolishing this barrier.

Several editions of my works are being prepared here in Germany. A translation of *Brand* has appeared in Cassel; but I am not happy with it. Another translation of the same work is announced from Berlin. *The Pretenders* and *The League of Youth* have also been published in Berlin, in a splendid German rendering by Dr. Adolf Strodtmann, the excellent translator of Byron and Tennyson. At present Dr. Strodtmann is busy translating my minor poems.

Having my works presented to the English reading public is, however, the matter of chief importance to me; and the sooner it can be done, the more I shall be pleased. Should you think of honoring me with a letter on this subject, my direct address is, and will be at least until the end of June: Dippoldiswaldaerstrasse, No. 7, Dresden.

If you should happen to come to Dresden in the course of your summer tour, it would give me great pleasure to talk to you.

Allow me to express once again my sincere appreciation for the cordiality and sympathy which you have displayed toward me and the literature of my country generally.

Yours very respectfully and gratefully,
Henrik Ibsen

To Georg Brandes

Dresden, April 4, 1872

Upon his return to Denmark from Italy, Brandes applied for a position at the University of Copenhagen. His education and the brilliant articles he had already written made him the natural choice to succeed the aging Professor Carsten Hauch in the chair of aesthetics. To demonstrate his qualifications for the position, Brandes was asked to give a series of lectures on a subject agreeable to both him and the university. The subject turned out to be "Main Currents in Nineteenth-Century Literature," and the first lecture was delivered on November 3, 1871, a momentous date in Scandinavian culture.

Brandes was not unknown when he made his debut on the lecture platform. As we have seen, the young man with the Jewish background had won fame, notoriety, and a considerable number of enemies in his controversy with the established philosophers and theologians in Denmark. His radical position was more clearly defined, at least for himself, after his recovery from typhoid fever, when his moral principles began to undergo a great change. The lecture hall was filled to overflowing before Brandes began to speak, and about one third of the audience consisted of women, an extraordinarily high proportion at that time. But, after all, the twenty-nine-year-old Brandes had translated John Stuart Mill's *The Subjection of Women* and was rumored, correctly, to have been in love with an older married woman who was the mother of six children.

From the very first words of his opening lecture—unfortunately not translated into English, although all the rest of the lectures of "Main Currents" have been—it was apparent that Brandes had accepted Ibsen's invitation to join with him in

bringing about a revolution of the human spirit, with literature helping to lead the way. Pointing to the French writers,
Brandes said the only living literature was the literature that
submitted contemporary social problems to debate. He declared that Danish culture was forty years behind the times,
that it was mired in the swamp of reaction, that Danish literature was unique in its naïveté, that it concerned itself only
with dreams and not with life, and that the current of abstract
idealism was so strong that even a fundamentally revolutionary nature such as Ibsen's could not withstand it—witness
Brand.

Brandes had made his position only too clear; and a satiric
little piece he wrote in November, 1871, about a modern
Little Red Ridinghood, a freethinking girl who is gobbled up
by the opposition press, did not help to smooth troubled
waters. The newspaper *Fædrelandet* took this to heart and
attacked Brandes. From then on the regular columns of every
newspaper in Copenhagen were closed to Brandes, and to
reply to *Fædrelandet* he had to insert a paid advertisement
in another paper. When the first volume of his lectures was
published in February, 1872, every newspaper in Denmark
expressed its disapproval of Brandes and all that he stood for.
The second volume was not reviewed at all. When Professor
Hauch died in March, 1872, his strong recommendation of
Brandes was ignored, and Brandes was not given a position
at the university until thirty years later. To gather support
for his views Brandes had already formed a literary society
in February, 1872. But a few years later, tired and dis-
couraged, he left Copenhagen for Berlin where he quickly
won international fame. Like Ibsen, Brandes had to go into
exile to fulfill his purpose in life.

Dear Brandes, I have just this moment received your
letter.

I cannot believe the incredible things you write! I have
been picturing you as joyful and triumphant! But I am
certain that you have an army behind you. Remember that
the men you are leading into the fire are only recruits.
The first time, they will retreat; the second time, they
will hold their ground; and after that they will follow you
into the attack and to victory.

So the liberal press is closed to you! Naturally! I once
expressed my contempt for political liberty. You contradicted me at the time. Your story of "Little Red Ridinghood" shows that you are now more experienced. Dear

friend, the liberals are the worst enemies of freedom. Freedom of thought and spirit thrive best under absolutism. We saw this in France, later we saw it in Germany, and now we see it in Russia.

But I must turn to what has been continually in my thoughts and has even disturbed my sleep. I have read your lectures.

No more dangerous book could fall into the hands of a pregnant writer. It is one of those works that place a yawning gulf between yesterday and today. After I had been to Italy I could not understand how I had been able to exist before I had been there. In twenty years one will not be able to comprehend how a spiritual existence was possible at home before these lectures. I have no clear conception of what it was that Steffens° accomplished in his day; but I presume that he gave a new form to conventional aesthetics. Your book is not a history of literature in the old sense, nor is it a history of civilization. I will not go to the trouble of finding a descriptive title for it. It reminds me of the gold fields of California when they were first discovered. They either made millionaires of men or ruined them. Is the spiritual constitution in the North robust enough? I don't know; but it makes no difference. Whatever cannot sustain the new ideas must fall.

You say that every voice in the faculty of philosophy is against you. Dear Brandes, how else would you want it? Are you not fighting against the philosophy of the faculty? You cannot fight your war as a paid employee of the King. If they did not lock you out, it would show that they were not afraid of you.

As regards the agitation against you, the lies, calumnies, etc., I will give you a piece of advice which I know from personal experience to be the best possible. Be dignified! Dignity is the only weapon against such assaults. Look straight ahead. Never reply in the newspapers. If you must wrangle, do not direct your polemics against this or that particular attack. Never show that your antagonists have had any effect upon you. In short, behave as though you had no idea that you had any antagonists. How much strength do you suppose there is in these attacks? In the old days when I read an attack on myself in the morning,

° The lectures of Henrik Steffens in 1802 marked the beginning of the romantic movement in Denmark.

I thought, "I am ruined; my reputation will never survive this!" But it did survive, and now no one remembers what was written—even I myself have long ago forgotten it. Therefore do not demean yourself by bandying words with this, that, or the other person. Begin a new series of lectures—unperturbed, unmoved, with an irritating equanimity, and displaying a cheerful indifference to and contempt for whatever is collapsing to the right and left of you. Do you really believe that what is rotten to the core has any power of resistance?

What will be the outcome of this mortal combat between two epochs, I do not know. But anything is better than the existing state of affairs. I do not promise myself that any permanent improvement will result from the victory. All development hitherto has been nothing more than a stumbling from one mistake into another. But the struggle itself is good, wholesome, and invigorating. To me your revolt is a great, emancipating outbreak of genius. When the men of the old school raise the cry of blasphemy, they ought to bear in mind that they, too, are blasphemers; the Great One in question has surely had a purpose in creating you.

I hear you have organized a society. Do not rely implicitly upon everyone who joins you. With an adherent, everything depends upon the reasons for his adherence. Whether you may be strengthening your position or not, I cannot tell. To me it appears that the man who stands alone is the strongest. But then I am sitting here under cover, and you are standing there in the midst of the storm. That makes a big difference.

Good-by for now, dear Brandes! Give a friendly thought to me and mine when you can spare it from all that must henceforth be of supreme importance to you, because in spirit and in truth it is your own.

Excuse haste and incoherence!

Yours ever,
Henrik Ibsen

To Edmund Gosse

Dresden, April 30, 1872

Honored Sir, Will you forgive me for not answering your friendly letter sooner? I shall consider myself most fortunate if you decide to translate one or more of my books. But I shall, of course, be equally indebted to you if you continue to draw attention to my works by means of articles in the English papers. I presume this would contribute in no small degree to removing the difficulties of finding a publisher. There can be no question of beginning a translation without some assurance of a reasonable compensation for the time and trouble spent on it. I leave the matter in your hands with the greatest confidence, convinced that you will choose the surest and most advantageous way of attaining our aim.

Last week I wrote to my publisher in Copenhagen, requesting him to send you *Love's Comedy*, a play in three acts, along with the two books you asked for. *Love's Comedy* should really be regarded as a forerunner of *Brand*, for in it I have represented the contrast in the present state of society between the actual and the ideal in all that relates to love and marriage. The book aroused a storm of anger in Norway when it appeared—the reason for which you will find explained in my preface to the second edition, which is the one being sent to you. *Peer Gynt* is the antithesis of *Brand*. Many consider it my best book. I do not know how you will like it. It is wild and formless, written recklessly and without regard to consequences—as I dare to write only when far away from home. It was created during my stay on the island of Ischia and in Sorrento in the summer of 1867.* . . .

To Georg Brandes

Dresden, May 31, 1872

. . . It surprises me that you have not thought of giving lectures in Sweden. In certain respects the Swedes are a

* See footnote, p. 102.

stage behind the other two Scandinavian nations in development. But this only results in their being nearer than us to what is coming. We have gone ahead of them, but in the wrong direction. . . .

To Michael Birkeland

Dresden, June 30, 1872

. . . I am not at all surprised by the way in which the grants have been distributed. I originally applied for the Schäffer Bequest, but afterward asked that my application might also be considered in the distribution of the funds for enabling artists and scientists to travel abroad. You may rest assured that I do not feel my honor affected in the least. It is not in the power of the Norwegian Ecclesiastical Department to affect my honor in any way. But I cannot agree with you that the reason I have been left out is that I have already been so long abroad. One of my more fortunate fellow-applicants, Mr. Stenersen (a close relative of Minister Riddervold), has also lived abroad for a long time and has already had at least one grant. Mr. Jonas Lie has, in the course of a little over a year, received four different grants, amounting in all to 1,050 specie-dollars. The explanation is quite simple: Mr. Lie belongs to the party which must not be offended, and I to the party which one must not do anything for "in fear of stirring up trouble." I would take the greatest pleasure in writing publicly about the mean behavior of our government; but since I regard Minister Riddervold as a personal enemy, I must of course, as a matter of honor, refrain from doing so. . . .

To Georg Brandes

Berchtesgaden, Bavaria
July 23, 1872

Dear Brandes, When you know my reasons, you will not take my long silence amiss. For once I am really blameless.

The fact is I have been roaming about in Bohemia and other parts of Austria. We are settling down at last here in the Bavarian Tyrol, where I have taken quarters for four or five weeks. Here I received your letter.

Nothing you wrote in previous letters had suggested you were thinking of coming to Dresden this summer; otherwise you may be sure I should have arranged my plans differently. But the summer is long down here, and if you come in September, you will be certain to meet me, and I shall receive you with open arms.

Far from feeling alarmed at the idea of contributing to your periodical, I have already made a list of subjects on which I would like to express my views and which should suit your purposes—to be handled in the form of rhymed letters concerned with present-day politics. literature, etc. They would form my confession of faith, so to speak. They would be of no direct assistance to you and your cause, but, dear Brandes, it is the only way in which I can collaborate. I must confine myself to what is my own, to what obsesses my thoughts. My domain is not an extensive one, but within it I do my best. Now don't put that down to egotism!

I do not know as yet how soon I can begin these letters; that monster *Julian* still has such a grip on me that I cannot escape. But we can enter into further particulars later —best of all, when we meet. I do not shrink in the least from being regarded as a partisan. I do not really understand why I am considered as belonging to no party.

I have long thought that you would need an organ of your own, but it would never have occurred to me that you would need it, as you say you do, "to live by." Is it possible that Denmark has no vacant place for you? One cannot blame the old fogies for wanting to keep you out. But who is there that would dare to take the appointment when you have been passed over? Who could dare to take your place as the preferred candidate without sinking into the earth in shame at the comparison? I don't understand it.

I am glad to hear that your lectures are to be published in German. The extracts from them which have already been translated in *Über Land und Meer* have attracted much attention. I heard them discussed in the Literary Society of Dresden. Come to Germany! It is abroad that we Scandinavians must win our battles. A victory in Germany, and you will be king of the mountain at home.

Hoping to see you again soon, I am,

Yours sincerely,

Henrik Ibsen

To Frederik Hegel

Berchtesgaden, August 8, 1872

Dear Mr. Hegel, I do not remember if I told you in my last letter that I was to be off soon to the Tyrol? At all events, we are now here in this lovely district, where we spent the summer of 1868 on our way from Italy and where we intend to stay until the end of this month. . . .

I am glad to be able to tell you that I have finished the second part of the trilogy. Part One, *Julian and the Philosophers,* a play in three acts, will come to about one hundred printed pages. Part Two (of which I am now making a fair copy), *Julian's Apostasy,* a play in three acts, is about the same length. The third play, *Julian on the Imperial Throne,* will be in five acts. I have done so much in preparation for it that I shall be able to write it much faster than the others. What is already finished forms a complete work in itself and could well be published separately. But for the sake of the over-all impression, I think it advisable that the three plays should appear at the same time. If you think differently, I trust you will let me know. . . .

To Johan Herman Thoresen

Dresden, September 27, 1872

For the thousandth anniversary of Norway's existence as a united kingdom Ibsen wrote a poem that was read at the festival at Haugesund in July, not at the unveiling of the memorial statue but at the banquet afterward. At the festival in Christiania on the same day it was not read at all, but copies were distributed. Criticizing the "separatist spirit working under the flag of pettiness" and calling for "a free, united, and powerful North," the poem could scarcely please the party seeking for Norway's independence. Bjørnson and Søren Jaabaek were among the leaders of the democratic and separatist movement.

Dear Brother-in-law, . . . Our holiday in the Tyrol this summer was a particularly pleasant one in every respect. Since our return we have been unusually sociable, as so many Scandinavians have been in Dresden. Goldschmidt* and G. Brandes came expressly to see us. The motive of the majority of the Norwegians who call on us is, I suspect, curiosity. I cannot reckon on any genuine sympathy from my countrymen when I think of the inconsiderateness, typically Norwegian, with which I was treated last summer by the so-called Harald Committee.

They asked me to write a poem to be read at Hauge-sund. I wrote the poem. Then they omitted it from the festival program and sold it instead like a hawker's ballad, without considering it necessary to offer me the slightest explanation for their remarkable behavior. If they rejected the poem because reference is made in it to the separatists of our day, then all I can say is that the cause of order, culture, and progress is in the hands of men who are incapable of furthering it and insuring its victory. And I shall regard it as my first duty, in my capacity of state satirist, to represent this party in all its wretched weakness, with all its lack of courage and determination, and with its absurdly naive belief that a sulky, passive resistance can possibly accomplish anything at all in the face of a well-organized, reckless, antagonistic party. In short, I should consider that I was doing a public service if I could make all those concerned ashamed of themselves. I imagine that you do not entirely disagree with me. I take for granted that you will admit the present situation at home is not so much the result of any great ability in the leaders of the opposition as of any absolutely indefensible, cowardly, complaint, and compromising spirit in nearly all of those whose task it ought to be to defend the foundations of our society. The reluctance of individuals in the past to place themselves personally in the breach is our country's misfortune. They retreat foot by foot, they lose ground bit by

* Meir Aaron Goldschmidt (1819–87) had been editor of the satiric, antiroyalist weekly *Corsaren* from 1840 to 1846. He was now finding it difficult to come to terms with the new radicalism represented by Brandes.

bit. That is what has brought us to the position we are in now; and it would require a superhuman effort of self-denial to let such material for epigrams and comedies slip through one's fingers.

In the meantime, however, I am too busy with *Emperor Julian,* which will probably be finished about Christmas. Nor do I imagine there is any need for hurry in carrying out the above-mentioned plans. The conditions are hardly likely to improve very soon—if they did, that would be the best that could be wished for. I often wonder what we may expect from our new king. A determined and fearless man in his position could accomplish a great deal; but it seems doubtful that he possesses these qualifications. This much is certain, however: if he is to accomplish anything useful it will not be with the help of the present royal advisers. People who permit Jaabaek and Bjørnson to be at large deserve to be locked up themselves. . . .

To Edmund Gosse

Dresden, October 14, 1872

Dear Mr. Gosse, It has taken me a little time after our summer outing in the Tyrol to settle down in our new house here in Dresden. But I must no longer postpone what is always a pleasant duty to me, namely, to write to you, and especially to thank you heartily and sincerely for those fresh proofs of your interest in me which I received at different times during these last months.

At Berchtesgaden I had the pleasure of receiving your friendly letter of August 1, together with *The Spectator* [of July 20] containing your review of *Peer Gynt.* A better, clearer, and more sympathetic interpretation of my poem I could not possibly hope for. I only wish that the praise you give it were fully merited. The objections you have to the work are certainly well founded; I see some of the defects of the work myself now. In the long interval that has elapsed since I wrote it, I have got so far away from it that I am able to look upon it as the work of a stranger.

I have also to thank you for the copy of *The Academy* [of August 1] containing the review of *The Pretenders.* My remarks on your review of *Peer Gynt* are equally applicable to your criticism of *The Pretenders*. However, I must make one small scholarly correction: A. Munch's drama *Duke Skule* did not appear at the same time as *The Pretenders* [October, 1863] but a little later [1864]. And *The Pretenders* has all along enjoyed, both on the stage and with the reading public, a far greater measure of favor than *Duke Skule*. Of course, this is a matter of no importance.

Then I had the pleasure a few days ago of receiving your excellent article on Norwegian poetry in *Fraser's Magazine* [of October, 1872]. Just as you have laid me personally under a great obligation to you by the two reviews, you have now by this longer article placed the whole Norwegian people under a debt of gratitude to you. I am certain that the Scandinavian press will understand and publicly recognize this. Perhaps it has already done so.

I was glad to learn from your letter that you had enjoyed your stay in Copenhagen. I hope that your visit to Christiania has been an equally pleasant one, although it was not made at the most favorable season of the year. In the middle of the summer many people whose acquaintance it might have interested you to make are out of town. I hope, however, that you saw our mutual friend, Mr. Løkke. I regret very much that circumstances forbade my visiting home this summer, and thus deprived me of the much desired opportunity of making your personal acquaintance.

I work every day at *Julianus Apostata* and hope to have the whole work finished by the end of the year. As soon as the book is printed, I shall take the liberty of sending it to you. I hope that it may meet with your approval. It is a part of my own spiritual life that I am putting into this book. What I depict I have, under different conditions, lived through myself; and the historical subject I have chosen has a much closer connection with the movements of our own time than one might at first imagine. I regard such a connection as imperative in any modern poetical treatment of such a remote subject if it is to arouse any interest as a creative work.

Once again, assuring you of my sincere and hearty gratitude, I beg to remain,

Your devoted friend,
Henrik Ibsen

P.S. I have forgotten to thank you especially for your translation of the little poem in *Brand,* which seems to me most beautifully done.

To Hartvig Lassen

Dresden, October 24, 1872

Hartvig Lassen was the newly appointed artistic director of the Christiania Theater.

Dear Mr. Lassen: Ever since I had the pleasure of hearing that you have taken over the artistic direction of the Christiania Theater, I have been quietly waiting and hoping to receive a proposal from you to produce *Love's Comedy* for a Norwegian audience.

Contrary to expectation, however, such a proposal has not been forthcoming, and I am therefore compelled to take the initiative, which I now do by asking you to consider that I have officially submitted the play to your theater by this letter. . . .

The apprehensions I had at one time about the play being produced have long since vanished. There are many indications that convince me the public has by now had its eyes opened to the fact that the deeper meaning of this work is based upon an absolutely moral foundation. As for the general artistic structure of the play, I am now more than ever convinced that it is irreproachable, and in any case, I have not surpassed it in my other works. I rank *Love's Comedy* among my finest creative efforts.

It is therefore only natural that I should want to see this play produced at home, nor do I think that the public would be altogether dissatisfied if that were to happen. In fact, I think my position in Scandinavian literature gives me a certain right to make this friendly request, a request that would be quite unnecessary for an author in a similar position in any other country. . . .

To Hartvig Lassen

Dresden, November 14, 1872

Dear Hartvig Lassen: Thank you most sincerely for accepting so readily my suggestion that you produce *Love's Comedy.* Let me say I fully appreciate the doubts and misgivings that have hitherto kept you from staging it. But I think that the approach it demands from the actors will be fairly obvious to them from its very nature. If during rehearsal, this proves not to be true, I hope you will be so good as to help with hints and advice.

It is a shame that *Mr. Wolf cannot be counted on to play Guldstad,* but it cannot be helped. *Casting Mr. Brun in this role* seems to me *dubious for many reasons.* What the play requires above everything else is perfect memorization of the parts. Now, is Mr. Brun capable of learning a role properly by heart these days? Or can he be persuaded to subject himself to the necessary inconvenience? And even if there is nothing to be feared from that side, I doubt that he will be able to give the part the right tone. If he plays it in his comic manner, then Svanhild's decision—that most dangerous point in the play—might easily come to stand out too crudely. If he plays it with dignity, without comedy, then he is in unfamiliar territory. Would it be possible to *try Mr. Reimers?* Mr. R. is an intelligent man, and if he can play the part at all, I think he could do it in such a way that the leap from Falk to the businessman would not seem incredible; and this would be a great gain. . . .

Love's Comedy proved to be a popular success when it was performed a year later. From November 24, 1873, to Christmas it was played twelve times, and at that time eight performances of a play in the course of a year was the equivalent of at least a hundred performances on Broadway today. The six performances of the play in November brought in one third of the theater's total receipts for the month.

To Frederik Hegel

Dresden, February 6, 1873

Dear Mr. Hegel, I have the great pleasure of informing you that my long work is finished—and more to my satisfaction than any of my earlier works. The title of the book is *Emperor and Galilean, A World Drama in Two Parts.* Part One is *Caesar's Apostasy,* a play in five acts (170 pages); Part Two is *Emperor Julian,* a play in five acts (252 pages). Do not let the subtitle "World Drama" alarm you! It is a descriptive subtitle like "folk drama," "family drama," "national drama," etc., and is quite appropriate, since the play ranges from heaven to earth.

Owing to the manner in which my thoughts have developed during the process of composition, I shall be obliged to recopy the first play once more. However, it will be no longer than it is now; on the contrary, I hope to shorten it by about twenty pages, so that the whole will come to four hundred. (Each of my pages is equivalent to about one printed page.)

In a week from now I shall begin the recopying. Thereafter I shall send you an installment of forty-eight pages every week. This is at the rate of seven pages per day, which I ought to be able to accomplish. The second play could quite well go into the hands of the printers as it is; but if you are in no hurry to publish, I will, for the sake of certainty, copy it also.

This drama has been a Herculean labor—not the writing of it; that has been easy—but because of the trouble it has cost me to revivify in my own mind an age so remote and alien. I am very glad to see from the letter before your last one that there is the prospect of a good sale, for several years of my life have been given to this book. I venture to predict that both of us will derive satisfaction from it.

Please decide the time of publication yourself. The reason why I do not at once begin recopying is that I have had to consult a learned friend in Christiania as to the proper manner of writing certain Greek names. I found out only a few days ago that these have been corrupted in the Latin works from which I have drawn my facts.

My best thanks for the 150 thalers [$107] enclosed in your letter of the twenty-sixth of November. Also for the very valuable package of books received at Christmas.

It was a great and unexpected pleasure to learn that new printings of *Brand* [the sixth] and *Love's Comedy* [the third edition] are called for. The former may be issued unchanged. In the latter, I am correcting the orthography and a few details. I devote my evenings to this. During the summer I shall rewrite *Lady Inger of Østraat* completely; I shall make it one of my best books. If you can let me have a copy of it, I shall be very much obliged to you. *The Pretenders* does not require many alterations. I think that these two books may be issued to advantage in the wake of the big new work.

I have still another favor to ask. I have 49 rix-dollars [about $25] in the savings bank and in my account with you. Will you advance what is needed to make up 150 Prussian thalers, and send that sum to me? Since the Christiania Theater has postponed the production of *Love's Comedy*, I did not receive the money I planned on, and I am now financially embarrassed. Please do not be upset. I would not ask this favor if it were not a case of necessity. With kindest regards to you and your son.

Yours most sincerely,
Henrik Ibsen

To Edmund Gosse

Dresden, February 20, 1873

. . . When *Emperor and Galilean* is ready, it shall be sent to you at once. No one shall read it before you! I have adhered strictly to the historical facts. I have seen everything happen, as it were, before my own eyes; and I have represented it as I saw it. But nevertheless there is a great deal of self-analysis in the book.

It is very natural that I should send it first to you, for I value your criticism more than that of any of my other friends—and this because of the real, intimate, poetic understanding revealed in everything that you have been good enough to write about me.

How can I thank you enough for your last exhaustive

article! * I shall not attempt to do so. I will only say that it made me very happy. The translations from *Love's Comedy* and *Peer Gynt* are excellent. I do not know of anything in them that I would wish changed.

And I also thank you warmly for the photograph you sent me. I shall be happy to send you mine in return. At the present moment I do not possess one, but as soon as I have a morning hour to spare, I shall pay a visit to my photographer. There you have another reason why I have so long put off writing to you.

I should like to tell you more about my work, but time does not permit. I hope and trust, however, that the book will not in any way tend to alter the good opinion you are kind enough to entertain of me.

Begging you to continue, in spite of my remissness, to show me the same favor as heretofore, I remain,

Yours most sincerely,

Henrik Ibsen

To Ludvig Daae

Dresden, February 23, 1873

Ludvig Daae was the "learned friend" (mentioned in the letter to Hegel of February 6) to whom Ibsen applied for information about the spelling of certain Greek names. Daae and Ibsen had been members of the same intellectual circle in Christiania.

. . . The work that I am now bringing out will be my chief work. It is entitled *Emperor and Galilean*, and consists of: 1. *Caesar's Apostasy*, 2. *Emperor Julian*. Each of these is a long, five-act drama. The play deals with a struggle between two irreconcilable powers in the history of the world—a struggle that will always repeat itself, and because of this universality I call the book "a World-History Play." In the character of Julian, however, as in most of what I have written in my riper years, there is much more of what I have lived through in spirit than I care to acknowledge to the public. But at the same time the work is an entirely realistic work. I have seen the characters

* "Ibsen, the Norwegian Satirist," in *Fortnightly Review*, January, 1873.

before my eyes in the light of their age—and I hope that
my readers will do the same.

. . . I am writing this late at night, as my whole day
is taken up with copying. Best wishes! I shall never forget
your readiness to help me in this matter.

Devotedly,
Henrik Ibsen

To Adolf Strodtmann

Dresden, March 20, 1873

Adolf Strodtmann was one of Ibsen's German translators.
Bjørnson in 1872 had called for a reassessment of Norway's
attitude toward Germany, and Ibsen had replied in a poem
"Nordens Signaler" ("Signals in the North") invoking the
memory of the Danes who had died when the Germans had
invaded Schleswig and Holstein while the Norwegians and
Swedes stood idly by, and casting scorn on "weather-vane"
politics in Norway and the new "pan-Germanism." When
Strodtmann read the poem, he construed it as violently anti-
German.

. . . Not one word of the poem is aimed at the Germans but at the Scandinavians who could bring themselves
to give up what belongs to them without a struggle. . . .

Actually, I have not changed my attitude toward Germany, and I never will. Like most Norwegian Scandinavians, I am a pan-Germanist. I look upon Scandinavianism
only as a transitional phase leading to the confederation
of the whole Germanic race. If I knew that we would
eventually end with an isolated Scandinavian union, I
would not even dip my pen in ink to further the cause. . . .

To Georg Brandes

Dresden, April 30, 1873

Dear Brandes, You certainly have good cause to complain
of my negligence in letter writing. The excuse I have to
offer is that my pen has scarcely been out of my hand since
we last saw each other, except while I was eating and
sleeping.

My best thanks for the books. I have read [Victor Cherbuliez'] *Ladislaus Bolstki* [to which Brandes had written an introduction] with great interest, although I must say that the description you gave me of it made a deeper impression on me than the book itself. Now, as to Stuart Mill's pamphlet! * I do not know whether I ought to express my opinion on a subject in which I am not an expert. Yet, when I remember that there are authors who write on philosophy without knowing Hegel, or without any knowledge of German scholarship in general, many things seem to be permissible. I must candidly confess that I cannot in the least conceive of any advancement or any future in the movement represented by Mill. I cannot understand your taking the trouble to translate this work, the sagelike philistinism of which reminds me of Cicero and Seneca. I am convinced that in half the time it took you to translate it you could have written a book ten times better. I also believe that you do Mill a gross injustice when you doubt the truth of his assertion that he got all his ideas from his wife.

You once remarked in a conversation with me that German philosophy set itself the task of defining the meaning of things, whereas English philosophy concerned itself with showing the laws of things. This remark made me want to read the English philosophers, but it does not seem to me that Mill has in the least accomplished what, according to you, was his task. "Things" are surely not all kinds of improper and fortuitous occurrences. There may be a great deal of acumen displayed in such a work; but if that passes for science, then "the ethics of Christianity" is also a scientific work.

I don't wish to get any more deeply involved in this subject in a letter, but when we meet to talk again I think I shall be able to defend my view.

I am looking forward with great pleasure to your book on the German Romantic School [the second volume of *Main Currents in Nineteenth-Century Literature*]—and with no less pleasure to meeting you again. But where are we to meet? I cannot possibly go to Munich this summer. Can you not travel via Dresden? About the middle of June I go to Vienna to stay there until the end of July. If you

* *Utilitarianism*, which Brandes had translated in 1869.

can arrange your plans to fit in with this, please try to do so.

Our mutual friend Adolf Strodtmann is offended by my poem "Signals in the North." In the preface to his book he called it a *Hohngedicht* [poem of scorn] directed against Germany. I wrote to him on the subject; but as he chose to remark in his reply that he had not imagined I wished them to remain ignorant in Germany of what I wrote in the Danish papers, I have had nothing further to say to him. Of course I have nothing against their knowing in Germany what I write in Denmark. What I protest against is the false interpretation of what I write. The poem is full of scorn, true enough; but it is not directed against Germany. There is too much in our own countries deserving of my scorn and derision for me to go out of my way to cast scorn on the Germans. Enough for today on Strodtmann's book, but I shall have a good deal more to say about it when we meet.

Come soon! I look forward with joy to having you here, in spite of all our differences of opinion. At all events, let me hear from you. I promise you to be more punctual in answering, since I now have much more time at my disposal.

With kindest regards from my wife and myself,

Yours ever,

Henrik Ibsen

To Suzannah Ibsen

Vienna, June 25, 1873

In the summer of 1873, Ibsen served on one of the committees at the International Art Exhibit in Vienna, and this was one of the few occasions when he was away from his wife Suzannah and son Sigurd.

Dear Suzannah, As the time approaches when for three days in succession there will be continuous cooking and baking, and the coffee kettle will be bubbling on the hob from early morning on, I send you these lines with all my good wishes for your birthday.

I can for the moment only afford to send you the enclosed bank note, which I beg you to accept and which you can change into Prussian money immediately. Had your brother Thomas not been invisible these last days, I would have sent some little thing by him. But he went off without saying good-by. So you must be patient, dearest cattttt!

The work on the committee is now in full swing, and long letters are therefore out of the question. As I have been asked to sit on two committees, one for painting and one for sculpture, I have to attend two sets of meetings. The following is my daily routine: I get up at six o'clock and by eight o'clock I have finished my toilet, had breakfast, read the paper, and smoked my morning pipe. Then I proceed to the exhibition where the judges of the pictures sit from nine till twelve. After that I go to a restaurant nearby, where I eat an excellent meat course and drink a glass of tasty beer. At 2 P.M. the judges of sculpture meet and this lasts until four thirty or five o'clock. The meetings are not always confined to sitting about. At present, for instance, we walk through the extensive exhibition halls inspecting the works of art. Since my arrival in Vienna my afternoon nap has been out of the question, so you can imagine that I am tired out by the end of the meetings. So I go and sit down in one of the many beer gardens in the Prater and watch the carriages passing by, while I have my supper, which consists of cheese and bread and excellent beer. At nine o'clock I return home and go straight to bed; this life suits me splendidly. So far the members of the committee have not met at social functions. I hear this is to follow later.

Thank you for your letter and the ragamuffin for his. I have received a copy of *Lady Inger*. Dietrichson is expected. Every day I meet many excellent men. The officials at the exhibition are instructed to show us all the greatest respect.

Write again soon. To the dear young student [another of Ibsen's playful names for his son] I can only send my visiting card today.

I shall celebrate the day tomorrow with something specially tasty.

And now my very best wishes for your birthday.

                                                    Your devoted
                                                    Henrik Ibsen

To Frederik Hegel

Pillnitz, near Dresden
August 8, 1873

When Oscar II was crowned King of Sweden and Norway at
Trondhjem in July, 1873, Ibsen was made a Knight of the
Order St. Olaf for his "literary contributions."

Dear Mr. Hegel: Do not take it amiss that I have put
off acknowledging the receipt of your kind letter of the
fourteenth of last month, with the enclosed 75 thalers
[$54] until my return from Vienna. I must also thank you
for your kindness in sending me the beautiful ribbon of the
Order that I was awarded; I am certain that I could not
have got anything like it here. Being made a Knight of
St. Olaf at the time of the coronation was a great surprise
to me since I had not written anything for the occasion
nor been asked to write anything. This mark of recognition
from the King and the government would have been very
much more acceptable to me if Bjørnson had shared in
the honor. But as you know, he has made anything of the
kind impossible, at least for the present. . . .

To Georg Brandes

Dresden, September 8, 1873

Dear Brandes, It is exactly a year since we were going
about together here in Dresden, and now that I have
moved into my winter quarters again after a nomadic,
restless summer, I think every day of the time last year
when you brought life and variety into our solitude. As I
sat thinking of you today, I decided to write you a few
lines to find out at least where and how you are, for I am
ignorant on both these points. First of all, I must clear up
a misunderstanding, or whatever it ought to be called. In
July you were here with your brother and sister-in-law.
Your sister-in-law, accompanied by Mrs. Falsen, was kind
enough to call upon us. Afterward, according to Mrs.

Falsen, you expressed surprise that my wife "would not receive" you! My wife begs me to tell you that such a supposition on your part must be the result of misunderstanding. She expected both you and your brother, but you didn't come. I don't know what you may have been told. Anyway, the whole affair is clear enough to me. During the latter part of your previous visit to Dresden, it seems that there was also someone here anxiously on watch lest you should be too much with us, and we should have too much undisturbed, intimate intercourse. You are rather free-spoken, dear Brandes, and it really looks as if someone dreaded this propensity of yours—I shall refrain from saying why.

I tell you all this because I want you to know that you have been misled, and because in us you have real friends, not mere acquaintances who are warm or cold according to circumstances.

I spent a couple of months in Vienna this summer as a member of the Art Jury. Afterward I was for some weeks in the country here in Saxony. Neither in Vienna nor in the country did I have time to keep up with our newspapers, and my correspondence with Denmark and Norway was purely on matters of business. So I have no idea what you are doing or where you are. Tell me, first of all, if anything is to come of your plans for a lengthy stay in Germany. There are no end of things I want to discuss with you, but a thorough discussion is possible only if we talk together. It seems to me that there are many signs of something new about to break on the horizon. Or how else do you explain the craze for pilgrimages in Renan's France? However, I shall not write anything more about this and other matters, lest I be misunderstood.

I expect my new book to arrive any day now. I am very anxious to know your opinion of it. I hear from Norway that Bjørnson, though he cannot know anything about the book, has spoken of it as "atheistic," adding that it was inevitable that I should come to that position. What the book is or is not I have no desire to investigate. I only know that I saw a fragment of the history of humanity plainly before my eyes, and that I tried to reproduce what I saw.

I hope that this letter will reach you, wherever you are.

If it does, please let me hear from you soon, unless you are going to give me the still greater pleasure of coming to see me. . . .

The "new book" was *Emperor and Galilean,* which was published on October 16, 1873 in a first printing of 4,000 copies, twice as large as the first printing of Ibsen's previous play, *The League of Youth.* As we can see from his letters, Ibsen had been working for years on a play about Emperor Julian, the first idea for such a play having come to him as early as 1864. Ibsen generally regarded *Emperor and Galilean* as his most important work.

To Georg Brandes

Dresden, October 16, 1873

Dear Brandes, In your last letter you express surprise at my not having written a single word about the second volume of your lectures [*The Romantic School in Germany*], which you were kind enough to send me this summer. I was as surprised as you when I was told I had not written about it. I was completely under the impression that I had written, and at great length, shortly before my departure for Vienna. Obviously, I must have forgotten to do it after all, and I entreat you to forgive my carelessness.

You seem to be in some doubt as to what impression the book made on me. Dear Brandes, if I had not been absolutely certain that you did not mean this seriously, I would have answered by return post. I felt quite sure you would understand that the second volume has made the same impression on me as the first. You know very well that I regard your work as epoch-making in our view of life, and I feel certain that this will be generally acknowledged at home, even though a few years must pass before that happens. You say that the papers in Denmark have killed the book with silence; but other Danes tell quite a different story. It may be true that the papers have kept silent, but it is not true that they have succeeded in killing the book. I can quite well understand that the second volume has not aroused the same storm of controversy as the first. The spirit of the work is not as rebellious. But this fact, if it is a fact, is no indication of the impression the book has made. There is no need for an outsider to tell you all this; you are a sufficiently able critic to know it yourself. To be quite honest, I have not felt that there was any necessity to address words of comfort to you. I can well understand your becoming despondent at times, surrounded as you are at home by all kinds of petty narrow-mindedness. But I also know that there are great, beautiful moments that come stealing on you when you see with joyful certainty what is right and what is bound to come.

Briefly, this is all I have to say to you. I do not feel I should offer any criticism. Criticism lies outside my sphere, and mine would be valueless to you. You have in me a pleased and grateful reader; that is all.

Proceed confidently with your work! I think the time is propitious for it. When we look back upon the history of Scandinavian development, it becomes apparent that we do not march forward in step with the other European nations. Every now and then they steal a march on us and catch us by surprise. One of these surprises is in store for us soon. Then everyone at home will see your book in the right light—and insist that they did so from the first. The reaction will be instantaneous. The book will be accepted at once. It will not be placed on probation.

By the time you receive this letter, *Emperor and Galilean* will probably be in your hands. The trend of affairs in Europe is making this work more timely than I myself had thought possible.

May I ask you to thank your brother [Edvard Brandes] for planning to call on me in Vienna. I am very sorry that I did not meet him. It would be a great pleasure to see you or him here in Dresden.

Best wishes, from

Your devoted friend,
Henrik Ibsen

To Edmund Gosse

Dresden, January 15, 1874

Dear Mr. Gosse, You must think it very ungrateful of me to keep silent for so long after receiving the splendid gift you sent me toward the end of last year. But I beg you to believe that you have been in my thoughts every day. I have not written sooner because I wanted to read your book first [Gosse's book of poems, *On Viol and Flute*]— and not merely read it through, but study it and assimilate its contents and spirit as completely as possible. This has taken time, for I have but an imperfect knowledge of the English language, which I have taught myself without anyone's help.

Allow me to congratulate you on your book, which will surely win a place of honor for you among the lyric poets of our day. Only in the work of a select few of those now writing do I find anything resembling the refinement and beauty which distinguish these poems. And it seems to me that these are qualities that ought to be specially appreciated by the English, whose characteristic practical ability is united with pure and noble sentiments and a depth of feeling in such a way as to make the English nation a nation of aristocrats—in the best sense of the word.

Allow me, in the second place, to thank you warmly for the friendly and flattering attention you have shown me by inserting a special greeting to me among your poems. Would that I might soon have an opportunity of thanking you for this personally, and more warmly and satisfactorily than I can in a letter.

I am greatly obliged to you for your kind review of my new play [*Emperor and Galilean*, in the December 27, 1873, issue of *The Spectator*]. There is only one remark in it about which I must say a word or two. You say that the drama ought to have been written in verse and that it would have gained by this. Here I must differ from you. As you must have observed, the play is conceived in the most realistic style. The illusion I wished to produce was that of reality. I wished to produce the impression on the reader that what he was reading was something that had actually happened. If I had employed verse, I would have counteracted my own intention and defeated my purpose. The many ordinary, insignificant characters whom I have intentionally introduced into the play would have become indistinct and indistinguishable from one another if I had allowed all of them to speak in the same meter. We are no longer living in the days of Shakespeare. Among sculptors there is already talk of painting statues in natural colors.

Much can be said both for and against this. I have no desire to see the Venus of Milo painted, but I would rather see the head of a Negro executed in black than in white marble. Speaking generally, the dialogue must conform to the degree of idealization which pervades the work as a whole. My new drama is no tragedy in the ancient sense. What I sought to depict were human beings, and therefore I would not let them talk the "language of the Gods."

I have a great deal more to say to you, both about this and other things, but I am always hoping for an opportunity of doing it by word of mouth. Therefore I shall say no more for today. Thanking you again most heartily, I remain

Yours very sincerely,
Henrik Ibsen

To Edvard Grieg

Dresden, January 23, 1874

In spite of the protests of the Norwegian Liberal Party, which was urging Norway to become independent of Sweden, Ludwig Josephson, a Swede, had been appointed head of the Christiania Theater in 1873. He began the 1873–74 season with a production of *The Pretenders,* and a little later in the season, on November 24, he staged *Love's Comedy,* which proved to be a popular success. This encouraged Ibsen to think of adapting *Peer Gynt* for the stage.

Dear Mr. Grieg, My object in writing to you is to ask if you would care to co-operate with me in a certain undertaking.

I am thinking of adapting *Peer Gynt*—of which the third printing is soon to appear—for the stage. Will you compose the music that will be required? Let me indicate briefly how I think of arranging the play.

The first act is to be retained in full, with only a few cuts in the dialogue. Peer Gynt's monologue [scene 2] I wish to have treated either as melodrama or in part as recitative. The wedding scene [scene 3] must be built up by means of a ballet into something more than is in the book. For this a special dance melody will have to be composed, which would be continued softly to the end of the act.

In the second act, the musical treatment of the scene with the three cowherd girls [scene 3] must be left to the discretion of the composer—but there must be lots of deviltry in it! The monologue [in scene 4] should, I think, be accompanied by chords, in melodramatic style, as also the scene between Peer and the Woman in Green [scene 5]. There must also be some kind of musical accompaniment to the scene in the Hall of the Mountain King; here, however, the speeches are to be considerably shortened. The scene with the Boyg, which is to be given in full, must also be accompanied by music. The Bird Cries are to be sung; the bell ringing and the psalm singing should be heard in the distance.

In the third act I need chords, but not many, for the scene between Peer, the Woman, and the Ugly Brat [scene 3], and I imagine that a soft accompaniment would be appropriate [for Aase's death].

Almost the whole of the fourth act will be omitted in performance. In place of it I think there should be a large-scale musical tone picture, suggesting Peer Gynt's wandering all over the world. American, English, and French airs might be used as alternating themes, swelling and fading. The chorus of Anitra and the Girls [scene 6] should be heard behind the curtain, jointly with the orchestra. During this music, the curtain will be raised, and the audience will see, like a distant dream picture, Solveig, now a middle-aged woman, sitting in the sunshine singing outside her house [scene 10]. After her song, the curtain will be slowly lowered again while the music continues, but changing into a suggestion of the storm at sea with which the fifth act opens.

The fifth act, which in performance will be called the fourth act or the epilogue, must be considerably shortened. A musical accompaniment is needed [for the scene with the Stranger]. The scenes on the capsized boat and in the churchyard will be omitted. [At the end of scene 5] Solveig will sing, with the music continuing afterward to accompany Peer Gynt's speeches and changing into that required for the choruses [in scene 6]. The scenes with the Button-molder and the Old Man of the Dovre will be shortened. [At the end of scene 10] the people on their way to church will sing on the path through the forest. Then bell ringing and distant psalm singing should be suggested by the music that follows and continues until Solveig's song ends the play. And while the curtain is falling, the psalm singing will be heard again, nearer and louder.

That is approximately the way I have imagined it. Will you let me know if you are willing to undertake the job? If I receive a favorable answer from you, I shall at once write to the management of the Christiania Theater, sending along the revised and abridged text, and making certain, before we go any further, that the play will be performed. I intend to ask 400 specie-dollars [$400] for it, to be divided equally between us. I am certain that we may also count upon the play being produced in Copenhagen and Stockholm. But I shall be obliged if you will keep the matter a secret for the present. May I please hear from you as soon as possible.

Yours most sincerely,
Henrik Ibsen

To Georg Brandes

Dresden, April 20, 1874

Dear Brandes, I certainly did not deserve to be remembered by you on my birthday and to be greeted by a kind letter. I thank you with all my heart. Rest assured that my thoughts are with you more frequently than you would suppose from my negligence in writing.

I did not answer your previous letter on the subject of the proposed periodical, because I wasted too much time considering what and how I should answer. You see, it became more and more evident to me that it was not merely a matter of replying yes or no. If I was going to be honest with you—and I did want to be—I would have had a great deal to say. But it seemed to me that it could be discussed best by word of mouth, and therefore I waited in the hope of seeing you soon again here. As it now seems unlikely that this hope is to be realized, I shall delay no longer in giving you my opinion. Please do not be offended by my frankness!

It was your and your brother's plan to publish a "magazine." But what kind—a Danish or a Scandinavian magazine? The Danish literary men like to have subscribers and readers in all the Scandinavian countries, but they live and move and think only in the atmosphere of Copenhagen. All the discussions in your periodicals and daily press refer to what is going on *with you Danes.* Only the Danish—strictly speaking, only the Copenhagen—point of view in philosophy, matters of philosophy, politics, etc., seems to you to be of any importance. In fact, you really know about no other, as far as Scandinavia is concerned—though you are remarkably well informed as regards foreign countries. The Danes regard it as almost an act of grace to acknowledge that what is strictly Norwegian has the right to express itself in literature. If they are in a friendly mood, they make excuses; if in a hostile, they sneer; but the supposition is always that Denmark sets the standard. What do the Copenhageners know about our domestic affairs, about our politics, and about our politicians? Nothing. We Norwegians, and a certain proportion of the Swedes, know all about your affairs; you hardly know anything of ours. The Copenhagen ignorance of Scandinavian affairs surpasses everything but Copenhagen arrogance.

This is (boiled down to a thousandth part of what I have to say) the reason why Copenhagen periodicals are unsuccessful. Your population of two million cannot support a periodical. If it is to succeed, you must not, in your Copenhagen superiority, overlook the four million Swedes, the two million Norwegians, the one million Finns, and the almost equally large Scandinavian population in America. This makes a public of about ten million in all. Give up your Copenhagen particularism. Write for them all. Then I will join you. But to tell the truth, I do not consider it worth while to address myself in literary style to the people who live within the walls and out in the suburbs of Copenhagen.

I am quite aware that you yourself are on many points openly antagonistic to this "Copenhagenism." Nevertheless you are unconsciously affected by it. The whole first volume of your *Main Currents in Nineteenth-Century Literature* is more an attack upon Copenhagen narrow-mindedness than upon the narrow-mindedness of Scandinavia in general. What you assail are the Copenhagen theories in literature, philosophy, and art, and it is this limited war, it seems to me, that an author in your part of the world, as elsewhere, must avoid if he is to be successful.

All this, dear Brandes, I beg you to regard in the light of a friendly invitation to come down here in order that we may make our war plans together. You must not give up the idea of the periodical. But it is absolutely necessary that it should be established on a wider basis than former Danish periodicals if it is to spread your ideas as widely as they deserve to be spread and secure for you an existence free from care.

I shall not take up anything else today. But think over what I have said, and write soon to

Your faithful friend,

Henrik Ibsen

Brandes visited Ibsen in Dresden for a few days in June, 1874.

Speech to the Norwegian Students
Christiania, September 10, 1874

In 1876 Ibsen finally made up his mind to visit his homeland and probably thought of resettling there. Except for a week in August, when he attended an international congress of archaeologists in Stockholm, he remained in Christiania from early July to the middle of September. On September 10, toward the end of his stay, he appeared in public to be honored by a torchlight procession of university students, and in the evening he attended a production of *The League of Youth* at which he was repeatedly called forth.

Gentlemen: When during the latter years of my stay abroad it became more and more evident to me that it had become a necessity for me to see my own country again, I will not deny that I felt considerable doubt and uneasiness as I prepared for my journey. To be sure, my stay here was intended to be only of short duration, but I felt that, however short, it might be long enough to destroy an illusion I should like to continue to live with.

I asked myself: in what sort of spirit will my countrymen receive me? The favorable reception which greeted the books I sent home could not quite reassure me. The question always arose: what is my personal relationship to my countrymen?

It certainly cannot be denied that at several points there has been a feeling of animosity. So far as I have been able to understand, the complaints against me have been of a twofold nature. People have thought that I have regarded my personal and private relationship to my homeland with undue bitterness, and they have furthermore reproached me with having attacked certain events in our national life that, in the opinion of many, deserved quite a different sort of treatment than mockery.

I do not think I could put this day, so honorable and joyful to me, to better use than to render an explanation and a confession.

I have never made this personal relationship the direct subject of any fictional work. In my early hard times it meant much less to me than I could ever explain to myself afterward. When the nest of the eider duck was robbed the first, second, and third times, it was robbed of illusions and of great aspirations. At festival gatherings when I, like a bear in the hands of its trainer, reacted to little hints and reminders, it was because I knew myself to be partially responsible for those days that buried a glorious ideal beneath songs and celebrations.

Now, what does it mean to be a poet? It was a long time before I realized that to be a poet means essentially to see; but mark well, to see in such a way that whatever is seen is perceived by his audience just as the poet saw it. But only what has been lived through can be seen in that way and accepted in that way. And the secret of modern literature lies precisely in this matter of experiences that have been personally lived through. All that I have written these last ten years I have lived through in spirit. But no poet lives through anything in isolation. What he lives through, all of his countrymen live through with him. If that were not so, what would bridge the gap between the creating and the receiving mind?

And what is it, then, that I have lived through and that

has inspired me? The range has been wide. In part, I have been inspired by something I felt on rare occasions and only in my best moments stirring within me, vividly alive, great and beautiful. I have been inspired by that which, so to speak, stood higher than my everyday self, and I have been inspired by this because I wanted to confront it and make it part of myself.

But I have also been inspired by the opposite, by what appears on introspection as the dregs and sediment of one's nature. Writing has in this case been to me like a bath from which I have risen feeling cleaner, healthier, and freer. Yes, gentlemen, no one can draw poetically anything for which he himself has not to a certain degree and at least at times served as a model. And who is the man among us who has not now and then felt and recognized within himself a contradiction between word and deed, between will and duty, between life and theory in general? Or who is there among us who has not, at least at times, been egoistically, selfishly, sufficient unto himself, and half unconsciously, half in good faith, sought to extenuate his conduct both to others and to himself?

I believe that when I say this to you, to you students, my remarks have found exactly the right audience. You will understand them as they are meant to be understood. For a student has essentially the same task as the poet: to make clear to himself, and thereby to others, the temporal and eternal questions that are astir in the age and in the community to which he belongs.

In this respect I dare to say of myself that I have endeavored to be a good student during my stay abroad. A poet is by nature farsighted. Never have I seen my homeland and the true life of my homeland so completely and clearly and at such close range as I did in my absence when I was far away from it.

And now, my dear countrymen, in conclusion a few words which are also related to something I have lived through. When Emperor Julian stands at the end of his career and everything collapses round about him, there is nothing that makes him so despondent as the thought that all he has gained was this: to be remembered by clear and cool heads with respectful appreciation, while his opponents live on, rich in the love of warm, living hearts. This thought was the result of much that I have

lived through. It had its origin in a question I had sometimes asked myself, down there in my solitude. Now the
young people of Norway have come to me here tonight
and given me my answer in word and song, have given
me my answer more warmly and clearly than I had ever
expected to hear it. I shall take this answer with me as
the richest reward of my visit with my countrymen at
home; and it is my hope and my belief that what I experience tonight will be an experience to "live through"
which will some day be reflected in a work of mine. If
this happens, if someday I send such a book home, then
I ask you students to accept it by way of a handshake
and a thanks for this meeting. I ask you to accept it as
having a share in the creation of it.

To Frederik Hegel

Dresden, November 23, 1874

The third printing of *The League of Youth* and a new
edition of *Lady Inger of Østraat* appeared in December,
1874.

. . . My wife brought me the pleasant news from you
about *The League of Youth* and *Lady Inger*. Is it really
true a great number of the new editions have already been
sold before publication? The time of publication is favorable. I only hope that the paper needed for these editions
will not arrive too late. Of course the publication of *Lady
Inger* must not be delayed until the play has been performed. The sooner it can be put on the market the
better. I shall take the liberty of sending to you at the
proper time the letters for the different theatrical managements.

I was glad to learn that you have no objection to en-
larging the volume of poems by some thirty pages. Everything that you need from me for this purpose will be
ready and dispatched about the end of February, or still
earlier, if possible.

Now I have another proposal to offer for your consideration. Next year will be the twenty-fifth anniversary not
only of my university matriculation but also of my debut
as an author. In March, 1850, [actually in April] there

appeared *Catiline,* a drama in three acts, which was the first book of mine to be printed. This play contains some good, along with some very immature, writing. Of late, critics have often remarked how characteristic it was of me to make my debut with this work. And I myself agree with them, for I feel now that it had a close connection with my life at that time, and that it contains the germs of a good deal that has since come to light in my poetry. My idea is to give some explanation of this and various other things in a preface to a new and revised edition of the book [see page 8]. I would make no change in the thoughts and ideas, only in the language in which they are expressed. The verse is, as Brandes has remarked, bad —one reason for this being that the book was printed from my first rough, uncorrected draft.

For my part, I believe that the work would be received now with considerable interest, and that it would be bought by those who possess my other works. The book is now known to the public only by hearsay, because at the time it was published not more than sixty to one hundred copies were circulated. I myself watched the remainder of the issue converted into waste paper.

Will you give me your candid opinion of this project? If you doubt the advisability of it, please tell me. If you agree with me, I shall be exceedingly obliged if you will procure me a copy of the book as soon as possible. Because of the many corrections and alterations that I propose to make, it will be necessary to rewrite the whole play for the printers; and it would be best if the new edition could appear at the same time of year as the first one did. The borrowed copy shall be returned undamaged. I imagine that it will be possible to borrow a copy from one of the large libraries. . . .

To Georg Brandes

Dresden, January 30, 1875

The magazine *Det nittende Aarhundrede* (*The Nineteenth Century*) was published by Georg and Edvard Brandes from 1874 to 1877. It never had any Norwegian contributors other than Ibsen. Swedish contributions were always translated into Danish. To the first issue Georg Brandes contributed articles on Ibsen and the German novelist Paul Heyse. He criticized Ibsen's *Emperor and Galilean* for its thoroughgoing determinism while remarking on, without condemning, the determinism of Heyse's novel *Kinder der Welt*.

Dear Brandes, In order to convince you—though I don't believe you really doubt it—that you enjoy the special favor of the gods, I am going to lay everything else aside today to answer the letter I received the day before yesterday.

My best thanks for the issues of the periodical published by you and your brother. I have found much in them of great interest. But I still cannot help thinking that your magazine is far too exclusively Danish, or rather Copenhagenish, when your aim should absolutely be to take in all of Scandinavia. No one here in Germany would dream of starting a periodical for Baden or for Hesse-Cassel, and Denmark by itself is just as little able to support one. Have you not thought of enlisting Professor Sars, or O. Skavlan, or F. R. Baetzman as Norwegian contributors? And in Sweden you should be able to count upon even more contributors than in Norway. I see you have already received one contribution from Sweden; and no stronger proof is needed of the exclusively Danish character of the periodical than the fact that the Swedish article is printed—in a Danish translation! Why? Do you not expect to find any readers in Sweden? And do you Copenhageners believe that the Swedes will read original Swedish articles in Danish translation? Are the Danes really still so ignorant of Swedish that communications from that country cannot be understood unless they are translated? If so, the outlook for the most important of all our causes is very bad. I have the feeling, dear Brandes, that in your heart you are not very much devoted to this cause. As for me, I could not have lived so long in Germany without seeing clearly that this cause is the chief thing, and that all the other aims are subordinate to it.

Why do you and all of us whose standpoint is a European one feel so isolated at home? Because the state we belong to is not a complete, united organism, and because the people at home are parochial, not Scandinavian or nationalistic in their thinking, their feeling, and their general orientation. I set very little store by political organizations, but all the more by the welding together of our national ideas. You call your periodical *The Nineteenth Century*—but at the present moment isn't the physiognomy of this century quite different in Denmark, in Sweden, in Norway! And do you believe that the fraction of Europeanism each branch of the Scandinavian people has assimilated provides a sufficient foundation for everything you dream of building? Only entire nations can join in great intellectual movements. Advancing the front line of our conceptions of life and of the world is not a parochial matter. Compared with the other European nations, we Scandinavians have not yet got beyond the point of view of the parish council. And have you ever heard of a parish council looking for and preparing the way for "the third kingdom"?

I won't dwell on this any longer. I want to give a direct answer to your letter.

It is quite true that I promised Councilor Hegel to send some poems as my contribution to the periodical. But in the first place, these poems treat of specifically Norwegian matters, which leads me to fear that they will be almost "Swedish" to the Copenhageners. In the second place, they have not yet been elaborated, but are still in the crude, formless shape of first drafts. There is, therefore, more than "revising" that has to be done. Of course, I have not thought of making them "unimprovable." This would be unnecessary, for my experience has been that people in Denmark, as elsewhere, are generally kind enough to put the best construction on what they do not understand. You shall have the poems, however, but to prevent disappointment I shall accept your utmost time limit, "in April or May."

I am unaware of having given occasion for your remark that it would not in any way "compromise" me to contribute to your periodical. Besides, it would be difficult for you, or for anyone except myself, to decide whether I should consider it more compromising to collaborate with Bishop Martensen [an orthodox theologian opposed to both Grundtvig and Kierkegaard] or with the late David Strauss.

It is incomprehensible to me how you could take offense at my observing that the periodical under given conditions would secure a carefree existence for you. I remember your letters quite as well as you seem to remember mine, and I assure you that the observation was made in direct answer to something you yourself had written. And I do not understand how anyone in our days can feel hurt by its being taken for granted that he expects to be able to live *by* what he lives *for*.

Accept my best thanks for having found a place in your magazine for [a review of] *Emperor and Galilean*. There are several points in your review I would like to discuss with you; but in writing I must limit myself to observing that it seems to me as if your condemnation of the determinism contained in my book were contradicted by your approval of something similar in P. Heyse's *Kinder der Welt*. I don't see any real difference, in writing of a person's character, between saying, "It runs in his blood," and, "He is free—subject to the laws of necessity."

In April I go to Munich to settle there. Do you not think of taking a trip abroad soon? It seems to me that it would be easier for you to edit the periodical from abroad than at home. Everything else that I have to say must wait until some other time. Write soon to

Yours ever,
Henrik Ibsen

Preface to the Second Edition of *Catiline*

Dresden, February 1, 1875

(See page 8.)

✳ EXILE IN MUNICH
1875–1880

To Hartvig Lassen

Kitzbühel, Tyrol, August 16, 1875

Lassen was literary consultant at the Christiania Theater.

Dear Lassen, It was not until yesterday that your kind letter reached me here among the mountains where I am spending the summer. I hasten to answer it.

Of course it is impossible to stage *Peer Gynt* except in an abridged form. The first time I wrote to Grieg with reference to the music, I explained to him my idea of substituting an orchestral tone picture for most of the incidents in the fourth act with one or two *tableaux vivants* representing the situations most suited for such in the act omitted—for instance, Peer Gynt and the Arab girls, Solveig waiting near her cottage, etc. I communicated this plan to Mr. Josephson [head of the Christiania Theater], but he did not agree with me. He submitted to me a proposal for cutting the speeches. The cuts seemed to me to have been made with great judiciousness, and I agreed to them.

I dare not decide here at a distance which of the two plans it will be best to adopt. I prefer that you and Mr. Josephson should discuss and decide the matter. He assures me that if his suggestion is carried out, the piece will become a popular favorite and draw large houses. I prefer not to interfere in the matter. I shall be satisfied so long as the piece is reduced to proper length; not to do this would ruin everything. I therefore beg the theater

157

authorities to do what they think best. There are advantages to each of the alternatives. In order to decide between them, one must be on the spot, must know the capabilities of the actors, the technical resources of the theater in the matter of decorations, machinery, etc.

I do have one special wish, however. I would like to see the première take place before Christmas—indeed, as early in the season as possible. Plays that do not get staged until springtime cannot be expected to attract much interest; and the reception of a play during its first year is crucial for its future life in the repertory. . . .

Peer Gynt did not open at the Christiania Theater until February 24, 1876. Grieg's music was used, and, in general, Josephson's suggestions for abridging the play were followed rather than Ibsen's as set forth in the letter of January 23, 1874. Even with the cuts, the play ran from 7:00 to 11:45. The play was a great success, being performed thirty-seven times in the first season, and could have run longer.

To Frederik Hegel

Kitzbüchel, August 22, 1875

Dear Mr. Hegel, I want to send you a few lines from my summer spot up here in the mountains to let you know, first of all, that I have just completed the full outline of the new five-act play about contemporary life which I have for a long time thought about writing, and which will be finished sometime this winter if nothing unforeseen happens to spoil my plans. . . .

To Frederik Hegel

Munich, October 23, 1875

Dear Mr. Hegel, Owing to the unexpected delay in the production of *Peer Gynt* at the Christiania Theater, I find myself obliged to ask you to advance me 675 marks [$161]; I trust you will not take this amiss.

My new work is progressing rapidly. I shall have the first act completed in a few days, and that is always the most difficult part of a play for me. The title will be: *The Pillars of Society, A Drama in Five Acts.* In one way, this work can be regarded as a counterpart of *The League of Youth.* It will probe into several of the more important questions of the day. For the present I should like to keep this between ourselves. A little later I shall have no objection to having some news of it come out, as I think that some talk among the public beforehand helps the sale of a work. . . .

To Frederik Hegel

Munich, November 25, 1875

Dear Mr. Hegel, While thanking you deeply for the 675 marks enclosed in your kind letter of the twenty-fifth of last month, I must unfortunately prevail on your kindness to ask for an advance of another 675 to prevent my being in difficulties at the beginning of next month. As for my previous request asking you to invest in government bonds the last installment due me by the Royal Theater [in Copenhagen] for *The Vikings,* please disregard that and apply the money instead against the payment you have advanced me. I am hopeful that it will not be long before the Royal Theater presents the play again.

I would like to take this opportunity to mention that I am not satisfied with Berner's [the treasurer of the theater] manner of remuneration. Plays that are offered and accepted in manuscript are, according to the regulations, to receive a certain percentage of the receipts. Now, both *The Pretenders* and *The Vikings* were offered in manuscript; and *The League of Youth,* too, was offered before it was published. If the procedure adopted in my case becomes general, the regulations will become meaningless. The management can make a practice of first refusing all the manuscripts sent in and thereby compelling the authors to have their plays printed—after which they can be had for performance at a much lower price. This is not fair, and I have no objection at all to Mr. Berner's being informed at the earliest opportunity of my opinion.

However, my real reason for writing to you today concerns another matter. Recently I subscribed for ten shares at a total price of 1000 specie-dollars [$1,000] in the recently reorganized Bergens Kreditbank, formerly a branch of the Kreditkasse of Christiania. On these shares 360 specie-dollars are to be paid sometime in December. I have also subscribed for shares in the new passenger steamship *Dronningen* to the amount of 500 specie-dollars, of which 250 must be paid *at once* to H. J. Preus in Christiania and for whom I enclose a letter. Therefore I require a total of 610 specie-dollars. What I want to ask you is, may I borrow this amount for a few months, say six, from some moneylending institution in Copenhagen at a reasonable rate of interest on the security of the bonds and shares which I already own, the vouchers for which are in your possession?

To procure the money in any other way would take too long. I have put it off until now, hoping that the production of *Peer Gynt* in Christiania and of *The Vikings* in Stockholm would provide me with enough funds. Please do not be annoyed with me for causing you trouble in this matter too. If, as I hope, things can be arranged in Copenhagen, please send the letter to H. J. Preus as soon as possible, and the amount due for the Kreditbank shares sometime during December to Mr. Lund,* bookseller in Christiania, who has my instructions.

The first act of my new drama is ready and fair-copied, and I am now working on Act II.

What do you say to this move of Stjernström's? I have not heard from him since last summer. The news of the performance took me entirely by surprise.†

With kindest regards to you and your family,

Yours most sincerely,

Henrik Ibsen

To Ludvig Josephson

Munich, March 5, 1876

. . . The success of the Christiania Theater's daring venture [of producing *Peer Gynt*] has exceeded all my

* In August, 1875, Nils Lund had become Ibsen's financial agent in Norway.

† Edvard Stjernström had opened the New Theater in Stockholm in January, 1875, and on November 3 he presented Ibsen's *The Vikings at Helgeland* to warm audience response.

expectations, although I never harbored any fears as to the outcome. I knew that the play was in good hands and that no one else in our country could carry it through as well as you. It has pleased me deeply that this is the unanimous general opinion at home.

May I ask you to convey my thanks to the whole company, not only to those who filled the rewarding leading roles but also to all those whose co-operation in the smaller supporting parts did so much for the production. The success of a play of this type depends to an unusual degree on having each person without exception do his part. And all the reports agree that such was the case. . . .

To Frederik Hegel

Munich, April 11, 1876

. . . Yesterday *The Vikings at Helgeland* was performed for the first time in the local Court Theater. The house was virtually full, and the play was received with a storm of applause. I, who witnessed the performance from the wings, was called forth five times. After the performance the Munich literati improvised a party for me that lasted long into the night. . . .

The Vikings at Helgeland was the first of Ibsen's plays to be produced in Germany and, indeed, the first of his plays to be produced outside Scandinavia. Productions outside Scandinavia meant a great deal to Ibsen because of the more favorable financial arrangements. Apart from interest on the investments he was beginning to make at this time, Ibsen's income consisted of an annual writer's stipend of 400 speciedollars paid by the Norwegian government, plus royalties from the sale of his books (see footnote, p. 47) and the production of his plays. But in the matter of royalties on plays, Norway and the rest of Scandinavia were rather backward, retaining the system of "author's night" or else paying sums based on the number of performances, whereas the German system was to pay the author a percentage of the gross receipts. When *Peer Gynt* was to be staged in Christiania, Ibsen was offered the receipts on author's night, as was customary. In a letter of February 21, 1876, Ibsen protested against this arrangement, saying that the author's night without a guaranteed minimum was unfair, since bad weather, festivities elsewhere on the same night, and other factors could reduce the playwright's income to a negligible sum. Instead he proposed that he receive 20 per cent of the receipts from the first five performances.

The contract that Ibsen drew up with the Bergen theater in October, 1876, probably represents the best terms that a rising playwright could get from one of the smaller theaters. According to his contract, Ibsen would receive (a) 100 specie-dollars the day after the first performance; plus (b) 10 specie-dollars for each of the next five performances; plus (c) 5 specie-dollars for each subsequent performance; with (b) and (c) payable at the end of the season. In contrast, German theaters paid 10 per cent of the gross receipts.

However, copyright laws in Germany and elsewhere offered no protection to Norwegian writers. In a letter of February 4, 1877, to Johan Sverdrup, leader of the Norwegian parliament, Ibsen called for increased state support of Norwegian authors on the grounds that their works were not protected when translated into other languages. For example, Ibsen was not collecting a cent from the three different German translations of *Brand*. The only way he could protect himself was to commission translations of his own works, as he did for *The Vikings at Helgeland* and *Lady Inger of Østraat*; but this cost money.

To Ludvig Josephson

Munich, June 14, 1876

. . . I have spoken to Dr. Grandaur [opera director at the Court Theater in Munich] about your receiving free admission to the Bayreuth Festival, but he says that you have no chance at all except by applying personally to Richard Wagner. He expects, however, that an endless number of similar requests will be received and has not much hope as to the result. The price of a ticket for the four performances is 300 marks [\$72].[*]

At the beginning of this month I went to Berlin to attend the première [on June 3] of *The Pretenders*, which was splendidly staged by the Meiningen Players. The play was received with great applause, and I was called

[*] The first Bayreuth Festival took place August 13–17 and was an unprecedented success with the public.

before the curtain several times. I do not think this pleased the Berlin critics very much, most of whom are playwrights themselves. The play, nevertheless, had a run of nine straight nights, and would have run longer if the Meiningen company did not have to end its season on the fifteenth.

After the première I was invited by the Duke [of Saxe-Meiningen, founder and director of the Meiningen Players] to visit him at his castle of Liebenstein near Meiningen, where I stayed until the day before yesterday. On my departure he decorated me with the Cross of the First Class of the House of Saxony-Ernestine. *The Pretenders* is now to be played at Schwerin, and *The Vikings* has been accepted by the Burgtheater in Vienna, where Charlotte Wolter is to play Hjørdis. If our mutual friend Winter-Hjelm would care for these particulars for his newspaper, please let him have them. And come soon! We remain at Munich till the first of August. . . .

To Frederik Hegel

Kaltern by Bozen,* Tyrol
September 15, 1876

Dear Mr. Hegel, After having given no sign of life for almost four months, I shall write a few words to you today chiefly because I doubt that the Scandinavian papers are as conscientious in publishing reliable good news about me as they are in spreading distorted accounts of bad news. They were eager to inform their public that at a rehearsal in Meiningen *The Pretenders* did not take the fancy of the public; but I suspect that they were in less of a hurry to report that in Berlin the same play was performed for nine nights in succession to wild applause with the author and the actors being recalled repeatedly. And this happened in spite of the fact that many of the journalists were, for obvious reasons, not well disposed toward me. After this victory, the Duke of Meiningen invited me to visit him at his castle of Liebenstein. I had a delightful time there and was decorated on my departure with the insignia of the House of Saxony-Ernestine. In the winter

* Now Caldaro, near Bolzano.

I am to visit the Duke again at Meiningen. In October *The Vikings* is to be produced at the Burgtheater in Vienna. I have received an official invitation to be present there, and I am also invited to Schwerin, where *The Pretenders* is to be presented in November. In the course of a week or two they will be performing *The Vikings* at the Court Theater in Dresden. It is also being rehearsed at the City Theater of Leipzig, and is having at the present time a very successful second run in Munich. From each one of these theaters I receive 10 per cent of the gross receipts from all representations; and my heirs will receive the same for fifteen years after my decease. These are undeniably more advantageous terms than Mr. Berner sees fit to offer me; and no one should find it surprising if from now on I devote my attention to getting my works produced here. An original German edition of *Lady Inger* is already completed in manuscript, and will be played first at Meiningen and Munich.

While engaged in attending to all these matters, I have of course been obliged to neglect my new play. But after my return to Munich at the beginning of next month, I intend to put the final touches to it, although I must confess there is little inducement to write for the theaters at home. How is *The Vikings* succeeding in Copenhagen? According to the agreement, I am to receive 500 kroner [$134] more after the twentieth performance. Does Mr. Berner really intend to avoid paying me this by putting aside the play after the nineteenth performance, as was done last year? I have never mentioned to you a very characteristic trait of this gentleman. In the letter in which he begins negotiations with me for *The Vikings,* he writes that the theater can only pay me so and so much, "because the play is too short to take up a whole evening." Yet I have since learned that it was given every time as the sole offering of the evening. But Mr. Berner has not by so much as a single word informed me of this. I would very much like to see his attention drawn to these facts at the earliest opportunity. Tricks of this kind are really beneath the dignity of the manager and director of a royal theater.

I have long been expecting to see the new printing of *Peer Gynt* advertised. I hope that it will be out soon. And possibly a new issue of one or more of my other books may be required before Christmas. I should be very glad if this were the case, for I am in need of money. The theaters here pay only every quarter or half-year. May I presume, in spite of my debt to you, to ask you to send me 450 marks [$107] to the address given above? You will be doing me a very great favor. And I have every hope that it will not be long before our accounts are balanced again.

The scenery is superbly beautiful here on the borders of Italy, and one could not wish for a more delightful climate. A Danish and a Finnish lady, and the young author John Paulsen of Bergen, are the people we see most of. We hear very little from home. Young Paulsen has, however, told us a good deal about his stay in Copenhagen which delighted him enormously. From what he tells, we conclude that all is well with you and yours. But we should be very glad to hear this confirmed by you directly.

Please do not see in my long silence a sign of decreasing interest in things and persons at home. Trusting that it has not occurred to you to do so, I remain, with kindest regards to you and your family,

Yours most sincerely and cordially,
Henrik Ibsen

To Frederik Hegel

Munich, July 29, 1877

. . . Please do not let any outside party get a look at my manuscript until the book is published. I believe I may say with certainty that we shall both be satisfied with this play of mine [*The Pillars of Society*]. It is modern in all respects and completely in tune with the times; and it is probably composed with more skill and artistry than any of my other works. Please excuse this illegible writing. I have been working since five o'clock this morning and now it is twilight. . . .

To Frederik Hegel

Munich, August 23, 1877

Dear Mr. Hegel, Enclosed you will find the letters which are to be sent (along with the play) to the Royal Theater in Copenhagen and to the Göteborg theater. I shall get in touch with the Stockholm theaters when I am there. The book must not be sent to the Bergen theater until nearly the time when it will be put on sale in the bookshops. I have a contract with that theater [see notes following letter of April 11, 1876], and by sending a copy as early as this, we run the risk of its being circulated among those for whom it is not intended, which would injure the sale in that locality. I do not at present intend to offer the play to the Christiania Theater. The new artistic director [Johan Vibe, actually head of the theater, 1877–79] is an absolutely incompetent man, and as soon as my play is on the market I intend to state in a Norwegian paper that I have broken off all connection with the theater for the period of his directorship.* I have reason to believe that Bjørnson will do the same. From my knowledge of circumstances in Christiania, I feel pretty certain that this procedure, far from injuring the sale of the book, will rather cause it to be more extensively read and bought. And I am also persuaded that united action on the part of Bjørnson and myself will go far toward forcing the resignation of the new manager.

In my opinion the book should be published as soon as possible, and simultaneously in all three countries. I expect that it will create a good deal of excitement; and if we get it out at the right time, it is not impossible that in spite of the size of the first printing [6,000] another will be called for before Christmas.† This is what I think we must keep uppermost in our minds. Getting a slightly better offer from any single theater cannot be compared in importance with the sale of the book.

From the letters I have written for the theaters you will

---

* However, *The Pillars of Society* was performed at the Christiania Theater on March 7, 1879, while Vibe was still head.

† Ibsen was right. A second printing of 4,000 was printed before Christmas.

see that I have for the time being confined myself to the question of acceptance or nonacceptance. This I consider to be the best plan. The terms can be discussed after this has been decided.

I am exceedingly busy with the preparations for my journey to Uppsala. I look forward with pleasure to seeing you on the return journey.

With kindest regards to all your family, I remain

Yours most sincerely,

Henrik Ibsen

To Sigurd Ibsen

Stockholm, September 12, 1877

Dear Sigurd, At Uppsala on Friday the seventh I received your and your mother's letter, just as I was about to leave in all my splendor for the ballet. You may consider yourselves fortunate that you escaped unscathed and without illness from your adventure on the Folgefond [an ice sheet in Norway]. I hope that in future you will be more careful.

My investiture as honorary doctor took place in the cathedral on the sixth with a very moving ceremony. Addresses were made in Latin by the archbishop and three professors. The three doctors from the other faculties were presented with hats, but we poets with laurel wreaths, which we had to wear for the rest of the day— first at the Gala Dinner, at the great popular-festival meeting in the Botanical Gardens, and finally at the festivities in the evening in Uppsala Castle.

The Pillars of Society has already been accepted for production both here and in Copenhagen.

Write soon, and under no circumstance must you miss the beginning of school term.

Your devoted papa,

Henrik Ibsen

To Suzannah Ibsen

Stockholm, September 12, 1877

Dear Suzannah, You may have read in the papers about the tremendous festivities in Uppsala, which are now over.

Last Monday *The Vikings at Helgeland* was given here. Full house. Repeated calls for the author and the greatest enthusiasm. But about all this by word of mouth. During my whole stay in Sweden I have only received one letter from you and Sigurd, the one in which you tell about your tour to the Folgefond. I hope to find letters from you in Copenhagen. I am going there today.

I feel tired now and am longing to be back in Munich. Every day there have been invitations and social gatherings. At Uppsala I talked with the King every day, and from the first he received me in the most cordial manner. This is just to inform you that I am well; let me hear the same from you.

Yours,
Henrik Ibsen

To Edvard Fallesen

Munich, October 5, 1877

Edvard Fallesen was head of the Royal Theater in Copenhagen.

Dear Sir, In my answer to your telegram I had to confine myself to a brief statement that it was impossible to delay the publication of my new play [*The Pillars of Society*] until November 30, and I should now like to explain why I must refuse your request.

Since the Royal Theater does not see its way to allowing me a certain percentage of the receipts, I am compelled to make the sale of the book my chief source of profit. A very large printing of the play has been published, and for this first issue Mr. Hegel has paid me a considerable sum. Taking into account besides this payment, his expenses for printing, paper, etc., it is evident that his outlay has been anything but trifling. I therefore owe it to him as well as to myself not to make arrangements opposed to our common interests. In our Scandinavian countries, as you are aware, the last two months of the year are the bookselling season, and in order that a book published in Copenhagen may be available at the proper time in the more remote districts of Sweden and Norway, not to mention Finland and America where a good many copies of my plays go, it is imperative that it should be sent off not later than the middle of October. If this is not done, there is no chance of the printing being sold out during the Christmas season, and the author must wait for a whole year before a new printing is called for. I dare not and cannot expose myself to the risk of such a financial loss—a loss that cannot nearly be compensated for by the payment I can expect to receive from the Royal Theater. Besides, numerous orders have come in from the booksellers throughout Scandinavia, and promises have been made that the book will be delivered at a certain time. And there is yet another consideration. We understand that this book is awaited by the public with considerable expectation; and it is always unwise on the part of an author to strain such expectation beyond a reasonable point. If he does, the interest is apt to dwindle sharply before the book appears.

Regarding the matter from another side, I consider it injurious to a dramatic work that it should first be made accessible to the public by means of a stage performance. I believe that the regulation of the Royal Theater to this effect has repressed and inhibited playwriting in Denmark. It is a fact, at all events, that playwriting has shown no tendency to increase since the regulation in question was passed. This is only natural. As things stand now, a new play can never be considered and judged on its own, purely and simply as a literary work. The judgment will always include both the play and its performance. These two entirely different things are mixed up together; and as a rule the public is more interested in the acting and the actors than in the play itself.

In justice to myself I feel this explanation is necessary, for it would grieve me if my refusal were regarded as a lack of co-operation on my part. Nothing would have pleased me more than to accede to the request if it had been possible. I can hardly believe that the position I am forced to take will in any way harm the theater. If it becomes known that the play is to be given as early as November, the result will merely be that a large proportion of the Copenhagen public will give up the idea of buying the book beforehand.

Allow me, for the sake of order, to return you the pass issued to me, along with my sincere and hearty thanks for the enjoyable evenings it gave me.

Hoping that the approaching production of *The Pillars of Society* will be to the satisfaction of all parties concerned, I remain

Yours sincerely,
Henrik Ibsen

The Pillars of Society was published on October 11 in a first printing of 6,000 copies, and a second printing of 4,000 copies was called for within two months. It was performed in the Danish provinces as early as November 14; at the Royal Theater in Copenhagen on November 18; and in 1878 it began its triumphal progress through the German and Austrian theaters. In February alone, five theaters in Berlin staged it in three different translations. By the end of the year twenty-seven German-speaking theaters had produced it.

But great as was the success of *The Pillars of Society* in Germany, another Norwegian play had had an even greater success a couple of years before: Bjørnson's *A Bankruptcy*, which, like Ibsen's play, was a realistic, social problem play of the type that Augier, Sardou, and Dumas *fils* were writing in France. Bjørnson had first conceived his play about 1868 but did not finish writing it until 1874. Ibsen read it hot off the press in March, 1875, and saw a performance of it in Munich in June of that year. Undoubtedly the form and realistic dialogue of *A Bankruptcy* contributed much to the tone and final shape of *Pillars*. Ibsen had made his first notes for his play in 1870; Brandes' lectures in 1871 had called upon Scandinavian writers to submit social problems to debate as the French writers were doing; financial scandals in Scandinavia in 1873 provided fresh material for Ibsen's proposed play; and the poem "A Letter in Rhyme" that he wrote in 1875 with its famous line, "I think we are sailing with a corpse in the cargo," bears witness to a sharpened awareness on Ibsen's part to the inhibiting and stultifying effect of social morality on the development of the individual. Yet, in spite of all these inducements and pressures from within and without, it was not until the appearance of Bjørn-son's play that Ibsen could set to work in earnest and complete *The Pillars of Society*. Once again, Ibsen had been anticipated by his younger and perennially successful rival. But this was to be the last time. From now on Ibsen was the pioneer.

To Christian Paus

Munich, November 18, 1877

Dear Uncle Christian, Although I am one of your nearest relatives, I have good reason to fear that when you receive these lines from a distant country you will think of me almost as a stranger. In the eyes of the world it may indeed seem as if I had deliberately made myself a stranger to my family, or at least completely separated myself from them. But I believe I may honestly say that it was mainly unalterable circumstances and conditions that separated us from the first.

I am sure you have already guessed, dear Uncle, my reason for writing you today. The foreign papers and a letter from Hedvig [his sister] have informed me of my old father's death, and I feel a need to express my heart-felt thanks to all those of the family whose affectionate assistance made life easier for him for so many years, and who have done in my behalf, or in my stead, what until quite lately I have not been in a position to do.

From my fourteenth year I was thrown upon my own resources. It has been a long, hard struggle to reach my present position. I seldom wrote home during all these years of struggle because I could offer no assistance of any kind to my parents. It seemed useless to write when I could not be of any real and practical use. I went on hoping that my circumstances would improve. But the improvement was very long in coming, and did not come until fairly recently.

It has been a great consolation to me to know all along that both my parents and more recently my aged father were surrounded by devoted relatives; and the thanks that I owe for all the kind assistance rendered to those who are gone, I also owe for the assistance rendered to me.

Yes, dear Uncle, I want you to know, and ask you in turn to tell the others, that taking upon yourselves, out of affection for my parents, the duties and obligations that I myself should have carried out was a great help during my years of struggle and striving, and furthered the accomplishment of what I have been able to achieve in this world.

During my last stay in Norway I felt a strong desire to visit Skien and my family. But at the same time I felt strongly disinclined to have any contact with certain tendencies that prevail there, tendencies with which I do not sympathize. A clash with them might have led to unpleasantness, which I preferred to avoid. But I have by no means given up the idea of seeing my childhood home once again. In a year my son will have finished his education here, and we shall be able to live wherever we choose. Probably we shall first go to Italy for a short time, and then take up our residence in Christiania, although I fear that I shall not be able to live or work permanently in Norway. Conditions here are far more favorable. They are the conditions of the big world—freedom of thought and a broader view of things. But on the other hand, these conditions demand considerable sacrifices of one kind or another.

I enclose a photograph of myself. It is twenty-seven years since we saw each other, and I am sure you will not recognize me. But I hope the day is not far off when the family will have an opportunity of seeing for themselves whether the picture resembles the original or not.

That is all I have to say for now. Please remember me kindly to all the family, and please accept my cordial wishes.

Your grateful and affectionate nephew,
Henrik Ibsen

To Emil Jonas, German translator

Munich, January 18, 1878

Mr. Emil Jonas: In reply to your letter I must remind you, although you must surely be aware of it, that as early as the beginning of last November I published a German first edition of *The Pillars of Society* at Theodore Acker-mann's company. A translation from your hand is there-fore quite superfluous; and the adaptation you propose to make I most definitely reject.

Your remarks about cutting the first act is nothing but nonsense and shows that you do not have the faintest understanding of the work you imagine yourself qualified to adapt. I should have thought it would be obvious to even the most naive hack writer that in this play nothing can be left out and not a single line of dialogue can be cut. Furthermore, the play has already been accepted by many German theaters in its uncut and ungarbled form.

If, in spite of what I have told you, you continue with your proposed adaptation and by your incompetence butcher and ruin my play, I hereby warn you that I shall notify the Scandinavian papers in order that you may get the publicity you deserve. I shall make you known in the highest circles, and what the consequences of that will be you shall learn in due course.

I do not feel it is right not to warn you. You still have time to stop the mistreatment of my play which you threaten in your letter. For your own sake I advise you to think twice about what you are doing.

At any rate, my play will be produced in its ungarbled form at least at two other theaters in Berlin that have already accepted it, and thus the public will have plenty of opportunity to make comparisons. If you still allow the botched-up play you advertise to come before the public, you might at least give me the satisfaction of having printed on the posters of the Stadttheater the words: "Butchered by Emil Jonas."

Respectfully yours,
Henrik Ibsen

To Markus Grønvold

Rome, January 22, 1879

In the autumn of 1878 Ibsen moved to Rome and lived there for a year. Grønvold was a thirty-year-old Norwegian painter who had become a good friend of Ibsen's in the summer of 1877 when Ibsen was alone in Munich for a while, working on *The Pillars of Society*.

. . . There are a great many of our countrymen in Rome this winter as well as in Munich, but, like you, I see little of most of them. We live very quietly. Our dinner is brought ready-cooked to the house, and the land-lady provides us with breakfast and supper. Everything is much cheaper here than in Munich. Wine in particular is to be had this winter at a ridiculously low price: in the Sabine towns an excellent wine is sold at 3 soldi (12 Pf.) [3 cents] a liter! I don't remember if I told you that I am taking advantage of every opportunity to buy old paint-ings. I have already purchased eleven, all good and valu-able, at comparatively low prices. I intend to buy more in order to decorate my future home at Munich entirely with works of art. Now all I need to do is to find a home. I shall probably come to Munich before the others to look for a house. This will give me a chance to see the art exhibition, which I look forward to with great pleas-ure. . . .

Henrik Ibsen

To Lorentz Dietrichson

Rome, April 18, 1879

. . . We have been here since the middle of September and will not return to Munich until October. Sigurd, who graduated last year (passed his final examinations with "ones" in every subject), is now studying at the university here. In the fall he will enter the University of Munich and take the general law courses for a year or so until it is necessary for him to go to Christiania to study Nor-wegian law. Whether or not we shall accompany him and settle down there for some time is still undecided. I have no great inclination to do so. We are all well and happy here. Just between us, I am preparing to write a new play this summer. Another piece of news is that I have taken to buying old paintings. I hope to bring twenty magnificent ones back to Munich with me. . . .

To Jonas Lie

Rome, May 25, 1879

The Norwegian novelist was looking for a place to live in Germany.

. . . But tell me, have you never thought of living in Munich? The climate is more severe there in the winter than at Dresden, but I know that many rheumatic people feel very comfortable in Munich. The air is healthy and fortifying, and one can feel keenly the nearness of the Alps. Munich is less expensive than Dresden. Also, there is a very good technical school there where many Norwegians study. It has been my experience that Munich offers more opportunity for social intercourse than Dresden, and a more varied and interesting social life. . . .

As for ourselves, we spent last summer in the Tyrol and came here in September. Next fall we shall be in Munich again. My son, who graduated from the Gymnasium there before we left and who has been studying at the University of Rome this year, will resume his studies in Munich in October and continue there for a couple of years. Afterward, of course, it will be necessary for him to complete them in Christiania. Whether we shall accompany him there is still uncertain. I do not feel any particular desire to do so. Life here in Europe is freer, fresher, and broader.

I am busy right now on a new play [*A Doll's House*] which I hope to finish in another month or so. I hear that you, too, are writing a new work.

We should be very glad if we could meet you in one place or another, and we hope that it will turn out that way. Until then we send our best wishes to you all. . . .

To Markus Grønvold

Rome, June 27, 1879

. . . It is now rather hot in Rome, so in about a week we are going to Amalfi, which is cooler, being closer to the sea, and offers opportunity for bathing. While there I intend to complete a new play I am working on. . . .

We intend to return to Munich in the beginning of October. Sigurd will be able to study there for a year; then he must go on to Christiania. It is still undecided whether or not we shall accompany him and stay in Christiania as long as he is at the university; probably we shall. But we will stay no longer than necessary. I already have the feeling that I shall have to get out again, and in all probably I shall once again choose Munich, which offers me so many advantages, and where I feel as if I were in my spiritual home.

I have bought a number of old paintings here—twenty or so, some of them fairly large, all valuable, and one or two of them particularly good. With the pictures I already have in Munich, these will suffice to decorate three large rooms in the manner that is most to my taste. We have a great mind to furnish the rooms ourselves, so as to have everything as we like it. But then we remember that we may soon have to move to Christiania, so we still have not made any definite decision. . . .

We are enjoying life here, but there are often times when I wish that I could be in Munich for a moment. Especially in this enervating heat I often think with a sigh of all that delicious bock beer you are reveling in, and which I must do without. Well, one can't have everything at once, and a change is good for one. . . .

To Edmund Gosse

Rome, July 4, 1879

. . . I have been living here in Rome with my family since September, and have been keeping myself busy with a new dramatic work [A Doll's House] that will soon be finished, and which will be published in October. It is a serious play, really a domestic family drama, dealing with contemporary problems in regard to marriage. The play will be divided into three rather long acts. . . .

To Bjørnstjerne Bjørnson

Amalfi, July 12, 1879

In the late 1870's Ibsen's attitude toward Bjørnson under-
went a change. The note that Ibsen sent Bjørnson in 1877
along with a copy of *The Pillars of Society* contained the
first words that he had addressed to the liberal leader in
eight years. Ibsen's political views also seemed to change
after his visit to Norway in 1874 when he had been hailed
by the conservatives. He canceled his subscription to the
right-wing *Morgenbladet* and subscribed to the Norwegian
left-wing paper *Dagbladet*. Ibsen's new political orientation
furthered the rapprochement between Bjørnson and himself,
but it did not carry him so far that he could support
Bjørnson in the campaign to separate Norway completely
from Sweden. One step in this campaign was to give Norway
its own flag.

Dear Bjørnstjerne Bjørnson: It was very good to hear
from you, but it would have been even better if your
letter had concerned itself with a matter on which you
and I could agree. However, such is not the case. To the
depth of my being I am opposed to your proposal about
the Norwegian flag, and I shall explain why briefly.

In the first place, I believe that this protest against the
symbol of union of the two countries should have been
lodged as soon as the insigne was placed on the flag,
or else not lodged at all. But now the insigne is a fact
and should be left where it is. You cannot take the idea
of the union out of men's minds; what satisfaction can
there be then in taking the insigne off the flag? I cannot
understand why this insigne should be taken as a mark
of Norway's dependence. It simply shows that we are no
more dependent on them than they are on us. Moreover,
I don't have any great liking for symbols. Symbols are no
longer up to date except in Norway. So much time is
spent on symbols and theories and ideas up there that it
is impossible to make any headway in practical matters.
And there is something enervating in this preoccupation
with unproductive tasks.

But the main reason I am unhappy to hear that this
proposal of yours has been brought to the attention of the

public is that I consider it a crime against our people to
make a burning issue of matters that are not truly urgent.
It is not possible for more than one issue at a time to be
brought before the public for their urgent consideration.
If there is more than one, they draw attention and interest
from each other. Now we do have a single, major, burning
issue before us, but unfortunately it does not give the
appearance of being one. There is only one issue in
Norway that is worth fighting for now, and that is the
introduction of an up-to-date public education system.
This issue includes all the others. If it is not carried out,
we might as well forget about all the others. Having our
politicians provide the social system with a few more
freedoms does not matter very much as long as they do
not provide the individual with freedom. It is said that
Norway is a free and independent country; but I don't set
much store by this freedom and independence as long as
the individual human being is neither free nor independent. And in Norway he is not. In the whole country there
are not more than twenty-five free and independent persons. Such people are simply not to be found. I have tried
to acquaint myself with our teaching methods, school
plans, schedules, courses, etc., and it is disturbing to see
how much of class time, especially in the lower grades, is
taken up with old Jewish mythology and saga history and
medieval distortions of a moral teaching which in its
original form was undoubtedly the purest and finest that
has ever been preached. Here is an area in which all of
us, acting as one, should show a "pure flag." Let the sign
of the union remain, but take the sign of monkishness out
of men's minds. Remove the sign of prejudice, of narrow-
mindedness and wrongheadedness and slavishness and the
groundless belief in authority, so that the individual human
being can sail under his own flag. The flag you sail under
now is neither pure nor your own. But of course this is a
practical matter, and practical matters have a difficult
time arousing any interest in our country. Our whole
educational system has prevented us from reaching that
stage of development. And that is also why our politics
create the false impression that we actually have a national
assembly. We are still discussing principles. Other countries have long ago got clear of principles and are battling
over the practical ways in which to realize them. If a new

task confronts Norwegians, it is greeted not with confidence and resourcefulness but with confusion. Our public education system has simply succeeded in confusing the Norwegian people. That was made all too clear in the flag affair—and on both sides. Those who live off the sea have undoubtedly the clearest view of the matter, which is only natural since their trade allows them a freer development of their personality. But when the farmers and peasants from the remote valleys declare in public speeches their urgent need to see the union sign removed from the flag, this cannot possibly be regarded as other than the purest humbug. For if there is not an urgent need to liberate one's own personality, there can scarcely be any urgent need to liberate a mere abstraction like a symbol.

I must limit myself to these random remarks on the flag affair. I cannot possibly go along with you on it, nor can I agree with you when you say in your letter that we poets are especially called upon to further this cause. I do not believe that it is our mission to be responsible for the freedom and independence of the state, but rather to awaken individuals to freedom and independence—and as many of them as possible. In my eyes politics is not the most important business of our people; and in Norway it takes up more of our time than is compatible with personal efforts at liberation. Norway is both free and independent enough; but a great deal needs to be done before we can say the same of Norwegian men and Norwegian women.

With best wishes to you and your family,

Henrik Ibsen

To Frederik Hegel

Amalfi, September 15, 1879

. . . I am in complete agreement with you that the publication of a play does not hurt theater attendance. In my letters accompanying the script to the theater managements in Denmark and the other Scandinavian countries I make it a special point that the publication of [*A Doll's House*] will under no circumstances be delayed beyond the first half of November.

May I express my warmest thanks for the large first printing you have announced and for the increased royalty on this issue. I hope that all will go well with the printing and that the book will meet with a lively reception. One thing is certain, anyway: I cannot recall any work of mine that gave me so much satisfaction during the working out of the details as this one has. . . .

The Danish Royal Theater accepted *A Doll's House* on condition that the book not be published until December 21. Since this would virtually remove the book from the Christmas market, Ibsen regarded the condition as tantamount to a rejection of the play, and sent a telegram to the theater saying so. The upshot was that the book was published on December 4, and the play opened on December 21. The large first printing of 8,000 copies was followed by a second of 3,000 on January 4, 1880, and a third came out in March. The book was an international success, with Finnish, English, Polish, Russian, and Italian editions all appearing within a few years. After its première at the Royal Theater in Copenhagen, the play was performed at the other Scandinavian capitals, opening at the Royal Dramatic Theater in Stockholm on January 8, 1880, and at the Christiania Theater on January 20.

To John Paulsen

Amalfi, September 20, 1879

John Paulsen, a young aspiring writer who spent many informal hours with Ibsen, was later to serve as Ibsen's Eckermann by publishing his conversations with the playwright (*Samliv med Ibsen*, 2 vol., Christiania and Copenhagen, 1906–13). But long before that, he was to earn Ibsen's wrath by publishing a novel in which the married couple were easily recognizable as Mr. and Mrs. Ibsen.

Dear Mr. Paulsen, A new play, which I have just completed, has occupied so much of my time during these last months that I have had absolutely none to spare for answering letters. This is why you have not heard from me sooner in reference to your letter of August 9.

It was impossible for me, while I was so busy, to read your manuscript and give a carefully considered opinion of it. It would have taken much more of my time than, with every wish to oblige, I could spare. Nor is it possible for me even now to be of service to you. We are leaving here immediately. Our first destination is still uncertain, but we are due in Munich early in October.

I must also tell you that I have had to make it a fixed rule not to act as intermediary between Hegel and authors who wish to have their works published by him. I have had no trouble committing myself to this rule since experience has proved to me that such intervention is absolutely useless. Hegel has himself a very sure instinct about what it pays to publish and what not; and to remind him of other considerations is, I am sure, not your intention, any more than it would be mine.

But, dear Mr. Paulsen, is it of advantage for your training and development in general to remain so long in Paris? I cannot believe that it is. You can study French literature just as well elsewhere, and the many other studies that are imperative if you want to get ahead can be pursued with much more advantage in Germany. You ought to go to Munich, and work hard there for a whole year, or even two, attending lectures at the university according to a fixed, well-considered plan. Nothing matures a man's mind so much as acquiring a thorough knowledge of some one subject. History would be the most suitable subject for you. You ought to make a thorough study of the history of civilization, of literature, and of art; and there are particularly good professors in Munich in these branches. An extensive knowledge of history is indispensable to a modern author, for without it he is incapable of judging his age, his contemporaries and their motives and actions except in the most incomplete and superficial manner.

Think it over. And if you can, come to Munich this winter. With kindest regards from all of us, I remain

Yours very sincerely,

Henrik Ibsen

To Lorentz Dietrichson

Munich, December 19, 1879

The poem by Dietrichson referred to in this letter was an ardent plea for the recognition of art and national traditions as civilizing forces.

Dear Friend, Let me first of all thank you for sending me your polemic poem and to congratulate you on it, as well as on the immediate demand for a second printing. I hope that others will soon be called for.

It gave me much pleasure to read the easy-flowing, deft verse which not many poets can imitate, and I found your idea of basing the whole poem on the Kivleslaat legend both original and effective. And I must say that the cause you are working for is unmistakably one of far-reaching import. But it seems very doubtful to me that it will be possible to arouse and reform our good Norwegian people gradually—bit by bit. I doubt that better artistic conditions can be attained until the intellectual soil has been thoroughly plowed up and the intellectual swamp has been drained.

As long as a nation considers it more important to build chapels than theaters, as long as it is more eager to support the Zulu Mission than the Art Museum, art cannot really thrive and cannot even be considered as one of the immediate necessities. I do not think it is of much use to plead the cause of art with arguments based on the nature of art, which is still so little understood by us, or rather, so thoroughly misunderstood. We need first of all to attack and eradicate all that gloomy medieval monkishness that narrows our horizons and stupefies our minds. My opinion is that at the present time it is of no use to wield one's weapons *for* art; one must simply turn them *against* what is hostile to art. First clear this away, and then we can build. Of course, I do not mean by these remarks that a poem like yours, ardent and full of conviction, will not stir up and arouse people; I only mean that it will hardly succeed in changing the attitude of the general public.

But, old *carissimo*, do not let me influence you. Continue to write and to speak and to fight for what you have chosen as your task in life. Even if not a single one of your attempts reaches its goal, there is something about the spectacle of a man devoting all his powers to one task that is stimulating and that encourages one to emulate him. We live in an age of rapid progress, and you are a determined man with, I hope, many years still before you, so you will be certain to accomplish something.

Briefly, this is what I have to say. I am sure that you will not misinterpret it. . . .

To the Editor of *Nationaltidende*, a Danish newspaper

Munich, February 17, 1880

Dear Sir: In No. 1360 of your esteemed paper I have read a letter from Flensburg, stating that *A Doll's House* or *Nora,* as it is known in German, has been acted there, and that the end of the play has been changed—the change having been made, it is asserted, at my orders. This last statement is untrue. Immediately after the publication of *Nora,* I received from my translator, Mr. Wilhelm Lange of Berlin, who is also my business manager for the North German theaters, the information that he had reason to fear that an "adaptation" of the play, giving it a different ending, was about to be published, and that this would probably be chosen in preference to the original by several of the North German theaters.

In order to prevent such a possibility, I sent to him for use in case of absolute necessity a draft of an altered scene in which Nora does not leave the house but is forcibly led by Helmer to the door of the children's bedroom. A short dialogue takes place, Nora sinks down at the door, and the curtain falls.

In a letter to my translator, I myself stigmatized this change as a "barbarous outrage" against my play. Those who make use of the altered scene do so entirely against my wishes. I trust that it will not be used at very many German theaters.

As long as no literary convention exists between Germany and the Scandinavian countries, we Scandinavian authors enjoy no protection from the law here, just as the German authors enjoy none with us. Consequently, our plays are exposed in Germany to acts of violence at the hands of translators and producers, of directors and actors at the smaller theaters. When my works are threatened with such outrages, I prefer, taught by experience, to commit the act of violence myself instead of leaving them to be treated and "adapted" by less careful and less skillful hands.

Yours respectfully,

Henrik Ibsen

To Heinrich Laube

Munich, February 18, 1880

Laube had become director of the Vienna City Theater, where *A Doll's House* was produced on September 8, 1881.

Dear Sir: It was a great pleasure for me to learn that my latest play, *A Doll's House,* is to be produced at the Vienna Stadttheater under your widely renowned direction.

You find that the play because of its ending does not fit properly in the category of *Schauspiel.* But, my dear sir, do you really attach much value to so-called categories? For my part, I believe that the dramatic categories are elastic, and that they must accommodate themselves to the literary facts—not vice versa. This much is certain, that the play with its present ending has had an almost unprecedented success in Copenhagen as well as in Stockholm and Christiania.

I prepared the alternative ending not because I thought it was required but simply at the request of a North German impresario and of an actress who is going on tour in North Germany as Nora. I enclose a copy of the altered scene. After reading it you will, I trust, acknowledge that the effect of the play can only be weakened by employing it.

I suggest that you disregard the altered ending and produce the play in its original form.

Yours respectfully,

Henrik Ibsen

To Ludwig Passarge

Munich, May 19, 1880

Passarge's translation of *Peer Gynt* into German was published in October, 1880.

. . . Let me first of all thank you warmly for the interest you have shown in my writings. Your view of *Peer Gynt* accords perfectly with what I had in mind when I wrote it, and naturally I rejoice that it has found a translator who penetrated so deeply into its meaning.

Nevertheless, I was surprised to learn that you consider the work suitable for translating and publishing in German. I must confess that I have my doubts on the subject. Of all my works I consider *Peer Gynt* the least likely to be understood outside Scandinavia. Please remember that most of your possible readers in Germany do not possess your qualifications for understanding the work. You yourself are familiar with Norwegian nature and the manners and customs of the Norwegian people, with our literature and our ways of thinking. You know Norwegian men and women and you understand the Norwegian character. And is not this necessary in order to relish this poem? It is in this regard that I have my doubts, and I do not want to conceal them from you, although I take it for granted that you thoroughly weighed all these considerations before deciding to undertake such a difficult and lengthy task. . . .

To Frederik Hegel

Munich, May 31, 1880

. . . I have plans for a new project on which I should like to have your frank opinion, and which I shall therefore explain to you briefly.

I do not think I am mistaken in my impression that the preface to the new edition of *Catiline* has been read with considerable interest. Suppose I now were to write a little book of 160 to 200 pages containing similar information on the inner and outer conditions under which each of my works was created? For *Lady Inger* and *The Vikings* I would discuss my years in Bergen; for *The Pretenders* and *Love's Comedy* I would describe the following years in Christiania; and after that would come my Roman years for *Brand* and *Peer Gynt*, etc., etc.

Of course I would not get involved in any interpretation of my works. It is best that the public and the critics be allowed to disport themselves as they please in that field —at least for the present. I would simply tell of the circumstances and conditions under which I wrote, observing the utmost discretion, naturally, and leaving the field wide open for all sorts of conjectures.

Do you advise me for or against this plan? Do you think it is a good idea, and do you think this is the proper time or would it perhaps be better to wait? Please let me have your expert opinion when convenient. But please let us keep this matter entirely to ourselves for the present. In any case, I intend to spend the summer getting the manuscript ready. I do not plan to write a new play this year and I have nothing else to occupy myself with. . . .

Hegel was not inclined to encourage Ibsen in this plan, unfortunately.

To Ludwig Passarge

Munich, June 16, 1880

. . . I am very glad to learn that you have found a first-class publisher for your translation of *Peer Gynt*. But, with every desire to oblige, I am not in a position to give explanations of the many allusions in the book that may be unintelligible to German readers. It is impossible for me as a foreigner to judge what needs to be explained and what does not. For the same reason, I consider that it would be useless for me to apply to Dietrichson or any other Norwegian. I believe that no one can be a better judge in this matter than yourself; and if there is any particular point on which you feel uncertain, it should be easy for you to obtain information during your approaching visit to Norway. But I have the impression that you know as much about Norwegian matters as any native.

Nor is it possible for me to describe the circumstances that gave birth to *Peer Gynt*. To make the explanation intelligible, I would have to write a whole book, and the time is not yet ripe for that. Everything that I have written has the closest possible connection with what I have lived through *inwardly*—even if I have not experienced it outwardly. In every new poem or play I have aimed at my own spiritual emancipation and purification—for no man can escape the responsibilities and the guilts of the society to which he belongs. Hence I once wrote the following lines by way of a dedication in a copy of one of my books:

> Living is a war with the trolls
> In the depths of the mind and heart;
> Writing means summoning oneself
> To court and playing the judge's part.

. . . The meaning of the verses [Act V, scene 10] which you ask about is this. Peer Gynt claims that he is entitled to be admitted to hell because he has been a slave dealer. The Lean One replies that there are many who have done worse things than that, for instance those who have enslaved the wills and souls and the spirit of those around them, but because they did it in a "twaddling way," that is, without demoniacal seriousness, they have not qualified themselves for hell but only for the "casting ladle."

This short answer is all I am able to give you at present. . . .

To Sigurd Ibsen

Berchtesgaden, August 30, 1880

Dear Sigurd, Only today I received your letter of the 21st inst. I had a communication from the Ministry of Education, saying that there is no legal way of exempting you from taking the intermediate examination on entering Christiania University. But from a letter written by the head of the department, V. Herzberg, which accompanied the communication, I conclude that it is a pure formality; it only concerns the subjects you studied at the Gymnasium abroad, that is to say: philosophy, mathematics, Greek, Latin, French, and German. You need not take an examination in natural science or any other subject but the ones mentioned above.

So you won't have to attend the lectures that lead up to the intermediate exam and you need not take it at once but at any time you like. It is only required that you take it sometime before you enter for your final law exams.

I am forwarding you the documents I received from the education authorities care of Mr. Lund, the bookseller, where you will receive them on your arrival in Christiania. You can study them thoroughly and make your decisions.

There is, of course, no question of taking another matriculation.

I hope you have by now received my letter of the 18th inst., which I addressed to the Victoria Hotel. Your Mamma's letter has arrived.

I much dislike the idea of your luggage being deposited at Anna Daae's Hospital; the children she attends are from a class of people among whom one might expect smallpox epidemics to be rampant. Therefore, on your return you must inquire whether there have been any cases of smallpox among the families concerned, and, if so, you must consult Biedenkap as to what precautions should be taken before using any of the articles contained in your luggage. I take it for granted that you will not be around the hospital on your return.

I was very glad to hear that you were well and I hope you still are. From Paris I heard through M. Emanuel Gonzales, the *presidente honoraire*, that I have been made a member of the Société des Gens de lettres de France, which is a great honor indeed.

Since I last wrote to you the weather has for the most part been excellent, but the evenings are of course long and tedious. I have midday dinner at the Gasthaus zur Post, where I am very comfortable. Altogether I am very well.

Greetings to your Mamma and write soon again to

Your devoted

Papa

To Sigurd Ibsen

Berchtesgaden, September 18, 1880

Dear Sigurd, From my telegram you will have seen that I approve of your wish to continue your studies in Italy.

Since I received that communication from the Ministry of Education I have, of course, thought a great deal about the matter and have come to the conclusion that your decision, brought about by this silly and out-of-date legislation of ours, is probably all for the best. What would you have gained by becoming *Candidatus Juris* in Norway? It was never your intention to become a government official up there. The type of post you want you can still obtain: you can be a professor or enter the diplomatic service without having to take the final law exam at home. We have foreign professors at the university and there are posts abroad in the diplomatic service. So nothing is lost. But I would advise you at present not to make plans beyond studying abroad. Let time decide whether you will find it expedient to become naturalized in Italy or not.

I hope that you have expressed yourself in strong and decisive terms regarding the resistance you have met with, but don't say anything about your future plans and have as little to do with people there as possible.

How is Mamma and how is her eye? No doubt she has consulted a doctor about it. If you need more money, you can get some at Messrs. Lund, or at Hegel's if you should return by way of Copenhagen, which seems the most sensible.

And then you must let me know as soon as possible when you will be back in Munich. I suppose your Mamma will remember that the new maid is arriving on the first of October. I must know whether you will be back then or whether I should send the maid a daily allowance through Frau Haggenmuller until our arrival; otherwise I would have to go back sooner, which I would rather avoid. I would prefer to stay here till I get a telegram from Munich informing me that you have arrived. Then I would leave here at once and would find the house in good order. As I say, I must soon get full details. . . .

Many greetings to you and your Mamma, but to no one else up there.

Your devoted Papa,
Henrik Ibsen

To Frederik Hegel

Munich, October 25, 1880

. . . As you have probably heard by now, the authorities, with true Norwegian spirit, have tried to make it as difficult as possible for my son to continue his study of law in Christiania. Two years ago he graduated with honors from the University of Munich, spent the following year studying in Rome, and the year after that he was studying here. But none of this counts in Norway. They insist that he study for at least another year in Christiania and then submit to another examination before he may be allowed to register as a graduate student of law in Norway. I do not want him to waste his time that way, nor does he want to. All the foreign universities are open to him, and we shall now return to Rome where he will complete his legal studies and be naturalized as an Italian citizen. That black gang of theologians who at present run the Norwegian Ecclesiastical Department [which had education under its jurisdiction] shall receive a fitting literary memorial as soon as I can get around to it. . . .

✳ EXILE IN ROME
1881–1885

Memories of Childhood

January 17, 1881

(See page 1.)

To Hagbard Berner, Norwegian State Comptroller

Rome, March 27, 1881
Via Capo le Case

Dear Sir, Although I unfortunately have not the honor of your personal acquaintance, I nevertheless venture to address you in Bjørnstjerne Bjørnson's✳ name and my own in a matter that is of very great importance to me and probably also to Bjørnson. It concerns an appeal to the Storting now in session. My observation of your journalistic career during a number of years leads me to believe that you are likely to be both more willing and able than most officials to support the cause which I am taking the liberty of putting before you briefly.

At the time when the Storting voted a state pension of 400 specie-dollars, first to Bjørnson and later to myself, everyone regarded this pension as public acknowledgment of and recompense for our literary labors; and as such it was gratefully accepted by us.

✳ Bjørnson was in America on a lecture tour from the autumn of 1880 to May, 1881.

The conception of an author's property rights in his own work was very imperfectly developed at that time in our countries, and to a considerable extent still is. Neither the Administration nor the Storting had then taken any measures to protect Norwegian authors—and more particularly, the dramatist—from piracy. In other words, the laws did not secure for us, as they did for other citizens of the state, the certainty of enjoying the fruits of our own labor. As a rule, we received from the Christiania Theater a small payment, once for all, for our plays. For *The Vikings* they offered me 30 specie-dollars, informing me at the same time that if I was not satisfied with this, they would present the play without giving me any compensation whatever since they were legally entitled to do so. The other theaters in Norway and the traveling theatrical companies naturally paid nothing; and the same situation prevailed throughout Sweden and Denmark, as far as the smaller theaters were concerned. Indeed, even the Royal Dramatic Theater in Stockholm, as you may remember, once produced a play of Bjørnson's without paying a single penny for it in spite of the vigorous protests. Thanks perhaps to the sensation this aroused, the Royal Dramatic Theater in Stockholm and the Danish Royal Theater have since made an agreement with us to pay us what they think proper— an arrangement that we are obliged to accept and even to be grateful for, since neither the Administration nor the Storting has protected our interests by means of literary conventions with Sweden and Denmark.

In this manner almost the whole series of Bjørnson's plays and my own have been plucked from our hands one after the other, without our having enjoyed the financial rewards invariably granted to authors in other countries. How great the loss that we have suffered really is I only learned after copyright conventions were finally concluded between Sweden and Denmark and Norway. For Bjørnson and myself, however, these conventions have come too late, seeing that almost everything we have written in the field of the drama has been either taken from us or acquired at a ridiculously low rate under the previous lawless conditions.

But this is not all. Indeed, what I have just explained is the part that affects us least seriously. What does us much more harm is the fact that Norway has not concluded a literary convention with Germany or any other country outside of Scandinavia. You must be aware that most of Bjørnson's and my books have been translated in Germany and that many of our plays are produced in the theaters there. But if people at home infer from this favorable reception that we are probably well paid, or even paid anything worth mentioning at all, they are, I regret to say, very much mistaken. It is the translators or their publishers who reap the benefit; and we Norwegian dramatists have absolutely no legal means of preventing this. Even if we have translations made of our plays at our own expense, we may be tolerably certain that within a short time cheaper translations will appear to replace ours.

That Norway should voluntarily take steps to bring about a general international copyright convention, or, to put it more correctly, should become a party to the convention already existing between most of the European states, is of course inconceivable. Indeed, as a good Norwegian I cannot even wish that such a step should be taken because it is plain that such a convention would greatly increase the cost of every foreign scientific or literary work that it might be desirable to make accessible to our public in translation. And this would be equivalent to obstructing a great number of those streams of enlightenment that now flow gratis into Norway. Gratis? Yes, as far as the state is concerned, but not as far as Bjørnson and I are concerned. For it is we two who for a number of years have been paying, and still are paying, most of the tax on our country's literary import of information and culture. And this tax amounts to a by no means inconsiderable sum. I can assert in good conscience that Bjørnson and I are, comparatively speaking, the two most heavily taxed men in Norway.

These are the reasons I venture to ask you to consider taking up this matter and calling the attention of the Storting to what I have here briefly touched on. The state grants that Bjørnson and I have hitherto received are very far from being equivalent to the losses that we have suffered and are still suffering both abroad and at home. Might not the Storting consider it equitable to grant us a reasonable indemnity by increasing our pensions? * Citi-

* In 1875 the Norwegian Storting had voted down by 54 to 42 a bill to increase the writers' pensions for Bjørnson, Ibsen, and Lie from 400 to 600 specie-dollars [$400 to $600].

zens are always being indemnified for losses suffered in cases where the state has been responsible. And in Norway authors, especially playwrights, have been suffering for a long time. It is characteristic that in our country game was protected by law long before authors were. And as far as foreign countries are concerned, we are still treated like destructive animals. Anyone who wants to can hunt us down without restriction, and the most galling thing of all is that we have to pay the hunting fees.

It is my duty to tell you that I have no authority from Bjørnson to write in his name. Distance has prevented me from obtaining his consent. But I am fully convinced that he will agree on all essential points with what I have written. To me personally the matter is of great importance at the present moment because the university legislation in force in Norway—and only in Norway—has forced my son to expatriate himself, and obliged me to extend my stay abroad for an indefinite period.

I shall not be so bold as to propose the amount by which our pensions should be increased. With all due respect, I shall only take the liberty of recalling the fact that Nordenskjöld and Palander, after having discovered the Northeast Passage,° were each granted a pension of 4,000 kronor [$1,072] by the Swedish Riksdag. I take the liberty of suggesting the possibility that Bjørnson and I, in the course of our poetic expeditions, have discovered both Northeast and Northwest Passages which will in the future be traveled by Scandinavians as much perhaps as that opened up by Nordenskjöld and Palander.

Requesting you to use this letter in any way that you may consider helpful, and again urgently recommending the matter to your favorable attention and, with your help, to the attention of the Storting, I remain

Yours respectfully,
Henrik Ibsen

Almost a year later, in a letter to Berner dated February 18, 1882, Ibsen attempts to estimate his loss of potential income due to the lack of copyright agreements. Before the agreement between Denmark and Norway, he received the following flat sums from the Danish Royal Theater: for *The League*

° In 1878–80 Nordenskjöld successfully accomplished the navigation of the Northeast Passage from the Atlantic to the Pacific along the northern coast of Europe and Asia.

of *Youth*, 1,200 kroner; for *The Pretenders*, 1,200 kroner; for *The Vikings*, 2,000 kroner; and for *Pillars of Society*, 2,000 kroner. His total income for these four plays at this one theater amounted, then, to 6,400 kroner [$1,715]. After a copyright agreement was reached between Denmark and Norway, *A Doll's House* at this same theater brought him about 9,000 kroner. Since each of the above four plays reached over the years approximately the same number of performances as *A Doll's House*, Ibsen figured he should have made 36,000 kroner from them. Making various allowances, he put his loss on these four plays as 25,000 kroner [$6,700].

To Frederik Hegel

Rome, June 18, 1881

Dear Councilor Hegel, Since I have to write you today about money, I shall take the opportunity to let you know that there has been a change in my writing plans for the summer. I have put aside for the time being the work I wrote you about before, and at the beginning of this month I began to work with some new ideas for a play that has been in my mind for a long time and that forced itself upon me now with such urgency that I could not let it alone. I hope I shall be able to send you the manuscript by the middle of October. Later I shall tell you what the title is to be. For now, let me simply describe it as "a domestic drama in three acts." It is needless to add that this play has absolutely nothing to do with *A Doll's House*. . . .

To Ludwig Passarge

Sorrento, August 17, 1881

Dear Sir: I was much grieved to learn from your esteemed letter that you had been greatly annoyed by a statement made in my letter to Comptroller Berner in Christiania. If I could have supposed that the statement would be thus misunderstood by you, I should certainly have worded it differently. In my letter I refer, as far as I myself am concerned, only to the payments made by the theaters; in mentioning publishers I had in mind the publishers of the different editions of Bjørnson's stories.

Peer Gynt is not intended for the stage at all, and you will remember that I myself was very doubtful as to the wisdom of publishing the work in Germany. The idea of its being a source of profit to you or your publisher would never have occurred to me; and you must not doubt that I feel indebted to you for bringing it out.

The same holds good with regard to the proposed translation of *Brand*. This poem is not intended for the stage either, and when, in spite of the fact that three German translations already exist, you see fit to make a fourth one, you evidence an interest in my writings that I can only regard as highly flattering.

I feel convinced that the passage of my letter in question has not been misunderstood by any Norwegian reader. But to make perfectly sure, I shall, when writing publicly again on these matters, as I intend to do before long, make a special reservation which I hope you will find satisfactory.

I am very eager to have a look at your translation of *Brand*, and also to hear how it is received in Germany. If you should think of honoring me with a few lines, my address until the end of October is Hotel Tramontano. After that I shall return to Rome.

I am engaged this summer in writing a new play [*Ghosts*], which will appear in the autumn, and which I shall be pleased to send to you.

I entreat you not to allow your temporary displeasure to affect the sympathetic favor which you have all along shown me as an author.

Yours sincerely and gratefully,
Henrik Ibsen

To Frederik Hegel

Rome, November 23, 1881

. . . I am already busy with plans for a new comedy in four acts [*An Enemy of the People*], a work which I had in mind before, but which I laid aside because *Ghosts* forced itself on me and demanded all my attention. *Ghosts* will probably cause alarm in certain circles, but that cannot be helped. If it did not, it would not have been necessary to write it. . . .

To Ludwig Passarge

Rome, December 22, 1881

. . . I was agreeably surprised yesterday by receiving your translation of *Brand.* I shall read it as soon as possible. In the meantime please accept my best thanks for this new proof of the good will you bear me.

My new play [*Ghosts*] has now appeared and has occasioned a terrible uproar in the Scandinavian press. Every day I receive letters and newspaper articles for and against it. A copy will be sent you shortly; but I see absolutely no possibility of getting the play produced at any German theater at present. I hardly believe that they will dare to play it in the Scandinavian countries for some time to come. Ten thousand copies of it have been printed, and it is very probable that a new printing will be required before long. . . .

Ghosts met with a hostile reception when it was published in December. Both the book-buying public and the theaters were reluctant to touch it. A great many copies of the exceptionally large first printing were returned by the bookshops to the publisher. It took thirteen years to sell out the edition.

To Frederik Hegel

Rome, January 2, 1882

. . . I am not in the least disturbed by the violence of the reviewers and all the crazy nonsense written about *Ghosts.* I was prepared for it. When *Love's Comedy* appeared, there was just as great an outcry in Norway as there is now. *Peer Gynt,* too, was reviled. So was *The Pillars of Society.* So was *A Doll's House.* The cry will die away this time just as it did before. . . .

There is one thing that does worry me, however, when I

think of the size of the first printing. Has all this uproar
hurt the sale of the book? . . .

To Georg Brandes

Rome, January 3, 1882

Dear Brandes, Yesterday I had the great pleasure of
receiving from Hegel your brilliant, perspicuous, and very
flattering review of *Ghosts*. Accept my warmest and harti-
est thanks for the invaluable service you have again rendered me. Anyone who reads your article must, it seems
to me, get to understand what I intended in my new book
—that is to say, if they have any desire to understand. For
I cannot get rid of the impression that a very large number of the false interpretations that have appeared in the
newspapers are the work of people who know better. In
Norway, however, I do believe that the blundering has
in most cases been unintentional; and the reason is not
far to seek. In that country a great many of the professional reviewers are theologians, more or less disguised;
and these gentlemen are as a rule quite unable to write
about literature in a rational way. That enfeeblement of
the judgment which, at least in the case of the average
man, is an inevitable consequence of protracted occupation
with theological studies betrays itself more especially in
judging human character, human actions, and human motives. Practical business judgment, on the other hand, does
not suffer so much from theological studies. Hence the
reverend gentlemen are often very excellent members of
local boards; but they are, unquestionably, our worst
critics.

And what can be said of the attitude assumed by the
so-called liberal press—of these leaders of the people who
speak and write of freedom of action and thought but who
at the same time make themselves the slaves of the supposed opinions of their subscribers? I receive more and
more proof that there is something demoralizing in engag-
ing in politics and in joining parties. It will never, in any
case, be possible to me to join a party that has the majority on its side. Bjørnson says, "The majority is always
right." And as a practical politician he is bound, I sup-

pose, to say so.* I, on the contrary, must of necessity say, "The minority is always right." Naturally I am not thinking of that minority of standpatters who are left behind by the great middle party that we call liberal; I mean that minority which leads the van and pushes on to points the majority has not yet reached. I mean: that man is right who has allied himself most closely with the future.

I have written this as a kind of apologia, if such should prove necessary.

I was prepared for the storm of protest against *Ghosts*. But I did not feel that I could take it into consideration; that would have been cowardice.

I have to thank you not only for the article in *Morgenbladet*, but also, and quite as much, for your lecture on me and my work, and your intention of having the said lecture printed. Hegel writes that you wish to make use of some passages in my letters to you. I have, of course, no objection to your doing so. I have perfect confidence in you in this matter as in every other. If you wish to quote from the present letter also, you are at liberty to do so.

When I think how slow and heavy and dull the general intelligence is at home, when I notice the low standard by which everything is judged, a deep despondency comes over me, and it often seems to me that I might just as well end my literary activity at once. They really do not need poetry at home; they get along so well with the *Parliamentary News* and the *Lutheran Weekly*. And they also have their party papers. I have not the gifts that go to make a satisfactory citizen, nor yet the gift of orthodoxy; and I prefer to keep out of what I have no gift for. For me, liberty is the first and highest condition of life. At home they do not trouble much about liberty, but only about liberties—a few more or a few less, according to the position their party adopts. I feel, too, most painfully affected by the crudity, the vulgarity in all our public discussion. The very praiseworthy attempt to make our nation a democratic community has inadvertently gone a good way toward making us a plebeian community. The aristocracy of mind and spirit seems to be decaying at home.

* Ibsen's remarks about Bjørnson the practical politician were quite evidently written before he had seen the December 22 issue of the Norwegian *Dagblad* where Bjørnson defended the play vigorously.

I must break off here today. Please give our very kindest regards to your wife, and assure her that we do not forget her. Thank you once more, dear Brandes, for everything that you have done and are doing for me.

Yours always,
Henrik Ibsen

To Sophus Schandorph

Rome, January 6, 1882

Sophus Schandorph, a writer, was a friend of Georg Brandes.

Dear Sir: Accept my sincere thanks for the letter that you were good enough to write me, and excuse my not having found time to answer it until today.

It came as a very welcome Christmas greeting at the time when my new play was being misrepresented at home and subjected to all kinds of foolish criticism.

I was quite prepared for the hubbub. If certain of our Scandinavian reviewers have no talent for anything else, they have an unquestionable talent for thoroughly misunderstanding and misinterpreting the authors of the books they undertake to judge.

Is it, however, really nothing but a case of misunderstanding? Have not many of these misrepresentations and distorted interpretations been presented to the public by writers fully aware of what they were doing? I can hardly think otherwise.

They endeavor to make me responsible for the opinions expressed by some of the characters in the play. And yet there is not in the whole book a single opinion, a single utterance, that can be laid to the account of the author. I took good care to avoid this. The method in itself, the technique which determined the form of the work, entirely precluded the author's appearing in the speeches. My intention was to produce the impression in the mind of the reader that he was experiencing something real. Now, nothing would more effectively prevent such an impression than the insertion of the author's private opinions in the dialogue. Do they imagine at home that I have not enough dramatic instinct to be aware of this? Of course I was aware of it, and I acted accordingly. And in none of my other plays is the author such an outsider, so entirely absent, as in this one.

And they also say that the book preaches nihilism. It does not. It preaches nothing at all. It merely points out that there is a ferment of nihilism under the surface, at home as elsewhere. And this is inevitable. A Pastor Manders will always provoke some Mrs. Alving into rebelling. And just because she is a woman, she will, once she has begun, go to great extremes.

I hope that Georg Brandes' article in *Morgenbladet* will be of great assistance in producing a more correct impression of the play. *Morgenbladet* has on several occasions shown good will toward me; and I trust you will be good enough to convey my deep gratitude to the editors. . . .

P.S. If any part of the above letter is likely to be of interest to readers of *Morgenbladet,* I have no objection to its publication.

After this letter appeared in *Morgenbladet* on January 14, Strindberg wrote to Edvard Brandes on January 18: "But does [your brother Georg] really believe that Ibsen stands by his ideas otherwise? Isn't Ibsen being a coward in his explanation?" Edvard agreed. (Letter to Strindberg, February 20.)

To Olaf Skavlan

Rome, January 24, 1882

Olaf Skavlan was editor of a new periodical, *Nyt Tidsskrift.*

. . . These last weeks have brought with them a wealth of experiences, lessons, and discoveries. I was quite prepared that my new play would provoke a howl from the camp of the standpatters; and that bothers me about as much as a pack of chained dogs barking at my heels. But the alarm which I have observed among the so-called liberals has given me cause for reflection. The very day after my play was published, the [Norwegian] *Dagblad* rushed a hurriedly written article into print with the evi-

dent purpose of whitewashing itself of any suspicion that
it approved of my play. This was entirely unnecessary. I
myself am responsible for what I write. I and no one else.
I cannot possibly embarrass any party, for I do not belong
to any. I stand like a solitary sharpshooter at the outpost,
acting entirely on my own.

The only man in Norway who has stood up frankly,
boldly, and courageously for me is Bjørnson. That is characteristic of him. He has in truth a great and noble soul;
and I shall never forget what he has done just now.

But how about all these champions of liberty who have
been frightened out of their wits? Is it only in the field of
politics that the work of emancipation shall be permitted
to go on? Must not men's minds be emancipated first of
all? Men with such slave souls as ours cannot make use
even of the liberties they already possess. Norway is a free
country peopled by unfree men and women.

I sincerely trust that I may find I have been mistaken
in the discoveries I have been making these last weeks as
to the nature of Norwegian liberalism. There must be
momentary circumstances of which I am unaware. I cannot believe otherwise.

I am sure you will understand me when I tell you that
I must refrain from any kind of collaboration. No one con-
tributor to a magazine ought to take a position totally
different from the others. In the present case could I avoid
doing so? I cannot say at this moment. I am very much
confused as regards the situation at home and need time to
get my bearings. Remember me to all those who are
silently my friends.

Yours most sincerely,

Henrik Ibsen

To Otto Borchsenius

Rome, January 28, 1882

Otto Borchsenius was editor of *Ude og hjemme,* a Danish
weekly.

Dear Sir, Although I see that the [Norwegian] *Dagblad*
is annoyed with me because I write letters to Copenhagen,

I shall no longer delay answering the letter that I had the honor of receiving from you last autumn at Sorrento.

You desired at the time some little poem in my handwriting, to be published in *Ude og hjemme* [*At Home and Abroad*] with marginal illustrations; and you referred me to the weekly in question for guidance in the matter of size of page, etc. I have looked in it in vain for similar contributions from other authors that could give me the hints required, and, concluding that the editors' plan has for some reason or other been given up, I have not sent you a contribution. However, if you still desire one, be good enough to let me know, and it shall be sent at once. Only please remember that I have nothing to offer you except what is already in print. It will simply be a copy of one of the small poems in my collection—for example the last poem, or any other which your artist might propose as more suitable for illustration.

Allow me to avail myself of this opportunity to offer you my warmest thanks for your favorable and instructive review of my latest play. By writing of it as you have done, you have rendered me a service for which I shall always feel indebted to you. It was a great consolation to me in the midst of the storm of excitement that has been raging both in Denmark and Norway to read your temperate judgment of the work, unaffected as it is by any party considerations.

It may well be that the play is in several respects rather daring. But it seemed to me that now was the time when some boundary posts had to be moved. And for that undertaking an older writer like myself was more fitted than the many younger authors who might desire to do something of the same nature.

I was prepared that a storm of protest would break over me. But a man cannot alter his course because of them; that would be cowardice.

It is not the attacks that have depressed me most, but the fear and trembling manifested by the so-called liberals in Norway. They would be poor fellows to man the barricades with. The Norwegian *Dagblad* has refused to print any more articles by Bjørnson. And if one looks carefully, there is much that indicates how isolated both he and I are in our own country. If we did not have Denmark, it would be a bad lookout for us and for the work of intellectual emancipation in Scandinavia generally. Once more my best thanks.

Yours most sincerely,
Henrik Ibsen

To Bjørnstjerne Bjørnson

Rome, March 8, 1882

Dear Bjørnson: For a long time I have been thinking about writing to thank you for having so forthrightly and honestly come to my defense at a time when I was attacked on so many sides [after the publication of *Ghosts*]. It was really no more than I might have expected from a man possessing a great and courageous spirit of leadership. But still, there was no compelling reason for you to step forward and express yourself as you did. And the thought that you did not hesitate to throw yourself into the conflict will always stay with me, I can assure you of that.

I am also aware that during your tour of America you wrote about me in kind and complimentary terms. For this I also thank you, and let me say at the same time that you were scarcely ever out of my thoughts the whole time you were away. I was extremely uneasy just at that time, and an American trip has always seemed an uncomfortably daring venture to me. On top of that, I heard that you were ill over there, and then, just when you were expected to return, I read about the storms on the ocean. It became vividly clear to me how infinitely much you mean to me—and to all of us. I felt that if anything should happen to you, if such a great calamity should befall our country, then all the pleasure would be taken from my work.

Next summer it will be twenty-five years since *Synnøve Solbakken* [Bjørnson's first novel] appeared. I traveled up through Valders and read it on the way. I hope this memorable year will be celebrated as it deserves to be. If things turn out as I wish, I too would like to go home for the celebration.

There is one matter I ought to mention. Through *Dagbladet*, or in some other way, you have probably become acquainted with the contents of the letter that I wrote to State Comptroller Berner about a year ago [March 27,

1881]. I did not have the opportunity to confer with you then, but I did not imagine that you would have any fundamental objection either to the contents of the letter or to the application itself. It seems a searing injustice to me that we should remain so long without legal protection for our literary property. I have now written to Berner again and given him a survey of the income that I, for one, have lost [see notes following letter of March 27, 1881]. Considering only the two royal theaters at Stockholm and Copenhagen, this amounts to about 25,000 kroner [$6,700]. A *Doll's House*, which was paid for according to the new convention, yielded 9,000 kroner [$2,412] in Copenhagen. Each one of your plays that was performed there would have yielded you at least as much if the convention had been in force. Count up what that amounts to! And then Germany!

In order to work with full force and undivided attention in the cause of spiritual emancipation, one must have a certain degree of economic independence. The standpat party obviously opposes the spread of our writings, and there are theaters that refuse to perform our plays. It would only be for the best of the people themselves if we did not have to pay any attention to this in our future writings.

That is why I hope you will not disapprove of the measures I have taken. I have simply asked for justice, nothing more.

Give your wife our best wishes. And please accept my repeated thanks.

Yours sincerely and gratefully,
Henrik Ibsen

To Frederik Hegel

Rome, March 16, 1882

Dear Mr. Hegel, I ought to have replied long ago to your kind letter of February 16. Of course, I have not the slightest doubt that it was written out of sincere regard for me, but I must entreat you not to lend an ear to advisers in my affairs, especially when they are persons who have no proper understanding of all the really new elements in the literature of the last twenty years.

I know quite well how greedy the gossips of our little provincial towns are for all kinds of information regarding the private affairs of authors and artists, but it seems to me that I am as cautious as anyone can possibly be. Indeed, some of my friends feel that I injure myself by being too reserved. Mr. Otto Borchsenius writes on the ninth of February that almost all my Copenhagen friends are agreed that this would be the right time for me to give a distinct and complete explanation of my position. He adds (I quote directly from his letter): "Your publisher, too, asked me explicitly if there was anybody who could make you (me) speak." I only quote this to show you the variety of opinions on the matter. Your last letter makes it clear beyond any doubt that he must have misinterpreted your words.

I long ago abandoned the literary plan [for an autobiography] that I once mentioned to you, and I am now completely occupied with the preparations for a new play [*An Enemy of the People*].

It will be a very peaceable play this time, one which may safely be read by the state councilors and the merchants and their ladies; and the theaters will not have to recoil in horror from it. It will be easy to write and I shall try to have it ready early in the autumn.

As regards *Ghosts*, I feel certain that in due time, and not very long at that, the real meaning of the play will penetrate the minds of the good people at home. All the decrepit old fossils who jumped in to attack my play will have a shattering sentence pronounced on them in future histories of literature. And the anonymous poachers and highwaymen who have showered me with abuse from their ambush in Professor Goos's* butchers' and bakers' journal and other such places will sooner or later be forced out into the open. My book belongs to the future. Those fellows who have bellowed so much about it do not even have any real connection with the living spirit of their own times.

Consequently, I have been very cold-blooded about this part of the affair. I have made many studies and observa-

---

* Carl Goos was at this time professor of jurisprudence at the University of Copenhagen, conservative member of the lower house of the Danish parliament, and publisher of the Danish right-wing paper *Dagbladet*.

tions during the storm—which I shall find very useful in my future works.

And now I have a favor to ask of you. Will you kindly again lend me 1,000 kroner [\$268]? I expressly say "lend"; for I wish to pay interest on any advance payments I receive from you. It would make no sense for me to put my own money in securities and then take advance payments from you gratis. Since I only require the money for a few months, I do not wish to part with any of my bonds. I hope you will see the matter from my point of view. . . .

To Frederik Hegel

Rome, June 21, 1882

. . . Yesterday I completed my new play. It is titled *An Enemy of the People* and is in five acts. I am still uncertain as to whether I should call it a comedy or a straight drama. It has many of the characteristics of comedy but it also has a serious theme. . . .

To Sophie Adlersparre

Rome, June 24, 1882

Baroness Adlersparre, a Swedish author, from 1859 to 1885 was editor of *Tidskrift för hemmet* (*Magazine for the Home*), in which she published in 1882 part of her lecture on *Ghosts* under the title "What Are the Ethical Conditions of Marriage?"

. . . In the midst of the storm of bad feelings and protests that sprang up from all directions against my latest play, and in the midst of all the misinterpretations it has been subjected to, nothing could have provided me with more welcome support than the views and statements of a richly gifted and highly esteemed woman.

I am certain that by means of this lecture you have made hundreds of listeners and readers look on my play with clearer eyes. The lecture takes up an extraordinary number of the points that I wished to have brought before the public, and it does so in a manner that gladdens me

greatly, while at the same time I feel deeply honored. It
would be a waste of words to discuss details. But there
is one point I want to mention: I am completely in agreement with you when you say that I dare not go further
than *Ghosts*. I myself have felt that the general conscience
in our countries will not permit it, nor do I feel any urge
to go further. A writer dare not alienate himself so far
from his people that there is no longer any understanding
between them and him. But *Ghosts* had to be written.
After Nora, Mrs. Alving had to come.

I have already begun to survey new fields. Just recently
I completed a new play in five acts, which deals with quite
different aspects of modern life and times in our countries.
I don't dare hope—nor would I wish it—that this new
work will escape being the target of protests and objections.
But they will be raised on quite other grounds than in the
conflict surrounding *Ghosts*. . . .

To Bjørnstjerne Bjørnson

Tyrol, August 4, 1882

Dear Bjørnson, You can imagine how overjoyed we all
were on receiving first your telegram and then your
two letters. If I have not replied before today it is because I had hoped till the last that I might be able to
do so by word of mouth. Unfortunately I must now give
up any idea of coming to Norway this year. We could not
leave Rome until Sigurd had finished his exam which was
not until the fourth of July.

Added to this I have been busy with a new play in five
acts [*An Enemy of the People*] which I am now writing
out in its final form. However much I would have liked to
have been present on the tenth of August, I cannot, for
compelling reasons which you will understand, put aside
this work; it would mean that it could neither be printed
nor played this winter.

So I will have to resign myself to being absent from the
festivities, but be assured we will celebrate the event down
here as best we can.

Through the newspapers I have been able to follow your
campaigns during these last months with the greatest in-

terest. The accounts of them have given me a great deal to think about; they have confirmed much that I already suspected regarding the social views at home. And again and again I had to ask myself: is it a good thing that politics should so completely take precedence over social problems? That is undoubtedly the case in Norway at present. Social problems seem of no importance with us; and yet the rest of Europe is so intensely interested in them; people are not so preoccupied with politics down here. It is clear to me personally that where progress is concerned, it is more imperative to liberate people than institutions. And you know how things are at home regarding the rights of man. You have had your experiences in that respect both in Drammen and in Larvik.

But I know well enough that you cannot look upon these things with my eyes. You have a powerful gift for politics and an irresistible urge to play a leading part in it, while I have not even a gift for citizenship; I am without any talent in that direction. Therefore it is just as natural for you to put yourself at the head of things as it is for me to remain outside.

Don't on any account think that I am unaware of the greatness and the importance of your actions; but to me the greatest and most important thing is that you put into the field the whole of your strong and truthful personality.

That is poetry put into practice. Your work has a first place in literature and this it will always retain. But should I have to decide what to inscribe on a monument in your memory, I would choose these words: "His life was his greatest poem." To express oneself in one's life is, I feel, something of the finest that man can achieve. We all try to do this, but most of us make a mess of it.

I am sitting here writing carelessly and disjointedly, but I hope you will understand me all the same.

Let me thank you for the past twenty-five years and send you my best wishes for your work as a poet in the next twenty-five years, whether you may express yourself chiefly by writing or by your way of living.

I hope that our wife is up and fully recovered so that she can celebrate the festive day with you in your home. I am sure she has had her share in what the past twenty-five years have yielded. If your son Bjørn is still with you, you must greet him from me and thank him for his two lively and courageous theater letters in the [Norwegian] *Dagblad*. No doubt he is a coming leader of the theater.

My son Sigurd will have to become an Italian, as our Ministry of Education would not acknowledge the validity of his German exams. In June he took with special honors the third and last of his law exams at the university in Rome, and on the fourth of July he took his doctor's degree in law and all the professors present on the occasion unanimously acclaimed him *Doctor Juris*.

The theme was: "The Function of an Upper House in a Representative Government." The faculty at home I dare say would have taken an adverse view of his opinions, but in Italy they are more liberal. He is the youngest doctor of law in Rome, twenty-two and a half years old.

Farewell, greetings, and hurrah for the tenth of August.

Yours,

Henrik Ibsen

To Frederik Hegel

Gossensass, Tyrol
September 9, 1882

Dear Hegel, I have the pleasure of sending you herewith the remainder of the manuscript of my new play. I have enjoyed writing this play, and I feel quite lost and lonely now that it is out of my hands. Dr. Stockmann and I got on so very well together; we agree on so many subjects. But the doctor is more muddle-headed than I am; and moreover he has other peculiarities that permit him to say things which would not be taken so well if I myself said them. I think you will agree with me when you have read the manuscript. . . .

Please have one word in Act IV corrected. A speech of Morten Kiil's reads as follows: "It will cost you dear." I wish it to read: "It may cost you dear." It probably occurs on the second page of the forty-third sheet of the manuscript. . . .

To Rasmus B. Anderson

Gossensass, September 14, 1882

Anderson, professor of Scandinavian languages at the University of Wisconsin, had inquired about permission to translate Ibsen's plays.

. . . I consider it most important that the dialogue in the translations be kept as close to ordinary, everyday speech as possible. All turns of speech and inflections that belong only in books must be very carefully avoided in plays, especially in plays like mine, which aim at making the reader or spectator feel that during the reading or performance he is actually experiencing a piece of real life. . . .

To Georg Brandes

Gossensass, September 21, 1882

Dear Brandes, I got my manuscript off my hands about a week ago, and now I can resume my long-neglected correspondence.

Naturally, you are the first to whom I write, for I have to offer you my sincerest thanks for the literary portrait of me which you have sketched with such a kind and friendly hand [in *Det moderne Gjennembruds Mænd,* which Brandes published in 1882]. I am, as you say, by no means indifferent to tokens of honor, but above all the others that I have received I place this careful and flattering analysis of my character and work, given to me while I am still here to read it, from you, the leading critic of our times.

When you read my new play, you will observe how it has interested and, I may say, amused me to recall many of the scattered and sketchy utterances in my letters to you; and you will understand how pleased I was that your portrait of me was published just before this new play appeared. Yes, my dear Brandes, you have lent me a helping hand this time, as always.

There is an inaccurate statement in your book I shall take the liberty of correcting. My parents both belonged to the most respected families of the Skien of their day. City Magistrate Paus, who for many years represented the town in Parliament, and his brother District Judge Paus* were my father's half brothers and my mother's cousins. And my parents were just as closely related to the Plesner, von der Lippe, Cappelen, and Blom families—that is to say, to almost all the patrician families who were at that time the most influential in the town and surrounding area. My father was a merchant with a large business and wide connections, and he enjoyed dispensing reckless hospitality. In 1836 he went bankrupt, and nothing was left to us except a farm near the town. We moved to this farm, and in consequence got out of touch with the society we formerly belonged to.

In writing *Peer Gynt* I had the circumstances and memories of my own childhood before me when I described the life in the house of "the rich Jon Gynt."

In your later letters you have repeatedly referred to two circumstances, the true and simple explanation of which I have not yet given you. On the occasion of my last two days' stay in Copenhagen, I was told that you were in the country; and as I did not see you and your wife at the dinner at Hegel's, the possibility of your being in the immediate neighborhood never occurred to me; and I can only believe that Hegel, too, was ignorant of your whereabouts. The explanation for my not having read your book on Lassalle† when we met in Munich is simply that Hegel had not as yet sent me the book; he always sends me those works published by him that he knows will interest me. Besides, I was occupied at that time planning *The Pillars of Society*; and under such circumstances I read hardly anything, and certainly not books that I know will engross me.

I do hope that you will find life in Copenhagen comfortable in all respects. I hope to meet you there next summer. There are so many things I want to say to you and to talk over with you.

---

* Actually Henrik Johan Paus was sheriff (*fogd*), not district judge (*sorenskriver*).

† *Ferdinand Lassalle* appeared in Danish in 1881, although it had been published earlier in German.

Our return to Italy is rendered impossible for the moment by great floods. We have no idea when we shall reach Rome. We must first get to Bozen, and there is no possibility of that yet.

With kindest regards to your wife.

Yours very sincerely,
Henrik Ibsen

To Frederik Hegel

Rome, December 2, 1882

Dear Mr. Hegel, After a fatiguing journey, during the course of which we were more than once in real danger, we arrived here on the twenty-fourth of last month, and have now settled down comfortably in our usual quarters.

I won't deny that I am awaiting the publication of my new play with nervous impatience. Its appearance has, I believe, been delayed by a combination of circumstances, and possibly also for prudential reasons. But I trust that it is out now; I hope to see it advertised in the Danish papers which arrive today. Generally speaking, November is a very good month for the publication of books; but it is not the best month for a play. It has no chance of being produced before the best part of the theatrical season is over. This is particularly true of Sweden where it must first be translated. But, on the other hand, since such a very large printing of my book has been published [10,000 copies], it is undoubtedly desirable for us both that it should appear at a time when it can count upon the full and undivided attention of the public, undistracted by other literary novelties. [*An Enemy of the People* was published on November 28.]

The immediate occasion of my writing to you today is, I regret to say, that I am obliged to ask you once more to send me a draft of 1,000 kroner [$268]. The last remittance came to hand duly at Brixen; my warmest thanks for it.

And I have another great favor to request. Will you put down my name for 4½ per cent mortgage bonds on the Norwegian bank to the amount of 4,000 kroner [$1,072] face value? I am informed that Norwegian government securities are at present regarded with distrust in the foreign money-markets, which makes it probable that this is a favorable time to purchase. I myself will not hesitate for a moment to invest in them. Being familiar with the ways of the political noisemakers in Norway, I know that they will never commit themselves to any serious action. . . .

To Leopold von Sacher-Masoch

Rome, December 12, 1882

In an album of over five hundred signatures presented to Sacher-Masoch in Leipzig on January 1, 1883, on the occasion of his twenty-fifth anniversary as a writer, Ibsen wrote:

In these times every piece of creative writing should attempt to move the frontier markers.

To Edvard Fallesen

Rome, December 12, 1882

Fallesen, head of the Royal Theater in Copenhagen, desired to stage *An Enemy of the People*. It was performed on March 4, 1883.

Dear Sir, It gave me great pleasure to learn from Councilor Hegel that you wish to produce my new play at the Royal Theater, and I trust that you have received my telegram.

My special purpose in writing today is to prevent a misconception and misinterpretation of one of the parts in the play. A Copenhagen newspaper in giving an account of the plot writes of Captain Horster as an "old man," an "old" friend of the doctor's, etc. This is a mistake. Captain Horster is a *young* man; he is one of "the young people" whom the doctor says he likes to see in his house. Horster must, especially in the brief dialogue between him and Petra in the fifth act, behave in such a way as to suggest the beginning of an intimate and warm friendship between these two.

Moreover, I would like to request that you will, as far as possible, give the minor parts in the fourth act to capable actors; the more figures you can have in the crowd that are really individualized and true to nature, the better.

I beg your indulgence in making this request, which is probably a perfectly unnecessary one.

Yours most respectfully,
Henrik Ibsen

To Camilla Collett

Rome, January 17, 1883

Collett's novel *The Governor's Daughters*, published in 1854–55, was a passionate call for a new attitude toward woman and her position in the home and community. It had a great influence on Norwegian literature in the nineteenth century. On January 23, 1883, Collett was to celebrate her seventieth birthday.

My dear and most esteemed Mrs. Collett, A notable day in your life is approaching—a day that deserves to be celebrated far and wide. I am certain that it will be, although the newspapers do not actually tell of preparations for it. But they are probably being kept secret.

You may be sure that in our little family circle here, the twenty-third will not pass without our drinking your health and wishing you all that is good in the new decade upon which you are entering.

On that day you can look back with pride on the literary accomplishments of your life. But I hope that it will be a long, long time before the list of your accomplishments is finished once for all. Your youthfulness of mind is unimpaired. Your thoughts, your ideas, and your interests keep you still, as of old, in the vanguard of the fight. You have kept pace with the changes that time has brought, and we are entitled to hope that for a number of years to come it will be in your power to go on making valuable additions to the long series of gifted works which we already owe to you.

Ideas grow and propagate themselves slowly with us in the North. But although unnoticeable, progress is being made. The Norway now being developed will bear traces of your spirit and of your pioneer work. To coming generations you will be regarded as one of the fighters without whom that progress could not conceivably have taken place.

But first of all I hope that gratitude and appreciation in full measure may fall to your share while you are still among the living. It is depressing, it is terribly disheartening, to notice how people always begin too late to make amends for long neglect. It is a matter of complete indifference to me, as far as I am personally concerned; but it annoys, embitters, and enrages me when I observe it happening in the case of those whom I esteem and admire.

I hope, however, that the approaching day will not give occasion for any such reflections. It will bring you sunshine and a breath of warm air in the middle of the cold northern winter. Let these lines from the South, from the Pincio [a hill of gardens in Rome], which you love so well, contribute a little to the warmth. Good luck and happiness that day and all the remaining days of your life!

Yours cordially and sincerely,

Henrik Ibsen

Preface to the Second Edition
of *The Feast at Solhaug*

Rome, April, 1883

(See page 15.)

To August Lindberg

Rome, April 19, 1883

As actor and director, Lindberg did perhaps more than anyone in Sweden during the 1880's to further the new drama represented by Ibsen and Strindberg. Reading *Ghosts* as soon as it appeared in the bookshops of Stockholm, Lindberg sensed the great potentialities in the role of Osvald Alving. But at that time no theater in Stockholm or in the rest of Scandinavia—or in all of Europe, for that matter—would touch the play. By 1883, however, Lindberg had organized his own acting company, which spent most of the time touring the provinces, and he set about acquiring the rights to two of Ibsen's plays.

. . . In reply to your letter, I beg to inform you that upon payment of 400 kroner [$107] to the publishing firm of Gyldendal in Copenhagen you will obtain the rights to have your theater company perform *The League of Youth* and *Ghosts* anywhere in Sweden with the exception of Stockholm and Göteborg.

I remember very clearly our meeting in Munich three years ago. I regret I did not get to talk to you longer then. But from having followed your artistic career through newspaper accounts, I have received the impression that my plays will find themselves in expert hands.

Hoping that the above condition will prove acceptable, I trust that the performances of the plays will have satisfactory results for all concerned.

Very respectfully yours,
Henrik Ibsen

To Lucie Wolf

Rome, May 25, 1883

Lucie Wolf was a comedienne at the Christiania Theater.

Dear Mrs. Wolf, At the beginning of this month we had the unexpected pleasure of receiving a letter from you. The letter was addressed to my wife; but as it chiefly concerns me, I am taking the liberty of answering it.

You wish me to write a prologue for the festival performance to be given at the Christiania Theater in June to celebrate the thirtieth anniversary of your debut on its stage.

I wish I could comply with your request. Nothing would please me more than to be able to do it. But I cannot; my convictions and my artistic principles forbid me. Prologues, epilogues, and everything of the kind ought to be banished from the stage. The stage is for dramatic art alone; and declamation is not a dramatic art.

The prologue would of course have to be in verse, since that is the established custom. But I will take no part in perpetuating this custom. Verse has been most injurious to the art of the drama. A true artist of the stage, whose repertoire is the contemporary drama, should not be willing to let a single verse cross her lips. It is improbable that verse will be employed to any extent worth mentioning in the drama of the immediate future since the aims of the dramatists of the future are almost certain to be incompatible with it. Consequently it is doomed. For art forms become extinct, just as the preposterous animal forms of prehistoric time became extinct when their day was over.

A tragedy in iambic pentameters is already as rare a phenomenon as the dodo, of which only a few specimens are still in existence on some African island.

During the last seven or eight years I have hardly written a single verse, devoting myself exclusively to the very much more difficult art of writing the straightforward, plain language spoken in real life. It is by means of this language that you have become the excellent artist you now are. You have never used smooth verses to delude anyone about your art.

But there is yet another argument, which I think is the chief one. In a prologue all kinds of agreeable things are said to the public. The public is thanked for its leniency and its instructive criticism, while the artist makes himself as insignificant as possible by crawling into the nooks and corners of rhymed verses. Is this honest? You know as well as I do that it is not. The exact opposite is the truth. It is not you who are in debt to the public; it is the public who are deeply in debt to you for your thirty years of faithful work.

In my opinion this is the point of view that an important artist has a duty to maintain out of respect for himself and his profession. And I am certain that you yourself will admit that, holding such opinions, I cannot very well undertake to compose a prologue for the occasion in question.

But though I am unable to serve you in this matter, I trust that you will, nevertheless, accept the tribute of thanks I herewith offer you, thanks for all you have meant and still mean to our stage, and my special thanks for the important share you have had in rendering so many of my own dramatic works.

Hoping and heartily wishing that there will be a long and bright artistic career still before you, I remain

Your attached old friend,

Henrik Ibsen

To Georg Brandes

Rome, June 12, 1883

Dear Brandes, Once again I must begin by asking you to forgive my long delay in answering your latest kind and friendly letter.

I was delighted to hear that your essay on me is about to be published in Germany. I wrote immediately to Hanfstaengl, the Munich photographer, requesting him to send direct to the office of *Nord und Süd* two different cabinet photographs of me—which I hope he did at once. I included on a visiting card my signature for the photographs.

Please accept my deep thanks for your great work on the Romantic School in France [the fifth volume of *Main Currents in Nineteenth-Century Literature*]. I need not tell you that I have read it with the keenest interest. While reading it, I had the feeling that I was actually living in the period you describe. But it is impossible for me to express my opinion of your book in a letter; I must tell you in person sometime. What strikes me again and again in your books is your feeling for the future. They introduce something into the art of writing history which I don't believe was there before. Your book on Disraeli in particular seems to me to be a profoundly original work. But, as I've said, I must talk about these things with you; my pen is not accustomed to dealing with such subjects.

Now that I think of it, it seems strange that I should never have told you how *The Feast at Solhaug* came to be written; but I really never attached any importance to the matter. However, when a preface was required for the new edition of that youthful production, I thought it was a suitable occasion to provide the true story.

As to *An Enemy of the People*, I think we should find

ourselves pretty much in agreement if we only had a chance to discuss it together. You are, of course, right when you say that we must all work for the spread of our ideas. But I maintain that a fighter in the intellectual vanguard cannot possibly gather a majority around him. In ten years the majority will possibly occupy the standpoint which Dr. Stockmann held at the public meeting. But during those ten years the doctor will not have been standing still; he will still be at least ten years ahead of the majority. The majority, the mass, the mob will never catch up with him; and he can never have the majority with him. As regards myself at least, I am quite aware of such unceasing progress. At the point where I stood when I wrote each of my books there now stands a tolerably compact crowd; but I myself am no longer there. I am elsewhere; farther ahead, I hope.

My head is full just now with the plot of a new dramatic work in four acts [*The Wild Duck*]. In the course of time a variety of crazy ideas are apt to collect in one's mind, and one needs an outlet for them. But as the play will deal neither with the Supreme Court nor the right of absolute veto, nor even with the removal of the sign of union from the flag, it can hardly count upon arousing much interest in Norway. I hope, however, that it may win a hearing elsewhere.

We were greatly pleased to read and hear of the reception you met with on your return to Denmark, and we sincerely trust that you may continue to find things there satisfactory in every way.

At the end of this month we go to the Tyrol, where we intend to spend the summer.

Our kindest regards to your wife and yourself. Thanking you once more for all that I owe you, I remain

Yours most sincerely,

Henrik Ibsen

In 1882 a group of Danish men and women sought to put an end to Brandes' exile in Germany by offering him an income of 4,000 kroner [$1,072] annually if he returned to Denmark. Brandes accepted the offer and resettled in Copenhagen in February, 1883.

To August Lindberg

Gossensass, August 2, 1883

. . . You must excuse me for not answering your letter of July 17 until now. But your letter was delayed in reaching me, and furthermore I have been unable to decide how to answer your request for the rights to perform *Ghosts* in Copenhagen and Stockholm.

I am fairly certain that in the not too distant future the rights of performance in these two capital cities will be much sought after. Obviously the conditions under which I would grant those future rights will be far less favorable to me if the play has already been performed there.

On the other hand, I can entertain the hope, strengthened by remarks in your letter, that if my play is entrusted to you, it will be given a stimulating and harmonious production; nor do I have any doubts that the spirit and tone of the play will be understood, respected, and rendered without any attempt to lessen its realism and ruthless honesty.

Consequently I will limit myself to setting the following terms: for the rights to perform in Copenhagen, a royalty of 500 kroner [$134]; for the same rights in Stockholm, 400 kroner [$107]. As per custom, the royalties are to be paid in advance to the Gyldendal publishing house (Councilor Hegel) in Copenhagen.

If you agree to these terms, no other producer or director will be given the rights to the play for as long as the granting of such rights might harm your interests.

It is extremely important to me that the translation [into Swedish] be prepared with the greatest possible care. This was far from true, according to what a competent and well-known Swedish critic informed me, of the translation of *An Enemy of the People* used at the Royal Dramatic Theater in Stockholm. The translator misunderstood many places in the Norwegian text, and other parts were rendered poorly, in heavy, unnatural speech, and using expressions and turns of phrase that do not occur in ordinary Swedish speech. The dialogue must seem perfectly natural,

and the manner of expression must differ from character
to character. Many changes in the dialogue can be made
during rehearsals, where one can easily hear what sounds
natural and unforced, and also what needs to be revised
over and over again until finally it sounds completely real
and believable. The effect of the play depends a great deal
on making the spectator feel as if he were actually sitting,
listening, and looking at events happening in real life.

You must excuse me for dwelling so long on this point.
But since this particular play, for which I have a special
liking, will be staged for the first time in translation, I
think you can understand why I concern myself so much
with everything that relates to it.

I have no firm idea how *Ghosts* will be received in the
provincial towns since I am not familiar with them. As for
its reception in Stockholm and Copenhagen, I have nothing to fear. Quite the contrary.

Hoping to hear from you in the near future, I remain

Very respectfully yours,

Henrik Ibsen

To August Lindberg

Gossensass, August 19, 1883

. . . You wish to perform *Ghosts* in Christiania also. I
can give permission for this only on certain conditions. In
the first place, I must insist that Mrs. Winter-Hjelm play
Mrs. Alving there as well. I can take that for granted. And
then I must absolutely insist that you do not use the
theater in Møller Street. This house is so cramped and
encumbered, and the distance between the spectators and
the actors so short that a completely effective performance
is impossible. . . .

I should also prefer that wherever my play is performed
there be no orchestra music either before the performance
or during intermissions. . . .

As royalty for the performance in Christiania I shall ask
no more than 500 kroner, which sum must be paid to
Nils Lund, bookdealer in Christiania, before the first
performance. . . .

The world première of *Ghosts* took place in Chicago, oddly enough, in May, 1882, when a company of Scandinavian actors performed it in the original Norwegian. But the credit for launching the play on the stages of Europe belongs to August Lindberg. His company performed it first in Helsingborg, Sweden, on August 28, 1883, and then played it at the three Scandinavian capitals, always, of course, at the secondary theaters. In Christiania Lindberg had to stage it at the Møller Street Theater in spite of Ibsen's explicit stipulation not to do so. The play was generally well received, and Lindberg's performance in the role of Osvald was a remarkable piece of realistic acting. On September 27, 1883, the Royal Dramatic Theater in Stockholm became the first major theater to produce the play. After that, there were very few productions of *Ghosts* in Scandinavia during the next fifteen years.

To Ole Andreas Bachke, Norwegian Minister of Justice

Rome, November 30, 1883

Dear Bachke, Although I know that your time and attention are probably fully occupied at present with important business, I nevertheless venture, emboldened by the good will you have shown me in the past, to write you on a matter that is of very great importance to me and my family.

As you perhaps remember, I applied in 1880 to the Department of Ecclesiastical and Educational Affairs for an order in council to the effect that my son, who had at that time been for a year and a half a law student at the University of Munich, should be permitted to continue his studies in Christiania without having to pass the "second examination" according to the Norwegian regulations. This application was refused on the grounds that granting it would be a breach of the existing laws. The proposal, which you were good enough to make at the time, that these laws should be changed, seems to have been ineffectual; at least we are not aware of any change having been made.

As my son was thus prevented from attending the University of Christiania, he continued his studies here in

Rome, and, as far as the university is concerned, brought them to a close by taking the degree of Doctor of Law in the summer of last year. While at the universities and since taking his degree, he has chiefly occupied himself with studies that bear on politics—constitutional law, international law, political economy, etc; and he is now in a position to present himself at any time for the so-called diplomatic examination here, which qualifies for appointments in the Foreign Office and in the diplomatic and consular services.

But before doing so, he must be naturalized. And this is a step that we have great difficulty in persuading ourselves to take. It is a very serious matter for a man to separate himself completely from his country.

Therefore, at my son's request, I am making a last effort to retain his Norwegian citizenship, by asking you to do what you can to obtain a promise from the government that his claim will receive due consideration the next time the post of an attaché falls vacant.

I may mention, as qualifying him for such a position, that in addition to his other acquirements, he speaks and writes German, French, and Italian like a native; and he will shortly be fluent in English also. He has special inclinations as an author—in the fields of sociology and politics —and he believes that an appointment at a legation would place him in the most favorable position for such work. At present he is engaged upon a treatise on "The Historical Development of the Conception of the State," the introductory part of which has appeared in *Nyt Tidsskrift*.

I have much more to say on the subject but dare not encroach further upon your time. I am reluctant to believe that I am—as some people have implied—*persona non grata* with a majority of the members of the government to the extent that I cannot reckon upon any consideration whatever. As to the head of the Ecclesiastical Department, I know quite well what to expect from him. Fortunately, his vote is not likely to be decisive in this case.

If you are able to send me a few lines in reply to this, please address care of our consulate here.

With kindest regards, I am

Yours ever,
Henrik Ibsen

In 1884 Sigurd Ibsen was given a position in the Norwegian consulate in Christiania, and the following year he entered the diplomatic service as an attaché at the Swedish Department of Foreign Affairs.

To Bjørnstjerne Bjørnson

Rome, January 9, 1884

Dear Bjørnson, Thank you for your New Year's letter. And pardon me for waiting until today to send you an answer. You must not think that in the meantime I have been in doubt regarding the matter. To me there was nothing to consider. As soon as I had read your letter, I had my answer ready, and here it is.

I neither can nor will take any leading position at the Christiania Theater. My theatrical experiences and the recollections of home are not of such a nature that I feel any inclination to revive them in practice. I might certainly feel a responsibility and a duty in the matter if I thought that as director I could do anything to advance the theater in Norway. But of this I despair greatly. Our theater staff is demoralized, will not submit to discipline and yield absolute obedience; and, moreover, we have a press that is ever ready to support the refractory ones against the leader. This is the chief reason why we cannot, as in other countries where the anarchistic tendencies are less developed, develop any real ensemble. I do not think I could manage to change these conditions for the better; they are too much a part of our whole national view of life. And, moreover, my inclination for the practical business of the theater is too slight. Therefore I would not under any circumstances undertake the job.

But dear Bjørnson, the main point, however, is this: it is not me at all whom the committee wants. It is you and no one else. Whether the hesitation you feel in accepting the offer is quite unconquerable I naturally cannot judge. But for the sake of the whole affair, I would be profoundly happy if it were not. I shall, of course, assume under all circumstances that you will reject the offer only after the closest consideration.

But whatever you make up your mind to do, the proper

authorities ought to arrange for your son to be attached to
the theater—that is, if he is willing. Last fall I exchanged
a couple of letters with him concerning other affairs, and
I gained still further confirmation of my conviction that in
him we would have exactly the technical director whom
we most of all need. Schrøder [the head of the theater]
might then remain, in case of need—that is, if you cannot
possibly see your way clear to accept the committee's
offer.

Besides, I must say that I am not quite sure whether the
Christiania public at present really feels the need of a
good theater. The audiences that the operettas and eques-
trian performances at Tivoli almost always can enjoy, and
the interest shown in the students' and businessmen's
amateur performances seems to me to suggest a stage of
culture incapable of appreciating dramatic art. For that
reason I regret that the opera at the Christiania Theater
was abandoned. The opera requires a less cultured public
than the drama. Therefore it flourishes in the large garrison
cities, in the mercantile cities, and wherever a numerous
aristocracy is gathered. But an opera public may gradually
develop into a legitimate-theater public. And also for the
theater's staff the opera has a disciplinary power; the
individual has to place himself in perfect submission under
the baton.

I shall return to the other points in your letter at another
time. Cordial thanks for the photographs. Best regards to
your wife from us. Also regards to the Lie family. I wait
with great anxiety to learn your final decision in the
theater matter. Thanks, thanks, and may success attend
[the plays] A Gauntlet and Pastor Sang [better known in
English as Beyond Human Power]. Stage them yourself
now. Farewell for this time.

Your truly,
Henrik Ibsen

Bjørnson did not accept the offer to manage the Christiania
Theater. However, his son Bjørn Bjørnson was engaged as
stage manager and technical director in September, 1884,
with Schrøder remaining as head of the theater.

To Frederik Hegel

Rome, January 17, 1884

. . . Holger Drachmann has been kind enough to send me his *Shadow Pictures*. It seems that the reviewers are almost unanimous in considering the last story in the book the best. As far as I am concerned, I cannot agree. I do not believe that the interest aroused by this story will be lasting. The world is not developing in the direction of nationalism and isolationism. Quite the opposite. Some of the other "shadow pictures" are much more to my taste.

On January 2 Lindberg and his company played *Ghosts* for the fiftieth time in Sweden. In Denmark and Norway he has performed it twenty-one times—in all seventy-one times in a little over four months. . . .

To August Lindberg

Rome, March 10, 1884

. . . I was especially pleased to hear that you are preparing to produce *Lady Inger of Østraat* with Mrs. Winterhjelm in the title role and with yourself, I believe I may assume, playing Nils Lykke.

The permission that you have requested of me you may have of course, and I am most happy to give it.

Since you ask me to set a royalty fee, permit me to suggest 400 kroner [$107] for all rights to perform the play wherever you like and for as long you care to exercise these rights. . . .

I am very happy to hear that *Ghosts* is still in your repertory. . . .

To Bjørnstjerne Bjørnson

Rome, March 23, 1884

In 1882 Hagbard Berner, one of the leaders of the Liberal Party, had presented a bill to the Norwegian parliament giving separate property rights to married women. The bill was referred back to municipal committees and was reported to the Storting again in 1884, at which time Ibsen, Bjørnson, Jonas Lie, and Alexander L. Kielland, the four major Norwegian authors, sent a letter to the Storting strongly urging the passage of the bill. Four years later it was passed.

Dear Bjørnson, The letter to the Storting that has been sent me has my entire sympathy. I herewith return it signed.

However, I must confess that I do not expect to see any results. If the majority of the Storting had honestly been in favor of Berner's motion, they would not have returned it to the committee chairmen for deliberation. In fact, they would not have asked men for an opinion on the matter at all; they would have asked women. To consult men in such a matter is like asking wolves if they desire better protection for the sheep.

No indeed, the minority of our nation that possesses all the political, communal, and social privileges will certainly not voluntarily give them up or share them with the unprivileged majority. Hence I also foresee what the fate of the proposals to extend the suffrage will be. None of them will obtain the necessary number of votes. Such things are not given away by their possessors; they must be fought for. And especially with us Norwegians where the decision really lies with a section of the peasant landowners. I have gotten to know the peasants of many countries, and nowhere have I found them to be liberal-minded and self-sacrificing. On the contrary, I have always found them to be extremely tenacious of their rights and very much alive to their own interests. Is it very likely that our peasants are different? I hardly think so. I do not understand why our men of the Left are called liberals. When I read the debates in our Storting, I cannot discover in the views expressed by our peasants an atom more of real liberalism than is to be found among the ultramontane peasantry of the Tyrol.

I am therefore very much afraid that social reforms with us are still far in the future. No doubt the politically privileged class may acquire some new rights, some new advantages; but I cannot see that the nation as a whole, or that the individual, gains very much by this. I admit, however, that in politics, too, I am a heathen. I do not believe in the emancipatory power of political measures; nor have I much confidence in the altruism and good will of those in power.

If I could have my way at home, then all the unprivileged should unite and form a strong, resolute, progressive party, whose program would include nothing but practical and productive reforms—a very wide extension of the suffrage, the statutory improvement of the position of woman, the emancipation of national education from all kinds of medievalism, etc. I would give theoretical political questions a long rest; they are not of much consequence. If such a party were formed, the present party of the Left would soon be seen for what it really is, and what it must be from its make-up—a center party of moderates.

But I have no more room for further pothouse politics. We are reading and rereading your splendid "old document";* I can guess what is coming and am eager to have the whole thing. Remember me to your wife, the Jonas Lies, and all other friends and fellow countrymen.

Yours,
Henrik Ibsen

To Frederik Hegel

Rome, June 14, 1884

Dear Councilor Hegel, I am pleased to be able to inform you that I finished the draft of my new play [*The Wild Duck*] yesterday.

It has five acts and, according to my calculations, it will fill some two hundred pages in print, possibly a little more.

I still have to make the fair copy, and I shall begin that tomorrow. However, as customary with me, this will mean not just copying the draft but a thorough revision of the dialogue. And that will take time. Still, providing no unforeseen circumstances prevent it, I would say that the

---

* The introduction to Bjørnson's novel *Det flager i Byen og paa Havnen* (translated as *The Heritage of the Kurts*) appeared first in the January, 1884, number of *Nyt Tidsskrift*.

complete manuscript should be in your hands by mid-September.

This play does not concern itself with political or social questions or with public matters in general. The action takes place entirely in the area of family life. It will certainly provoke discussion, but it cannot possibly give offense to anyone. . . .

To Georg Brandes

Rome, June 25, 1884

Dear Brandes, Many thanks for your letter, which I ought to have answered long ago, especially as I know that you keep strict accounts in the matter of correspondence—although you assure me that you have changed somewhat in this respect.

I would most willingly have written sooner, but for these last months my time has been entirely taken up with a new play. And writing a letter is not as easy for me as it is for you.

Like you, I have the distinct feeling that we stand much closer to each other now than we did during the first years of our acquaintance. I believe the reason for this is that we have both changed and developed, and that that change has tended to bring us together. I should like to talk to you about this and other related subjects. But I can't put it into a letter.

A tone of despondency pervades your account of your experiences since your return home. I am not surprised. I thought it perfectly natural that you should choose to go back, but I had an idea that your experiences would not all be pleasant. You returned to Copenhagen with a European reputation. And intellectual rank does not harmonize with democratic principles. Moreover, it is much easier to manage a party and lead a movement from a distance than on the spot. One's personal presence proves to be a source of irritation for various reasons and in various ways. I have had opportunities to observe this, and I have made use of my observations "in sundry wars."

I have been following with careful attention the literary comedy the press at home has been acting out for the last year or so.* I have not been surprised by the change in the part of the hero. But I shall not enlarge on that at present. Instead, I will thank you once more for your pleasant, frank letter, and also for the German version of my biography. I have not seen the magazine, but I have seen a separate reprint of the essay. Thank you again and again!

We have read in the German newspapers and heard from Danish tourists of the crowded attendance at your lectures. You see that your countrymen are proud of you after all, even if they cannot refrain from tormenting you at times. I know the situation.

I have finished the rough draft of my new work, a play in five acts, and am now engrossed in elaborating it—molding the language more carefully, and individualizing the characters and speeches more thoroughly. In a day or two I go to Gossensass in the Tyrol, expecting to put the finishing touches to it there in the course of the summer. My wife and son are going to Norway.

Please excuse this hurried letter. Remember us most kindly to your wife and your little girls.

Your devoted friend,
Henrik Ibsen

To Theodor Caspari

Rome, June 27, 1884

Caspari, a Norwegian poet, had spent the winter of 1883–84 in Rome.

Dear Mr. Caspari, I do not remember whether I told you when we were together here, that one of my faults was dilatoriness in the matter of answering letters. At any rate you have now been made aware of it by experience. I have had your kind letter and your beautiful, warm-hearted poem ["To Henrik Ibsen"] lying on my table since

---

* At the end of 1883 Brandes became the center of another literary controversy when the Danish writer Holger Drachmann, a former member of the "literary left," aligned himself with the Danish nationalists and the anti-French school, and turned his back on Brandes and all that he stood for in literature: "Europeanism, alcoholism, syphilitism, adultery-ism, pauperism, bestialism."

the middle of April, and have looked at them every day with the good intention of writing to you "tomorrow." But not until today have I acted on my good resolution. Don't be too harsh on me for the delay, and please accept my deepest and most cordial thanks for the poem, which moves and affects me each time I read it. And I read it often, for there is something in it that reminds me of home.

But you are greatly mistaken in thinking I want you to smash your poetic lyre. On the contrary. There is not a single poem of yours that I know of which I would wish unwritten; and I hope that in the future you will produce much more in the field of meter and rhyme, for that is your natural realm. I have not forgotten certain disrespectful utterances of my own on the art of verse, but they stemmed only from my own momentary attitude toward that art form. I gave up making universal demands of everybody long ago because I no longer believe that they can be applied with any inherent right. I mean that the best and only thing anyone of us can do is to realize oneself in spirit and in truth. In my opinion, this constitutes true broad-mindedness, and that is why I am so deeply opposed in many ways to the so-called liberals.

I spent all this winter spinning some new follies in my brain until they assumed dramatic form, and in the last few days I completed a play in five acts—that is to say, the rough draft of it. Now comes the elaboration, the more energetic individualization of the characters and their mode of expression. In order to find the quiet and solitude necessary for this work, I am going in a day or two to Gossensass in the Tyrol. My wife and son are going to Norway. How I wish I could have gone with them! But that is not possible. At my age a man must devote his time to his work. The work will never be finished. One "will not find time to write the last verse";* but still, one wants to get as much done as possible. . . .

* The hero of Holberg's *Jacob von Tyboe, or The Braggart Soldier* needs just one line, rhyming with "fool," to finish his poem to his beloved.

To Sigurd Ibsen

Gossensass, July 20, 1884

Dear Sigurd, It was a great relief to receive your two letters from Trondhjem yesterday afternoon. I see from them that you are well, and I hope you will continue to have a good journey. I had read in *Dagbladet* [probably the Norwegian newspaper] about your visit to Sverdrup and therefore was all the more pleased to get a detailed account from you. . . .

The second act, which is eight pages longer than the first, I finished on the 12th instant; the third act I started on the fourteenth and hope to have it completed this week. I see now that the whole of it will be finished in ample time. My daily routine is on the whole the same. . . . Punctually at 7 A.M. I drink my tea; I get up every day at 6 A.M. at the latest, sometimes earlier and it agrees with me splendidly, although I don't go to bed before 11 P.M. I thoroughly enjoy everything I eat. This year I am only charged 60 kreuzer [about 30 cents] per day for my comfortable, quiet, and well-isolated room. . . .

Right up to the fourteenth we have had beautiful, clear weather with a fresh breeze, but then it began to get oppressively sultry and in the evening of the sixteenth while we sat at the dinner table a terrific thunderstorm broke right above us. The rain poured down in torrents for an hour, and then it turned into an unbelievably heavy hailstorm. Hailstones crashed right through the window-panes into the dining room; their force was so great that they did not smash the glass but made bullet holes through it of their own size. And what size do you think that was? Many of them were bigger than the biggest hens' eggs that I have ever seen. We picked up some of them; they were as hard as ice and as smooth as polished glass. I took down the circumference of some of them on a piece of paper.

At midnight another thunderstorm broke out, the church bells rang incessantly and most people were up all night. At three o'clock I got up too, but went to bed again later. The two following days we had heavy rain showers and yesterday, Saturday morning, a veritable cloudburst. The Eisack [Isarco] toward midday burst its banks and up at Pontigal tore away the road over a stretch of between two and three hundred yards. It also threatened Gossensass, but in the end all was well there.

Farther down it was worse. You remember the little stream that comes down from the *Wasserfall* and runs away below the road to Sterzing, near the curve where there is a cross in memory of a murdered man? This stream became a big raging torrent that swept away the road so that the whole of that curve is now one gaping precipice. The railway line below was covered with rubble and the trains from the North could not proceed. All southbound passengers had to stay at Gröbner's, so we had a great disturbance here. Tonight the connection will be restored. A sweeping north wind is blowing and the good weather has returned.

Give many, many greetings from me to your Mamma. The next time I will write to her. Tell her that I send you both my wishes for an enjoyable and happy journey.

                                          Your devoted Papa,
                                          Henrik Ibsen

To Suzannah Ibsen

Gossensass, August 19, 1884

Dear Suzannah, . . . Yesterday I finished Act IV, which is about the same length as the others.

Now I am working on Act V, and as this will be the shortest, I hope to be able to send off the manuscript by the end of the month. Bjørnson and his wife and daughters are at Schwaz.

Bjørnson writes that he is working on the last chapter of his story, and suggests that when we have both finished I should come over to them on a visit. He will suggest the same thing to Jonas Lie, who is at Berchtesgaden, so that we can have a "Three-Poets Meeting." It would be impossible for Bjørnson to come here as all the rooms are still occupied or reserved, and it would also make a longer journey for Jonas Lie.

I have promised to go across for a few days. It will be

a relaxation from work and we may not chance to be so near to each other for a long time to come. It is now twenty years since we last met. . . .

Passarge's book about me, and Brandes' article in the *Nord und Süd* periodical, accompanied by my portrait, a masterly etching, are circulating in several copies among the guests here. My plays in German are known to most of them.

In the evenings I often sit and chat with Dr. Spitzer from Vienna. He is a quiet and charming person; no one would believe he could write with such an acid pen.

Give my greeting to Sigurd and tell him on no account to get at the back of any horses in Trøndelag. They have a reputation for kicking. Also, that I am looking forward to reading his essay, only he must not give all day to working.

Let us hope you will have a good time in every respect. I am as well as I could wish, eat and sleep excellently, and am in good form for my work. The weather is now cool, but healthy and invigorating.

The Scandinavians here send their good wishes. Farewell for the present. Write soon again to

Your devoted
Henrik Ibsen

To Sigurd Ibsen

Gossensass, August 27, 1884

. . . Work on my play is rapidly nearing an end. It will be all finished in three or four days. Then I shall read it through carefully and mail it. I am very happy when I work on this play. I keep putting in more and more details all the time; and I hate to part with it—but I'll also be glad. . . .

The German sculptor Professor Kopf from Rome has brought his thirteen-year-old daughter with him. She is as nearly perfect a model for Hedvig in my play that I could hope for. She is pretty, has a serious face and manner, and is a little *gefrässig*. . . .

To Suzannah Ibsen

Gossensass, August 30, 1884

Dear Suzannah, Although I do not know when and where my letters will reach you who fly about from one place to another, I must send you the good news that I have just completed my manuscript. The play is of considerable length, longer than any of my later ones. I have been able to put everything I wanted into it and I don't think it could easily be improved. Now it only remains to read it through, which will take two or three days, and then it goes to Hegel. Now I have to send him a preliminary note which must be done before midday, therefore only these lines.

I wrote to Sigurd on the twenty-seventh. The weather here is fine but chilly. Everything goes well. Your letter arrived on the twenty-second. Many greetings to you both from

Your devoted
Henrik Ibsen

To Frederik Hegel

Gossensass, September 2, 1884

Dear Mr. Hegel, Along with this letter, I am sending you the manuscript of my new play *The Wild Duck*. For the last four months I have worked on it every day, and it is not without a certain feeling of regret that I part with it. Long, daily association with the characters in this play has endeared them to me, in spite of their manifold failings. And I hope that they may find good and kind friends among the great reading public, and more particularly among the actor tribe—for all of them, without exception, are rewarding roles. But the study and representation of these characters will not be an easy task; and therefore the book should be offered to the theaters as early as possible in the season. I shall send the necessary letters, which you will be good enough to dispatch along with the different copies.

In some ways this new play occupies a position by itself among my dramatic works, its plan and method differing in several respects from my former ones. I shall say no more on this subject at present. I hope that my critics will discover the points alluded to. At any rate, they will find several things to squabble about and several things to interpret. I also think that *The Wild Duck* may perhaps entice some of our young dramatists into new paths, which I think is desirable.

I shall now take a complete rest, until new ideas come importunately knocking at the door. I do not know as yet where we shall spend the winter. If cholera breaks out in Rome or in that vicinity we shall not be able to go there for some time. For the present I am staying on here where, in spite of the altitude, we are still having real summer weather.

As you probably know, the Bjørnsons are at Schwaz, two or three hours by rail north of Gossensass. I have accepted an invitation to go and see them. It is more than twenty years since we last met. Perhaps Jonas Lie will come from Berchtesgaden at the same time to visit them. But this is quite uncertain.

Please accept my deep thanks for all the kindness and attention shown by you and your family to my wife and son during their stay in Copenhagen. They have been at the North Cape, and are now spending the summer at Selbu Lake near Trondhjem. It is uncertain yet when they will come south. . . .

To Suzannah Ibsen

Gossensass, September 17, 1884

. . . The reason for my not having written to you again until today is that I have been on a three-day visit to the Bjørnsons at Schwaz. I would not have missed that meeting for anything. The details of it are better told by word of mouth.

I will just give you the outline of it here. Bjørnson and his son met me at the station. They had a room ready for me at the Gasthaus in which they are staying; but I preferred to stay at another one where—just in case—there was also a huge big room at my disposal—very beautiful and comfortable.

At the Gasthaus of course I paid for my own bed and breakfast but I had dinner and supper with the Bjørnsons and was in their company practically all the time. They couldn't do enough for me.

B. has gone gray, but otherwise looks well and strong. Mrs. B. has also tinges of gray and is slightly deaf, but otherwise was as animated as ever and is a splendid character.

Both daughters are unusually pretty, well brought up and unself-conscious; I also like Erling, the son, very much.

Jonas Lie did not turn up as he was somewhat behind with his story. Bjørnson and I could therefore talk all the more undisturbed; we talked on political, literary, and many other subjects.

B. was much struck by some of my observations and later returned to them time and again. In one respect I have through this visit been able to ward off a veritable catastrophe for Norway, but about this I won't put anything on paper.

From all the Bjørnsons I have the warmest greetings to you both. It would be dear to me if Sigurd and Bjørn could see something of each other in Christiania.

But I must tell you a little about Schwaz itself. The place with its six thousand inhabitants has the character of a small town. It had become known there that I was to visit Bjørnson and the inhabitants greeted me wherever I went, whether with him or alone.

One family sent Mrs. B. a magnificent venison, another some wildfowl, others the best Moselle wine, and others again the finest old rum and many other good things. Everywhere, at windows and in shop doors, I saw friendly, welcoming faces. For there has been a lot about me in the Innsbruck and other Tyrolese newspapers during this summer.

Let me soon hear that you yourself are as well as I am down here. Fraulein Grøbner looks after me untiringly. Miss B. and Miss S. have now joined up with six other formidable eagles, all women painters. They meet at the dinner table every day and seem to have endless communications to make to each other, which they do in whispers and with heads stuck together so that it is impossible to say whom they malign.

The printing of *The Wild Duck* I hope will now proceed quickly.

Greetings to Sigurd and many to yourself from

Your devoted

Henrik Ibsen

To Karoline Bjørnson, Bjørnson's wife

Gossensass, September 23, 1884

. . . I trust you will not think me ungrateful, or more forgetful than the average person is in regard to hospitality shown to him, for not having sent you any word of thanks until now for all your kindness during my visit to Schwaz. . . .

You must not mind it too much if this letter is a little disconnected and jumps from one thing to another. As I've said before, letter writing isn't my strong point. I'm afraid that I've busied myself for such a long time now with the drama, in which the author must to a certain degree drown and kill his own personality, or at least hide it, that I have probably lost much of what I value highest in a letter writer. But I assure you that is only on the surface. . . .

To Bjørnstjerne Bjørnson

Gossensass, September 29, 1884

Dear Bjørnson, I was to write you about the theater, but I have not done so until now because of some unexpected letters I had to answer.

When a man has had as much to do with the management of theaters as I have, and has been occupied as long and exclusively as I have been in writing plays, he cannot help at times to want to take an active part in the practical side of the theater. There is something peculiarly attractive about the theater; and ever since you suggested the idea, a feeling of restlessness and desire has come over me. Besides, I cannot deny that I sometimes feel the need for a settled and responsible occupation. So there are motives which might be sufficient to induce me to go home and take charge of the [Christiania] theater, if it were practicable.

But, unfortunately, it is not practicable at present. The party in power at the theater is certainly no more favorably disposed toward me than toward you. My wife writes to me from Norway, "I could never have believed that we were in such utter disrepute with the Right as numberless signs prove us to be." I do not doubt for a moment that her observations are correct. To offer me the directorship of the theater would therefore be equivalent to placing the management and the theater in a hostile attitude toward many wealthy families and persons whose support is essential to the institution. And that is why it will not be done. You may be quite sure that I shall never be the director of the theater as long as it is controlled by the present board of governors.

But you will perhaps argue that I ought to go home all the same and do what I can in the meantime as a private reformer—speed the erection of the new theater, and thus help make conditions favorable for my appointment as director. All this might be practicable if I had sufficient means of subsistence. But I have not. I have not yet saved nearly enough to support myself and my family if I were to give up my literary work. And I should be obliged to give it up if I were to live in Christiania. In affirming this I am not thinking principally of all the worries connected with the theater. I simply feel that I would not be able to write freely, frankly, and without reservations there. And this means that I would not write at all. When ten years ago, after an absence of ten years, I sailed up the fjord, I felt a weight settling down on my breast, a feeling of actual physical oppression. And this feeling lasted all the time I was at home. I could not be myself under the gaze of all those cold, uncomprehending Norwegian eyes at the windows and in the streets.

In any case, I must have another year to think the matter over. If the government and the Storting see fit to increase the pension sufficiently to place me in an independent financial position, I might, for the sake of the theater, let one or two plays remain unwritten for a time. And it seems to me that the politicians who are in power ought to show us justice and grant us some indemnity for the great losses we have suffered and are still suffering on account of the lack of copyright agreements with foreign countries. The honorable gentlemen should remember that they certainly would never have held the position they now hold in the estimation of the Norwegian people but for the work done by us modern authors in awakening men's minds. And I notice that they are not so very reluctant when it is a question of compensations and remunerations for themselves.

Then there is another consideration. Do you think it would be desirable for Bjørn [Bjørnson's son] that I should come to Christiania? I am not sure that it would. I believe that as a stage manager and designer he can work freely and unhindered under Schrøder [the present head of the theater]. And of what real use could I be as long as they play in that old, horrible, narrow box of a building? The artistic reforms that I might wish to introduce would be impossible in the present theater. Bjørn will soon recognize this, if he has not done so already. He will feel so unable to carry out his plans for improved staging that he will soon agree with me that if theatrical art in our country is not to perish altogether, we must have an up-to-date playhouse.

No more today, except hearty greetings to you all.

Yours ever,
Henrik Ibsen

To Hans Schrøder

Rome, November 14, 1884

The Wild Duck was published on November 11 in a first printing of 8,000 copies and proved so popular that a second printing appeared on December 1. The major Scandinavian theaters staged the play during the 1884–85 season, the Bergen theater opening first on January 9, and the Christiania Theater only two days later. The unusual demands that the play made of the actors prompted Schrøder, the head of the Christiania Theater, to write the author for advice.

Dear Mr. Schrøder, On my return here last night I found your telegram; as a reply to which allow me to note the following.

I myself have no desire to cast my new play, nor could I very readily assume that responsibility, since several members of the company are unknown to me, and, in regard to others, I have no way of knowing their development except through newspaper reviews, which very often do not give a reliable picture.

However, I have supposed that Hjalmar will be played by Reimers. This part must definitely not be rendered with any touch of parody nor with the faintest suggestion that the actor is aware that there is anything funny about his remarks. He has a warm and sympathetic voice, as Relling says, and that should be maintained above all else. His sentimentality is genuine, his melancholy charming in its way—not a bit of affectation. Confidentially, I would like to call your attention to Kristofer Janson who, frankly, can be charming when he's talking the worse nonsense. This is a hint for the actor in question.

Gina, I think, could be acted well by Mrs. Wolf. But where can we get a Hedvig? I do not know. And Mrs. Sørby? She is supposed to be attractive, witty, and not at all vulgar. Could Miss Reimers solve the problem? Or can Mrs. Gundersen? Gregers is the most difficult character in the play as far as acting is concerned. Sometimes I think Hammer could do it, or perhaps Bjørn B. Old Ekdal can be given either to Brun or to Klausen; Relling perhaps to Selmer. I would prefer to get rid of Isachsen, because he always carries on like a strange actor and not like an ordinary man; but he might perhaps make something out of Molvik's few lines. The two servants must not be neglected. Pettersen could perhaps be given to Bucher, and Jensen to Abelstad, if he is not needed as one of the gentlemen at the dinner party. The guests! Simple supernumeraries cannot be used of course without destroying the whole act. And what about the merchant Werle? There is Gundersen, of course. But I do not know if he is capable of evoking what I want and in the way I want it evoked.

In both the ensemble acting and in the stage setting, this play demands truth to nature and a touch of reality in every respect. The lighting too, has its significance; it differs from act to act and is calculated to correspond to the basic mood that characterizes each of the five acts. . . .

To August Lindberg

Rome, November 22, 1884

More than the other Scandinavian directors, Lindberg appreciated the theatrical richness of *The Wild Duck*. After reading it, he said, "I get dizzy thinking about it. Such great opportunities for us actors! Never before have we been faced with such possibilities." To the playwright he wrote, "With Doctor Ibsen's newest play we have entered virgin territory where we have to make our way with pick and shovel. The people in the play are completely new, and where would we get by relying on old theatrical clichés?" Preparing to put the play into rehearsal immediately, he wrote to Ibsen about some details of the staging and got the following reply.

Dear Mr. Lindberg: In reply to your inquiry I hasten to inform you that *The Wild Duck*, just like all my other plays, is arranged from the point of view of the audience and not from that of the actor. I arrange everything as I visualize it while writing it down.

When Hedvig has shot herself, she should be placed on the couch in such a way that her feet are downstage, so that her right hand holding the pistol can hang down. When she is carried out through the kitchen door, I have imagined Hjalmar holding her under her arms and Gina carrying her feet.

I lay much stress in this play on the lighting. I have wanted it to correspond to the basic mood prevailing in each of the five acts.

I am especially delighted to learn that you yourself are likely to take a part in the play. . . .

To August Lindberg

Rome, February 18, 1885

Lindberg's production of *The Wild Duck* went into rehearsal at the Royal Dramatic Theater in Stockholm in December and opened on January 30. Recognizing Lindberg's innova-

tions, professional theater people felt that this production
was the first in Scandinavia to utilize fully the new "natural-
istic" approach to stage direction. The stage was treated as a
room with one wall transparent; the actors moved as if they
were in a real room; there were real doorcases; the doors had
knobs; and there was even a commode with chamber pot and
wash basin on stage. Indeed, Lindberg's commode became
as famous in Scandinavia as Robertson's doorknobs in England. But the critics were unable to agree on the merits of
the production. Their confusion stemmed in part from the
fact that Lindberg in trying to avoid "theatrical clichés" in
the various roles had slighted some of the leading actors at
the theater. They protested to the head of the theater, the
charges were echoed in the newspapers, and the reverbera-
tions soon reached Ibsen in Rome. Lindberg himself played
Hjalmar Ekdal, and though his performance was as much
censured as praised by the critics, their accounts suggest that
Lindberg's performance was actually a masterpiece of acting
and that it was the character as conceived by Ibsen that
perplexed the critics.

. . . When I submitted *The Wild Duck* to the management of the Royal Dramatic Theater in Stockholm, I was
absolutely certain that the part of Gina would be entrusted
to Mrs. Hwasser.

When I learned from the newspapers of the final distribution of parts, I was quite surprised. But it never
occurred to me to take exception to the decision of the
theater, since I was not familiar with the actress who had
been assigned the role of Gina, and naturally I assumed
that the management's choice was the best one.

Since then, however, all the reports that have come to
me from Stockholm agree that neither Gina nor Mrs.
Sørby is being represented in an altogether satisfactory
manner.

Whether the Royal Theater has another actress at the
moment who would be capable of giving a better interpretation of the latter role I cannot state positively, although I rather suspect it.

But I do feel absolutely convinced that the part of Gina
will not be handled properly until it is given to Mrs.
Hwasser.

Head of the theater Willman states in the newspapers
that such a change in the parts might be possible after
the play has been performed a number of times. On the

basis of this remark, I hope and trust that *The Wild Duck* will soon be brought before the public in Stockholm in the best production possible.

I beg you not to misunderstand me, my dear Mr. Lindberg. I certainly do not doubt that the present distribution of parts was arranged with the best interests of the play in mind. But it cannot be denied that this was an experiment which did not succeed completely in all respects.

I believe I should make it clear that Mrs. Hwasser is entirely unaware that I am writing this letter to you. I have not heard a single word from her in a long time, either directly or through other persons; nor has she heard from me.

Please accept my warmest thanks for your performance as Hjalmar as well as for all your work in rehearsing and staging the play. From the reports I have heard, all this seems to be exemplary. The triumph of young Miss Seelig [as Hedvig] gladdens me especially. Please convey my regards to her and my best wishes for the future. . . .

To Frederik Hegel

Rome, March 2, 1885

Dear Mr. Hegel, Please accept my thanks for the copy of *The Wild Duck*, as well as for the newspapers with reviews of the first performance and especially for the telegram that you were thoughtful enough to send me.

I see that there was some hissing at the first performance, and possibly there has been more since. I am not at all surprised when I consider the strained relations existing between the literary parties in Copenhagen at present. At all events, I do not for a moment imagine that the demonstration was intended as a personal insult to myself.

Mrs. Thoresen has written to us about the performances, which she thought were excellent, and she singled out the brothers Poulsen for special praise. I know Emil P. personally.* If you should happen to see him, please re-

---

* Emil Poulsen, who played Hjalmar Ekdal, excelled in the portrayal of Ibsen's characters: Bishop Nicholas in *The Pretenders*, Lundestad in *The League of Youth*, Bernick in *The Pillars of Society*, and Helmer in *A Doll's House.* His younger brother, Olaf, a character actor, played Old Ekdal.

member me to him, and give him my warmest thanks.

There have been disquieting rumors in Norway of late regarding Bjørnson's health; but I have not been able to find out what is really the matter with him. I hope that whatever he is or has been suffering from is of a passing nature. I only wish he would abstain for a time from all the excitement of participating in political controversies.

The immediate occasion of my writing today is that I find myself obliged to ask you to let me have a draft for 1,000 kroner [$270]. I have some money deposited at Mr. Lund's bookshop in Christiania, but I dare not touch this until I know how much Sigurd will require in Stockholm before the month of August. After that he will, presumably, be able to support himself.

We are having beautiful warm spring weather here now. This year we shall probably go to the country earlier than usual. We live more economically there, and it is quieter for my work. But we have come to no definite decision yet. . . .

To Ludvig Josephson

Rome, April 9, 1885

Josephson, now director of the New Theater in Stockholm, was the first to stage Ibsen's dramatic poem *Brand*. The première on March 24, 1885, lasted six and a half hours, with the final curtain being rung down at 12:30.

Dear Mr. Josephson, I have received letters from Stockholm and a number of newspapers, all of which express themselves with extraordinary unanimity on the subject of the performance of *Brand* at the New Theater.

I was very much surprised to hear that the play had already opened. I had no idea that it was to be staged so soon; in fact, I had begun to fear that it would have to wait till next year.

Therefore it pleased me all the more to receive the telegrams from you and my son announcing that your courageous, I may say rash, undertaking had been so remarkably successful.

It is more than ten years since you first mentioned to me the plan you have now carried out. In the interval I had almost forgotten about it. But you have kept firmly to your intention until it was possible to realize it. And I have several reasons for thinking that you could not have chosen a more propitious moment than the present.

I thank you most cordially and sincerely for having devoted your great talents and skill as a theatrical manager to a task that will once more join our names together in the history of Scandinavian theater. It is not the first time we have been linked together in this way, and I hope that it will not be the last. I have still a bunch of crazy ideas in my brain, out of which I think some pretty good plays can be made.

You must please convey my thanks to all your fellow workers at the New Theater—especially to Mr. Hillberg, without whose assistance you would, I suppose, hardly have been able to produce the play this winter.

I would gladly send my thanks to the Stockholm theatergoing public and the Stockholm press, if it were possible. But it is not. All I can do is tell you that their cordial approbation, of which they have now given me a fresh proof, is a source of great pleasure to me. It has effaced the impression made by all the cold, uncomprehending eyes which you yourself no doubt remember in a certain other city up there in the North.

May fortune attend you in your present sphere of activity! All best wishes!

Yours most sincerely,
Henrik Ibsen

P.S. My thanks for the royalty fee paid to Councilor Hegel.

To Frederik Hegel

Rome, April 25, 1885

. . . This year we intend to leave Rome about the end of May, rather earlier than usual. I still don't know where we will spend the summer, but it will be probably in the Tyrol or on Lake Constance, in a place where I can work undisturbed on my new play so as to have it ready in the autumn, about the usual time.

Whether or not we shall return to Rome afterward is doubtful. For several reasons it would be advisable for me to spend a year in Germany again, where I could attend to a great many literary matters better than I can down here. Besides, being in Germany brings me closer to home, and lately I have begun to think seriously about buying a little villa, or, rather, a small country house, in the neighborhood of Christiania—on the fjord—where I could live in seclusion and give myself up entirely to my work. The sight of the sea is what I miss most here, and my longing for it increases year by year. Besides, I have acquired with the years a small art collection, chiefly paintings, and all these things are now stored in a garret in Munich and give us no pleasure at all.

The successful production of *Brand* in Stockholm has given me great pleasure. But there was very little financial gain for me, as you know, since the great expenses involved in staging the play obliged me to let Josephson have the rights to the play for a single payment of 400 kroner [$108]. But this aspect of the matter is indeed of less importance to me now than it was twenty years ago at Ariccia when I began to write *Brand*. . . .

Speech to the Workingmen of Trondhjem

Trondhjem, June 14, 1885

The political tension between the Left and Right had reached the breaking point by 1885 when Ibsen visited Norway. Sensing the hatred and animosity all about him, he felt extremely uncomfortable and quickly abandoned any intentions he may have had to settle there. He made his own political position clear by speaking to the workingmen in Trondhjem, by rejecting the honor of a torchlight procession proposed by the conservative student organization of the University of Christiania, and by accepting an invitation to attend a banquet given by the radical students at the University of Copenhagen.

Eight days ago I returned home again to Norway after an absence of eleven years.

During these eight days at home I have experienced more of the joy of life than during all the eleven years abroad.

I have found immense progress in most fields, and I have seen that the nation to which I have the closest ties has brought itself considerably nearer to the rest of Europe than it formerly was.

But this visit to my home has also brought disappointments. My experience has shown me that the most indispensable individual rights are not as yet as safeguarded under the new form of government as I might have hoped and expected.

A ruling majority does not grant the individual either freedom of belief or freedom of expression beyond a certain arbitrarily fixed limit.

So there is still much to be done before it can be said that we have attained real liberty. But I fear that it will be beyond the power of our *present* democracy to solve these problems. An element of *nobility* must enter into our national life, our administration, our representative bodies, and our press.

Of course I am not thinking of a nobility of *birth*, nor of that of *wealth*, nor of that of *knowledge*, neither of that of *ability* or talent. I am thinking of a nobility of character, of a nobility of will and spirit.

Nothing else can make us free.

This nobility that I hope will be granted to our nation will come to us from two sources. It will come to us from two groups that have not as yet been irreparably harmed by party pressure. It will come to us from our women and from our workingmen.

The reshaping of social conditions now under way in Europe is concerned chiefly with the future position of the workingman and of woman.

This is what I hope for and what I wait for. It is what I intend to work for and what I shall work for all my whole life so far as I am able.

It is with these words that I take pleasure in extending to you my most hearty thanks for all the honor and joy which the Trondhjem labor union has given me tonight. And while extending my thanks I propose a toast: long life to the laboring class and its future!

Speech at the Danish Students' Banquet

Copenhagen, October 3, 1885

On his way from Norway to Germany, Ibsen stopped for a few days in Copenhagen. While there he was invited to a banquet in his honor given by the Union of Radical Students at the University of Copenhagen, a group that had been organized in opposition to the officially nonpolitical, actually conservative Students' Union. Georg Brandes and Professor Høffding lauded Ibsen with speeches at the banquet, and, reluctantly, Ibsen replied:

I do not like it at all to hear my praises sung so loudly. I prefer solitude, and I always feel an inclination to protest when the health of an artist or a poet is proposed with a motive such as: there he stands, and there far away stand the others. But the thanks given me contain also an admission. If my existence has been of any importance, as you say it has, the reason is that there is a kinship between me and the times. There exists no yawning gulf between the two. I thank you for the kinship I have found here among you.

✳ EXILE IN MUNICH
1885–1891

To the Managing Committee of the Norwegian Students' Union

Munich, October 23, 1885

The fact that Ibsen had refused the honor of a torchlight procession offered him by the conservative students at the University of Christiania and had accepted the invitation to a banquet in his honor given by the radical students at the University of Copenhagen was bound to have repercussions. In Christiania Ibsen's old friend Professor Lorentz Dietrichson brought the matter before the Norwegian Students' Union at its next meeting. He declared that "the great poet has on this occasion shown himself to be a small man," and he composed a poem, which was set to music and sung by the students, casting scorn on Ibsen. Inevitably, the affair received a great deal of newspaper publicity. After settling in his new Munich apartment on Maximilianstrasse, the still fuming Ibsen sent an angry letter to the Norwegian students. This was to be the last time that he allowed himself to be drawn into Scandinavian politics.

Sirs: You have seen fit to write to me and enclose in your letter a copy of a speech made by the president of your union, Professor Lorentz Dietrichson, on Saturday, October 10, on the subject of my refusal to receive a torchlight procession planned in my honor by the union. You lead me to understand that a majority of the members of the union have seen fit publicly to signify their general approval of the president's address as an expression of their feelings in the matter.

This expression of approval given in advance was, I must say, much too precipitate, and the most suitable proceeding on my part would perhaps be to return both the documents sent me without any comments whatsoever.

But out of regard to the members of the union who are friendly to me, I will offer an explanation, as short as I can make it, of my true position in the matter.

When Mr. Lorentz Dietrichson, accompanied by one of his colleagues, called upon me on the morning of Monday, September 28, to offer me the honor of a torchlight procession, he expressed himself in terms that led me to believe the proposal had emanated from the Managing Committee in its meeting on the previous Saturday.

This surprised me, for the Managing Committee had never shown any signs of good will toward me before, neither upon my arrival in the summer—when I returned to Christiania after an absence from Norway of eleven years—nor during the earlier part of the autumn.

Of course, I did not for a moment doubt that the supposed initiative of the committee was due to pressure of some kind from without. Still, I regarded it as courtesy on their part to have yielded to this pressure. Therefore I said "no thanks," politely but firmly and tersely. In the course of the interview I remarked that, since I had not noticed that my presence gave the union any great pleasure, I did not care to have it expressing any great joy on the occasion of my departure. No doubt I said this jokingly, but my joke concealed a serious point, which most people will understand. I am only surprised that a serious person like Mr. Lorentz Dietrichson did not get the point.

Later I referred to the fact that I had also refused the Workmen's Association; but this was used by me as an answer to Professor Dietrichson when he muttered something about getting me to change my mind in regard to the torchlight procession. I am sure he was being sincere, but his suggestion left a bad impression on me.

I requested the two gentlemen to convey my thanks and greetings—not to "the students," as the professor has reported—but to "my friends among the students." From his speech I learn that he has appropriated these thanks and greetings to himself, to his colleagues of the committee, and to all the members of the union. This is a misunderstanding. Not even at the moment when the torch-light procession was offered to me was I so foolish as to flatter myself with the belief that I had nothing but friends in Mr. Lorentz Dietrichson's Students' Union.

This includes everything essential that happened during the interview between the deputies of the committee and myself. From the professor's speech I see that I was right in presuming, as I did in my telegram from Copenhagen, that his report of my refusal must have been incomplete. It was incomplete and—no doubt unintentionally—mis-leading.

Later in the day on which I received the deputation, I learned from various quarters that there was a story be-hind the torchlight procession—a story which the two gentlemen had forgotten to tell me. I was informed as a matter of absolute fact that it was not the committee at all that had initiated the matter but that the proposal had been made quite unexpectedly by a section of the union that is in the minority as a rule, but which on Saturday, September 26, happened to be present in such numbers that it was able to carry the proposal.

I also learned from different sources that such a proposal could not possibly have been carried, given the present membership of the union and the present committee, if the ruling party among the students had known about it in time.

It was with all this in view, and mindful of all I had heard about the preponderance of reactionary elements in the Students' Union, that I gave utterance before a number of callers, one of whom was a student, Mr. Rode, to my sentiments regarding the union and the spirit dominating it at present. What I said seemed to interest the young student, and he exclaimed that he would be delighted if he might repeat my words to his "friends"—possibly he said to "the young students." To this I answered that he was welcome to repeat them to anyone he chose, in the union or out of it.

But it never for a moment occurred to me that what he had in mind was an official communication from me. This should be clear from the fact that in my telegram from Copenhagen I asked the president himself to inform the students of my real meaning.

During my absence from Norway, an absence of many

years, I have never had any official deputy or spokesman in that country. Had it been my intention to choose one on this occasion, I should certainly have selected one of the older and more experienced men of my acquaintance, and should also have told him precisely what I wished to have communicated. But, as I said, such a proceeding never occurred to me.

In itself, it is a matter of tolerable indifference to me whether my utterances were repeated at a formal meeting or over a bowl of punch. But what I am not at all indifferent to is the fact that Mr. Rode neither repeated my words nor reproduced my meaning.

If I may rely upon Professor Dietrichson's account of the matter as given in his address, Mr. Rode expressed himself to the following effect: "Henrik Ibsen desires that the party of the Right, which has a majority in the Students' Union, will do him the pleasure of unseating Dietrichson and his colleagues and electing a liberal central committee."

What I really said during the conversation was approximately as follows: "I have no wish for a torchlight procession or anything of that kind. The greatest pleasure the Students' Union could give me would be to have the leftist element, the minority, grow so large and strong as to become a majority, when, as a matter of course, it would unseat Lorentz Dietrichson and his colleagues in the committee and choose liberal-minded men in their stead."

It seems to me there is some sense in this. But in what Mr. Rode is reported to have conveyed there is no sense at all.

However, I do not blame the young student. He no doubt believed himself justified in behaving at the meeting as if he were my official representative; and though he has reported my words in a misleading manner, I have no doubt that he believed he was repeating what he had heard me say. He is probably not yet skilled in making logical distinctions.

The gentleman whom I do blame very much is the president of the Students' Union. He himself refers in his speech to his having known me for many years. Yet he puts on the appearance of seriously believing that I wished the students to be addressed in my name with these or similar words: "Listen! good students of the party of the

Right in this union, what I expect and demand of you is that at the next election of committee members you shall vote against your own convictions. I want you to unseat Professor Dietrichson and those other members who belong to your own party and to choose a new committee, entirely composed of adherents of the party to which you are opposed."

Can Professor Dietrichson bring himself to declare on his honor that he really believed me capable of such a line of argument?

Dare he, who has known me for so many years, deny on his honor that there occurred to him a hidden thought that I had actually expressed a desire to see so many students of the Right become so liberal in their views as to force them to get rid of the standpatters and to appoint in their stead a committee that would be in touch with the thought and aspirations of the age.

Dare Professor Dietrichson assert that this or a similar thought never occurred to him?

But now I come to think of it, if he had put such an idea into words, the union would have bethought itself to procure an authentic explanation directly from me—in which case Mr. Lorentz Dietrichson might have missed the opportunity of showing off before the freshmen just in from the provinces.

And the opportunity was certainly too good to let slip.

It was an opportunity to insult a creative writer. And creative writers are not popular in Norway just now.

And they are least popular in the circles whose point of view and whose taste set the tone for Mr. Lorentz Dietrichson's banquet speeches.

It is therefore quite understandable that Mr. Lorentz Dietrichson should at this particular time have seized on an opportunity to make a speech against me, especially since I was absent. And I consider that his introducing into the speech all kinds of low innuendoes and charges was particularly well timed and opportune. It seems to have pleased the Students' Union so much that the speech is recognized by it as an expression of the feelings of the union in this matter.

But now I have made it plain that "this matter" is actually quite different from what Professor Dietrichson assumed and from what the Students' Union evidently used

as a basis for its actions. The premises do not exist and
never have existed. Consequently Mr. Lorentz Dietrichson's speech has no foundation. It hangs in mid-air. The
whole thing is nothing but an oratorical paper kite which
this serious man has let fly into the air.

But what stands as firm as if it had been nailed to the
ground is the union's approval of the speech.

I must, therefore, repeat my opening remarks. The Students' Union has on this occasion acted much too pre-
cipitately.

Neither the union nor its president will succeed in doing
me any enduring harm, except that this episode will leave
behind a certain feeling that will remain with me for the
rest of my life. I shall be the same man I was the day
before Mr. Lorentz Dietrichson's assault. During the whole
course of this torchlight procession affair, I have had no
opportunity of proving myself either "small" or "great,"
either "narrow-minded" or "broad-minded." The "spiritual
tyranny" which has been imputed to me is an empty
phrase, and my behavior during the whole affair has not
at any point been (nor could it have been) a contradiction
of my "theory" or my writings.

But after what has happened, I ask the Students' Union
to say whether or not my instinct was correct in bidding
me to act according to my "real feelings" in the matter
and to decline an honor that unwilling persons had been
tricked into offering me. For it must be acknowledged now
that I had fairly good grounds for my suspicion of the
genuineness of the good will displayed by the Students'
Union with its present views and representatives.

I expect that the contents of this letter will be communicated by the committee to the students and to the
general public.

I demand that on the first Saturday after its arrival—
previous announcement having been made—this whole
letter shall be read from the same place in the hall of the
union from which I was insulted, without any provocation
on my part, by the president of the union and with the
approbation of the majority of its members.

I believe that is all I have to say, both for the present
and for the future, to the Managing Committee of the
Students' Union.

                                        Henrik Ibsen

The following month the Students' Union split into two groups, and the Union of Liberal Students was formed.

To Bjørnstjerne Bjørnson

Munich, December 22, 1885

Dear Bjørnson, Once again you must pardon my negligence as a correspondent.

I will not sign a second application to the Storting for a writer's pension for Kielland, and I advise you to think twice before you concern yourself further with the matter. I fear that such interference will injure and possibly even defeat the cause.

As you no doubt remember, I was present [on June 10] when the proposal was last debated in the Storting. The whole ministry absented itself, and the explanation and excuse offered was that the motion was a private one; that application had not been made to the government but directly to the House; that the State Council had thus had no opportunity of submitting the matter to preparatory discussion and consequently did not feel called upon to take part in the debate, etc., etc.

This excuse was actually regarded as genuine by some people.

My feeling is that next time the ministry itself must be made to bear this heavy cross. We ought not to do anything to lighten the burden of the Ecclesiastical Department. It might help if you can get the liberal newspapers to exercise pressure. We should then see if the government is favorably disposed toward this pension. I doubt it very much. I believe that our present government sets far too high a value on the opinion of the priest-ridden section of the population.

I am aware that what I have said does not apply to the motives which impel you to act. Nevertheless I cannot help believing that it would be for the good of the cause to wait and see what the government will do. I am also of the opinion that henceforth—or at least as long as we have parliamentary government—these direct applications to the Storting ought not to be made. In times past they may have been suitable and necessary, but they are so no longer. . . .

To Carl Snoilsky

Munich, February 14, 1886

Count Snoilsky, the Swedish lyric poet, is generally regarded as the model for Pastor Rosmer in *Rosmersholm*. In 1879 Snoilsky, then thirty-eight years old, had broken completely with his conservative family background by resigning his diplomatic post, divorcing his wife, marrying another woman, and leaving Sweden. In the summer of 1885 he returned to his native country for a brief visit, but he found himself more isolated than before. From August 11 to August 15, Snoilsky and Ibsen, another exile on a disappointing visit home, were together constantly in the beautiful small town of Molde in Norway. Lorentz Dietrichson was also there.

. . . My wife and I want to thank you not only for the books you sent us but also for the pleasure of your company in Molde. Seeing you again and making the acquaintance of your beautiful and noble-minded wife have been very rewarding experiences for us. The time spent in your company provides by far the finest memory of our stay in Norway. . . .

Being together with Professor Dietrichson had a fateful influence on our relations to each other. Seeing him day after day, I became more and more aware of a smallness of mind, a weakness of character, a cringing respect for other people's ideas and opinions, all of which could not help but affect me adversely. That is why I stood up against him and did the good deed, and I believe it was a good deed, of seeing to it that he was removed from his post as leader of the Students' Union. But in one way he is to be excused. He is constantly subjected to the influence of petty and narrow-minded people whom a spineless character such as he is cannot stand up to. . . .

I am engrossed in writing a new play [*Rosmersholm*] that I have been thinking about for a long time, and for which I made careful studies during my visit to Norway last summer. We have our son with us right now. Next month he goes to his post as attaché at the legation in Washington, and then we shall be all alone again. . . .

To Georg Brandes

Munich, November 10, 1886

Dear Brandes, I hardly know whether I dare count upon your willingness to receive a letter from me, now that more than a year and a day have passed without my giving any direct signs of life. But I rely on your good nature and on our old friendship, which I do not believe could ever really be destroyed. At least as far as I am concerned that would be impossible.

The reason for my obstinate silence is that I am getting more and more into the habit of occupying myself with one thing at a time, circling round and round one set of ideas, and as long as this is going on, I set everything else aside. Ever since I returned to Munich I have been tormented by an idea for a new play [*Rosmersholm*], which gave me no peace until I had got it out of my system, and that did not happen until the beginning of last month. That is to say, I got the manuscript out of the house then. But afterward came all the unavoidable correspondence that goes along with the publication and translation of a new book.

Also, I started work on this play quite late. Not till well on in June did I begin to write in good earnest. The impressions I received from my journey in Norway last summer and the observations I made disturbed me for a long time. And not until I had come to a distinct understanding of my experiences and had drawn my conclusions could I think of transforming my thoughts into a work of fiction. Your visit to Christiania, and your experiences there, also gave me much to think about. They were of valuable assistance to me in my characterization of our progressives. Never have I felt myself further from understanding and sympathizing with the *Thun und Treiben* of my Norwegian compatriots than after the lessons taught me last year. Never have I been more repelled. Never more disgusted. However, I do not abandon hope that all the crude immaturity of Norwegian life may someday be transformed into a culture with both form and substance. But

such a possibility is for the moment of no interest to anyone in Norway. Nor do I believe that the forces at present
operating in the country would suffice to accomplish any
more radical reforms than those that are now the order of
the day. And perhaps hardly even those. It was a bad hour
for progress in Norway when Johan Sverdrup came into
"power"—and was muzzled and handcuffed.

I have paid sufficient attention to what has been happening in the outside world this year to know that you
were at Warsaw again last spring, lecturing. We half
hoped that you would return by way of Munich. But of
course you did not. I do not believe you know how many
warm admirers you have here among those interested in
literature.

Please accept our thanks for your articles on the state
of Poland and on Luther's utterances on the subject of
celibacy. It was kind of you to send them. That on Poland
made a deep and lasting impression upon us, while the
other amused us immensely.

Please thank your wife for the letter of introduction she
kindly sent Sigurd. He will probably have an opportunity
to make use of it in the course of the winter.

We often talk of our visit to your peaceful, comfortable
home. Please remember us to your wife and the girls. We
shall perhaps come to Denmark next summer. We both
have a great fancy to spend some months at Cape Skagen.
I hope we shall see you in Copenhagen. Best wishes.

Yours sincerely and gratefully,
Henrik Ibsen

Rosmersholm was published on November 23, 1886, in a
printing of 8,000 copies and first performed on January 17,
1887, in Bergen. The Christiania Theater staged it on April
12. Several other Scandinavian and German theaters produced
it in 1887, but nowhere did it meet with any great success.

To Duke Georg II of Meiningen

Munich, November 13, 1886

Except for the Royal Dramatic Theater in Stockholm, none
of the major theaters in Scandinavia or on the Continent
would produce *Ghosts*. The first performances outside Scan-

dinavia were given privately in Germany to circumvent the police ban on public performances of the play. In April, 1885, Ibsen attended the first of these private performances at Augsburg. In December the Meiningen Players staged the work at the Duke's own Court Theater, a production that was transferred to Berlin the following month.

Your Grace, I have received with great pleasure your Grace's communication in regard to the impending production of my play *Ghosts*.

Allow me to express my very deepest thanks to your Grace as well as to your distinguished lady consort for your gracious invitation. I will certainly not fail to appear in time for the performance in Meiningen.

The interiors of Norwegian country houses usually show no specially marked national characteristics nowadays. The living rooms of the oldest family house of this type are sometimes covered with colored, dark wallpaper. Below the paper, the walls are lined with simple wainscoting. The ceiling as well as the doors and the window frames are all made in the same way. The stoves are big and massive, generally of cast iron. The furniture is kept to the style of the First Empire; however, the colors are consistently darker.

This is roughly the way I have imagined the living room in Mrs. Alving's house. . . .

To Suzannah Ibsen

Meiningen, December 22, 1886

Dear Suzannah, Let me tell you briefly. I arrived at 1:30 A.M. at Würzburg. Left there at 1:15 P.M. the next day. Arrived here at 4:15 P.M. and was met at the station by the Lord High Steward and was driven in the court equipage to the castle, and there I was received most cordially and charmingly by the Duke and his wife. They both accompanied me to my magnificent and gaily illuminated suite, consisting of four enormous salons with every kind of comfort. A court flunky is entirely at my disposal. P[aul] Lindau, R[ichard] Voss, and Hans Hopfen are also here as guests. They are on the floor below and their quarters are nothing like as splendid as mine.

At 5 P.M. dinner was served. Prince Ernest had arrived from Munich by another train. In the middle of the meal everybody was taken by surprise when a young couple entered in traveling attire. The Erbprinz and Princess of Meiningen had traveled from Berlin to see *Ghosts*. They were placed at the table, the Princess at my side, and she talked with great enthusiasm about her tour to the North Cape. She is incredibly well informed about our latest literature. After the meal there was a theater performance of P. Lindau's translation of a Spanish play. This was an ordinary performance with paid tickets of admission, as Voss's *Alexandre* will also be tomorrow.

Only *Ghosts* tonight is given before a specially invited audience. For this occasion people are pouring in from all directions, especially from Berlin. After the performance, which starts at six o'clock tonight, there will be a great soirée at the castle. Dinner today is to be at two o'clock. I feel very well here. The whole atmosphere is as easy and unforced as one could imagine and both the Duke and Duchess cannot be attentive enough. On Thursday I shall be back in Munich.

12:30 P.M. I was interrupted. The Duke came in and stayed for a long time. I must hurry to finish this letter if it is to be in time for the train. I enclose the draft of a telegram to Sigurd, which you must ask Lina to send off on Thursday morning [Sigurd's birthday]. I may even send a telegram to him from here myself.

And how is your eye? I sincerely hope it is not any worse? But don't be afraid. It is in no way dangerous, although of course very uncomfortable. I shall try to get away by the morning train on Thursday.

I hope that the knock against your mouth no longer hurts nor troubles you; it was too bad it should happen during my absence.

I hope that you are well on the whole. We've had a big snowfall. I haven't been out, although I have a carriage at my disposal. The Lord High Steward has sent me his card and I have sent mine to all the court officials. Personal visits are not necessary.

Well, now I will end this for today. Perhaps there will be a letter from you!

I seem to have been away a long time. However excellent it is here, in the long run it suits me best to be at home.

Your devoted
Henrik Ibsen

To Frederik Hegel

Munich, January 5, 1887

Dear Mr. Hegel, Will you be so kind as to send me 1,000 kroner [$268], either in German bank notes or by check?

I am at present leading a kind of wandering life to which I am not accustomed. I was just beginning to settle down after the week of festivities at Meiningen, but now I must be off again. I leave the day after tomorrow for Berlin, where *Ghosts* is to be performed on the ninth at the Residenz-Theater. I would much rather remain at home, but I have received so many urgent invitations that I can hardly refuse to put in an appearance, especially since *Ghosts* has become a hot literary and dramatic subject in Germany.

In Berlin I shall expect a considerable amount of opposition from the conservative press. That gives me one more reason for being on the spot.

At Meiningen the Duke conferred on me an almost ostentatious honor by investing me the day after the performance—*"als Zeichen seiner Verehrung und Bewunderung,"* as it says on the certificate—with the insignia of a Knight of the "Sächsisch-Ernestinisch" Order, First Class with the Star.

Please do not think that it is vanity that makes me tell you this. But I do not deny that the honor gives me a certain pleasure when I think back to the stupid denunciations hurled at the play for such a long time in Scandinavia.

With many thanks for the books sent me, and with our kindest regards to yourself and your family, I remain

Yours most sincerely,
Henrik Ibsen

Speech at a Banquet in Berlin

Berlin, January 11, 1887

Ladies and Gentlemen, you must not expect me to deliver a speech. I cannot make speeches, and I cannot find the words to express my thanks to you, for my thanks would not suffice for what I have experienced here.

This is not the first time that I have received great encouragement from Berlin. It was here that I found my first publisher; it was from here that I heard the happy news of the first performance of one of my plays. And from the press, magazines, and literary circles of Berlin I have received nothing but constant encouragement. But I still could not believe that I stood in such high favor with you; and when I look around me here in this circle of writers and artists, I feel that it is all a fairy tale. But in spite of this cordiality, or precisely because of it, I feel that I am a guest, a stranger, because one never does such honor to one of the children in the house. And that is why I wish that the day may come when I shall actually be at home here, when I shall no longer be a stranger in the great house of Germany. I shall never forget the love and cordiality that has greeted me today. It is not only happiness I feel but also melancholy; and I believe that this mood will also find its way into my future writings. I shall never forget this evening!

To Bjørn Kristensen

Munich, February 13, 1887

Bjørn Kristensen, Bjørnson's nephew, was a student in grade school at this time.

Dear Master Kristensen: Kindly accept and convey to the Debating Club my sincerest thanks for its friendly letter of December 4 of last year.

I should have answered it before now, but I have been away from home and overburdened with business that could not be postponed.

The call to work is undoubtedly one of the themes running through *Rosmersholm*.

But the play also deals with the struggle which all serious-minded human beings have to wage with themselves in order to bring their lives into harmony with their convictions.

For the different spiritual functions do not develop evenly and abreast of each other in any one human being. The acquisitive instinct hurries on from gain to gain. The moral consciousness—what we call conscience—is, on the other hand, very conservative. It has its roots deep in traditions and in the past generally. Hence the conflict within the individual.

But the play is, of course, first and foremost a story of human beings and human destiny.

With a friendly greeting to each one of the members of the Debating Club, I remain

Yours sincerely,
Henrik Ibsen

To Sofie Reimers

Munich, March 25, 1887

Sofie Reimers was an actress at the Christiania Theater.

Dear Miss Reimers: I feel unable down here to answer your inquiry, which is put in quite general terms and without mentioning certain definite points.

In order to be able to give you some guidance, I would have to be present and see how you had handled the part.

The only piece of advice I can give you is to read closely the whole play over and over again and carefully observe what the other persons say about Rebecca [in *Rosmersholm*]. In earlier times our actors often committed the great mistake of studying their parts in isolation and without paying sufficient regard to the character's position in and connection with the whole work.

I have already expressed myself briefly on Rebecca in a letter to the theater manager and will ask him to communicate these hints to you, if he has not done so.

Furthermore, you should bring to your assistance your studies and observations of real life.

No declamation! No theatrical emphases! No pomposity at all! Give each mood credible, true-to-life expression. Do not ever think of this or that actress you may have seen. But stick to the life that is going on around you, and give us a true, living character.

I do not think it is difficult to penetrate into Rebecca's character and understand it.

But there are difficulties in rendering and representing this character because it is so concentrated.

However, I am certain that you will master those difficulties, if you only take real life, and exclusively that, as the basis and point of departure for creating Rebecca. . . .

Speech to the "Gnistan" Literary Society

Göteborg, September 12, 1887

Ibsen spent the summer of 1887 vacationing and traveling in Denmark and Sweden. During July and August he was in Jutland. In September he went to Sweden, spending half the month in Göteborg and the other half in Stockholm, and in both cities he was warmly feted. According to a newspaper report of the banquet given in his honor in Göteborg:

Dr. Ibsen replied with a few words with which he desired to express, "as modestly as possible," his thanks for the friendship and good will shown him in Göteborg. He knew that he would cherish this good will all the more now that his polemical interests were waning, and he felt that he was about to strike off into new forms. And to achieve the proper mood for those new forms, the friendliness and the sympathy, which showed that he had been understood and appreciated, would be of great help and significance; and he expressed his thanks for all that he had received in this respect.

Speech at the Banquet in Stockholm

Stockholm, September 24, 1887

Ladies and Gentlemen: I thank you most deeply for all the friendliness, for the welcoming spirit and the understanding that I have once again received proofs of here. It is a great joy to feel that one belongs to a greater country. But to reply fully to all the words of praise that I have just heard lies outside and beyond my power. There is, however, one point in particular that I should like to consider for a moment. It has been said that I, too, have contributed, and in a prominent way, to bringing about a new era in our countries. I believe, on the contrary, that the time in which we now live might with quite as good reason be described as a conclusion, and that something new is about to be born from it. For I believe that the teaching of natural science about evolution is also valid as regards the spiritual aspects of life. I believe that the time is not far off when political and social conceptions will cease to exist in their present forms, and that from both of them there will arise a unity, which for a while will contain within itself the conditions for the happiness of mankind. I believe that poetry, philosophy, and religion will be merged in a new category and become a new vital force, of which we who are living now can have no clear conception.

It has been said of me on different occasions that I am a pessimist. And so I am insofar as I do not believe in the everlastingness of human ideals. But I am also an optimist insofar as I firmly believe in the capacity for the propagation and development of ideals. Especially, to be more definite, I believe that the ideals of our time, while disintegrating, are tending toward what in my play *Emperor and Galilean* I designated "the third kingdom." Therefore, permit me to drink a toast to the future—to that which is to come. We are assembled here on a Saturday night. Following it, comes the day of rest, the holiday, the holy day—whichever you wish to call it. For my part I shall be content with my week's work, a lifelong week, if it can serve to prepare the spirit for tomorrow. But above all I shall be most content if it will serve to strengthen the spirit for that week of work that inevitably follows.

Thank you.

Speech at the Private Party Given
by Frederik Hegel

Copenhagen, October 5, 1887

From Stockholm Ibsen journeyed to Copenhagen where he irked Georg Brandes by speaking on October 1 to the old Student Society at the University of Copenhagen instead of to the Union of Radical Students, the group he had addressed two years previously. A few days later he was honored at a dinner given by his publisher Frederik Hegel. According to the newspaper account:

Dr. Henrik Ibsen expressed his thanks in an extraordinary speech. He described what he owed to Denmark because of his summer here. The mountains he had long known, but this summer he had "discovered the Sea." The calm, mild Danish sea, that you could walk right out into, without mountains closing the road to it, had given his soul peace and quiet. He said he would take with him memories of the sea that would be of significance in his life and writing.

To H. Österling

Munich, November 15, 1887

H. Österling was a bookdealer in Helsingborg, Sweden

Dear Sir: During my stay in Stockholm last September you were kind enough to send me a copy of Strindberg's then newly published tragedy *The Father*, and I beg you to accept my deep thanks for this valuable gift.

One is reluctant, however, to read a new work by a writer like Strindberg during the turmoil and constant interruptions of travel.

Consequently I put off reading and studying this work until now, when I am back in the peace and quiet of my home.

Strindberg's experience and observations of that area of life with which *The Father* is most closely concerned do not agree with mine. But this does not prevent me from acknowledging, and being gripped by, the violent force of the author in this new work.

The Father is soon to be performed in Copenhagen. If it is performed as it should be, with ruthless realism, it will have a shattering effect on the audience. . . .

Actually, the world première of Strindberg's play had taken place in Copenhagen on November 14 at the Casino Theater, a house ordinarily devoted to farce. But H. R. Hunderup, manager of the theater, wanted to promote the higher drama. Georg Brandes helped to stage *The Father*, and the play was kept in the repertoire for several years, even though it failed to draw an audience. When Hunderup's troupe presented the play in Christiania in the summer of 1891, Ibsen received a special invitation. The house was virtually empty, and Ibsen sat all by himself in the front row.

To Julius Hoffory

Munich, February 26, 1888

Hoffory was a Danish-born professor of philology at the University of Berlin. A popular member of Berlin literary circles, he did much to make Ibsen known in Germany. He was also to serve as a model for Løvborg in *Hedda Gabler*.

. . . *Emperor and Galilean* is not the first play I wrote in Germany but it is the first work which I wrote under the influence of German intellectual thought. In the autumn of 1868, when I came from Italy to Dresden, I brought with me the outline of *The League of Youth* and wrote the play in Dresden during the winter. During my four years' stay in Rome I had occupied myself with all kinds of historical studies with a view to writing *Emperor and Galilean*. I had made notes for it, but I had evolved no distinct plan or plot, much less written any part of the drama. My point of view was still that of the Scandinavian nationalist, and I could not accommodate myself properly to the alien subject. Then came the experience of Germany's great era. I was in Germany during the war and the events following it. In many ways all this acted on me with a force that transformed me. My view of history and of human life had until then been a national view.

Now it expanded into a racial view, and with that change I could write *Emperor and Galilean*. The play was completed in the spring of 1873. . . .

To A. T. Schibsted

Munich, March 27, 1888

Schibsted was editor of the Norwegian newspaper *Aftenposten*.

Dear Mr. Schibsted: Allow me herewith to offer you my warmest thanks for the attention you have been good enough to show me by including in your paper for the twentieth of this month the series of articles published on the occasion of my sixtieth birthday.

I wish to assure you that I shall always be grateful for the pleasure you have thereby given me. And this pleasure was so much the greater since it was unexpected.

One of the things that have pained me most in my literary relations to my home country is that for a number of years, as far back as the appearance of *The League of Youth*, I have been appropriated by one political party or the other. I, who never in my life have busied myself with politics but only with social questions! And then the supposed opponents' unwillingness to understand! It is not praise or devotion I thirst for. But understanding! Understanding! The hand you have so kindly extended to me I am delighted to grasp.

Yours respectfully and gratefully,

Henrik Ibsen

To Oscar Nissen

Munich, March 29, 1888

Dear Dr. Nissen, It was with special pleasure that I received the telegram you sent me on my sixtieth birthday, conveying a greeting from the Workmen's Association of Christiania. I send my most cordial thanks for it.

It is unfortunately not in my province or power to do anything directly for the benefit of the working class.

But will you tell the members of the association that of all the classes in our country theirs is nearest to my heart. And will you also say that in that future time which I believe in and hope for the working man will gain those conditions and that social position I earnestly desire for him.

With kindest regards, I remain

Yours respectfully,
Henrik Ibsen

To Christian Hostrup

Munich, April 2, 1888

During the 1840's the Reverend Christian Hostrup had been a writer of popular Danish vaudevilles. After reading *A Doll's House*, Hostrup started to write serious plays, such as *In the Snowstorm*.

The Reverend Mr. Hostrup, Kindly forgive me for not thanking you sooner for the telegram with which you and Mrs. Hostrup gave me so much pleasure on my birthday.

And I am no less grateful to you for the copy you sent me of *In the Snowstorm*. It was a real joy to read the beautiful work and actually to live in and with it. Jutland, which has had a strong fascination for me ever since I first got to know it, was marvelously present in my mind as I was reading, although I have never seen it in winter. I hardly ever go to the theater here, but I enjoy reading a play now and then in the evening, and as I have power-ful imagination where anything dramatic is concerned, I can see everything that is really natural, authentic, and credible actually happening before my eyes. Reading a play produces in me almost the same effect as seeing a performance. This has made the reading of your new play a great pleasure for me. . . .

To Georg Brandes

Munich, October 30, 1888

Dear Brandes, After many months of incessant work upon a new five-act play [*The Lady from the Sea*], which is now completed, I once more have some time at my disposal and can think of a little letter writing that is not purely business correspondence.

Allow me now, late though it is, to thank you for the telegram which gladdened me on my birthday. Also for your essay "Temperament and Reality in Émile Zola" [in the September issue of *Tilskueren*], which you were good enough to send me at the time of its publication, and which I have repeatedly read with great interest. And, lastly, for your new, long work *Impressions of Poland*, which is beginning to absorb all of my attention to the neglect of everything else. In it a whole "dark continent" is opened up to the eyes of Western Europe! Thanks for this new treasure trove.

We have learned from the newspapers of the large attendances at your last course of lectures. But except for this we know very little of how things are with you and how the life at home suits you. I myself feel as if it might be possible to live very happily in Copenhagen. But then I have only tried it for short periods at a time.

It would be quite impossible for me to settle for good in Norway. Nowhere would I feel less at home than there. A man of some intellectual development can no longer be satisfied with the old conception of nationality.

We can no longer let ourselves be content with the political community we belong to. I believe that national consciousness is on the point of dying out, and that it will be replaced by racial consciousness. At least that is the evolution I have gone through. I began by feeling myself a Norwegian; I developed into a Scandinavian; and now I have arrived at Teutonism.

I follow with attention and interest all the activities in the old home country. The observations one has the opportunity of making are not particularly pleasant. But I cannot say that the political development has been a disappointment to me. What has happened is exactly what I expected. I knew beforehand that precisely this would inevitably be the course of events. But the leaders of our party of the Left are altogether lacking in experience of the world, and consequently they had been cherishing the most unreasonable illusions. They imagined that a leader of the Opposition would and could remain the same after he got into power as he was before.

November 4

Dear Friend, I had to leave this letter unfinished for I have not been well for some days, and besides, I have been overburdened with theatrical business matters that could not be postponed.

Today, just as I was sitting down to continue where I left off, there arrived a packet from Copenhagen addressed in your well-known writing. How good of you to send me your *Impressions of Russia* too! I dare not now continue to hold forth upon affairs at home. This letter, conveying my sincerest thanks, must go at once. The pencil inscription in the book, too, warns me that I must not put your friendship and your indulgence to a more severe test by my continued silence. I acknowledge that I fully deserve the silent but eloquent reproach. But it does not cause me any real alarm; it only awakens the conscience of the bad correspondent. A serious and lasting misunderstanding between us is unimaginable to me.

While I am on the subject of my sins as a correspondent, may I ask you to convey to your brother [Edvard Brandes] my warmest thanks for his review of *Rosmersholm*. It made an ineffaceable impression on me. The first time I read it I felt as if I were reading a beautiful, profound, sympathetic poem about my work. . . .

To Julius Hoffory

Munich, November 16, 1888

Dear Professor, It was a very great pleasure and no less a surprise to learn yesterday from your kind letter that you already have completed your translation [of *The Lady from the Sea*]. So there is all likelihood that it can appear at the same time as the original, that is, at the end of this month or at the beginning of the next.

It has not been an easy task to translate this play and I know of no one except yourself who could possibly have all the qualifications for carrying the task through with complete satisfaction. What is needed is an intimate familiarity with the Danish-Norwegian language to grasp the hesitant and schoolboyish semieducated quality in

Lyngstrand's mode of expression, or the slight touch of
pedagogic pedantry that now and then reveals itself in
Arnholm's speech and turn of phrase. And similar subtle-
ties and difficulties in respect to the language present
themselves also for the other persons involved. On that
account I owe you more thanks than I can express for
having taken the matter into your skilled hands.

Your kind statements about the play were a great joy
and reassurance to me. For it has been disturbing to think
that the pages were being sent to you piece by piece at
long intervals, and I have been afraid that this way of
assimilating the work might have an unfavorable effect
on your general impression of the work. However, I now
feel reassured.

I do not know what you have done with the beginning
of the second act where Ballested in his capacity of guide
is speaking broken German. However, I suppose that this
has been changed into a similar kind of English and that
he then lapses into French. Then there are the expressions
Geburtsdag and *födelsedag*. The former is now considered
old-fashioned and not good parlance. But since I cannot
imagine how this shade could be rendered in translation,
I suppose you have to drop it, to which I have not the
least objection.

The word *lugar* I think corresponds to *Volks-Kajüte*,
Mannschaftscraum, or something similar. I do not know
the appropriate German word for *påmønstre*. But in the
line in question it can be avoided by the use of the word
anwerben, which as far as I know, is the German sailor's
word for our *forhyre*. . . .

To Emanuel Hansen
Munich, November 27, 1888

Emanuel Hansen was a translator living in St. Petersburg.

Dear Emanuel Hansen: Please accept my sincere thanks
for sending me a copy of your translation of Leo Tolstoy.
I have read *The Power of Darkness* with great interest.
I have no doubt that if it is given a ruthlessly honest production, it will produce a deep effect. However, it seems
to me that the author does not have a full understanding

of the technique of the drama. There are more conversations than scenes in the play, and the dialogue seems in many places to be more epic than dramatic, the work as a whole to be less a drama than a narrative in dialogue form. But the main thing is indeed present. The spirit of a genius lives and breathes through all of it. . . .

To Julius Hoffory

Munich, February 14, 1889

The Lady from the Sea was published on November 28, 1888, in a printing of 10,000 copies. The first performances were given simultaneously on February 12, 1889, at the Christiania Theater and at the Court Theater in Weimar. The following letter concerns a later production at the Royal Theater in Berlin, which opened March 5.

. . . I must object to having the character listed on the program as "Ein Seeman" or "Ein fremder Seeman" or "Ein Steuermann." Actually he is none of these. When Ellida met him ten years ago, he was second mate. Seven years later he signed on as a simple boatswain, that is, in a decidedly lower position. And now he appears as a passenger on a tourist ship. He does not belong to the ship's crew. He is dressed as a casual tourist, not in traveling clothes. No one is supposed to know what he is, just as no one is supposed to know *who* he is or what his real name is. This uncertainty about him is the essential element in the method I have deliberately chosen.

Please be so kind as to direct the attention of Mr. Anno [the director of the play] to this point during rehearsals; otherwise the basic mood of the performance could easily be lost. . . .

To Suzannah Ibsen

Hotel du Nord, Berlin
March 5, 1889

In the first half of March, 1889, Ibsen attended a series of performances of his plays in Berlin and Weimar. On March 5 he was present for the opening of *The Lady from the Sea* at the Berlin Theater. Although the play met with a mixed reception, the audience called Ibsen forth repeatedly to applaud his total achievement as a playwright. On March 6 he saw *The Wild Duck* given at the Residenz-Theater, and the following night *A Doll's House* at the Lessing Theater. On the ninth of March he arrived at Weimar. There he was honored with a sumptuous banquet on March 12, and on the fourteenth he attended the Court Theater production of *The Lady from the Sea,* where he was applauded after each act of the play and at the end of the evening presented with a laurel wreath. The sixty-year-old Norwegian playwright had conquered Germany.

Dear Suzannah, There isn't time here for a proper letter as I have visitors every moment I am at home. I hope you have received my telegram. I arrived on Sunday morning to find a message at the hotel that the dress rehearsal had been postponed till the next day. At midday Hoffory, [Otto] Brahm, and [Paul] Schlenther arrived. With them was young [Helge] Rode from Copenhagen, who is staying here at the expense of [the Danish newspaper] *Politiken* to send them news about the first night.

I asked them all to an excellent dinner which lasted almost till evening.

Yesterday morning [Monday] was the dress rehearsal, which was to my full satisfaction. In the evening there was a men's party in my honor; some sixteen to seventeen people were present, [Paul] Lindau, Bülow, and [the actor Josef] Kainz among them.

Tomorrow evening *The Wild Duck* is to be given at the Residenz-Theater and the day after *Nora* [*A Doll's House*] in [Oskar] Blumenthal's Lessing Theater. I don't know yet when I shall get away from here nor whether I will go by way of Weimar, which is what they are trying to persuade me to do.

I hope you are writing to Sigurd. I shan't have time. Do send word to me, too, so that I know how you are.

It will be good to be quiet again. I am already pretty tired, although I am otherwise well. Good-by for the present. Today I am having dinner with Kainz.

Your devoted
Henrik Ibsen

To Julius Hoffory

Munich, March 26, 1889

Dear Professor Hoffory: Since my return home I have thought every day of you and my other friends in Berlin and have had the intention of sending you a few lines. But while I was away from home such a stack of business letters piled up on my desk that I have not even made a dent in it as yet.

Nevertheless I want to write a few words to you to offer you my deepest thanks and to ask you to convey them to all our mutual friends who helped make that week in Berlin the high point in my life. When I think back on it, it all seems like a dream. It almost frightens me.

I spent the following week in Weimar. *The Lady from the Sea* was quite well performed there also. The conception and the rendering of the parts had a remarkable similarity to the Schauspielhaus production. But Wangel was not as finely conceived in all details. Nor was Lyngstrand so perfectly felt and individualized. However, as for the Stranger, I could not wish for, or even conceive of, a better performance—a long, thin figure with a hawk face, piercing black eyes, and a wonderfully deep and soft voice. . . .

I have received several letters from Vienna from which I can see that Dr. Schlenther's lecture made a deep impression down there. And the most notable thing is that these statements and remarks do not originate from the Germans there but from Magyar and Polish circles, whose whole attitude toward life and toward art and the role it must play in progress would appear to be absolutely alien to our German attitude. The explanation for this certainly lies in the universality of the German mind and spirit, which predestines it to be a world power in the future. The opportunity of being a part of these movements I feel clearly and profoundly I owe to my entrance into contemporary German life. . . .

To Camilla Collett

Munich, May 3, 1889

Dear Mrs. Collett, A deeply interesting letter from you
has been in my possession for more than two months without my giving you a sign of life. What can you think of
me?

I can only say that a great deal has been happening
since it came—all of which has kept me from the writing
desk. First I had to go to Berlin, and then, quite unexpectedly, to Weimar. Only now am I beginning to get
settled again.

Permit me, then, to send you today a few words of very
sincere thanks for your sympathetic and understanding
response to *The Lady from the Sea.*

I felt pretty certain that you, and you in particular,
would understand it. But it gave me an inexpressible
pleasure to be confirmed in my belief by your letter.

Yes, there are suggestive resemblances [to your life].°
Many, I might say. And you have felt them and responded
to them. I mean things that could be for me only vague
premonitions.

It is many years now since you, by virtue of your spiritual and intellectual development, began in one form or
another to play a part in my writings.

You may be sure that my wife and I do not forget you;
we think and talk of you always. We heard during the
winter that you were in Berlin, and we felt certain that
we should have the pleasure of seeing you here in Munich
again. But it was not to be, at least not this time. As yet,
we have not been able to make any plans for the coming
summer. But it is not impossible that circumstances will
lead us northward, in which case we are sure to meet.

My wife sends you her warmest regards. And so do I.

Yours,

Henrik Ibsen

° Camilla Collett thought that she was the model Ibsen used in creating
"the lady from the sea," which seems unlikely.

Letter to Jens Braage Halvorsen

Munich, June 18, 1889

(See page 14.)

To Emilie Bardach

Gossensass, September 20, 1889

As he had so often in past years, Ibsen and his wife spent the summer of 1889 in Gossensass near the Brenner Pass. But this summer was destined to be different from the others. He met and spent much time in the company of two young girls, the twenty-four-year-old Helene Raff and the eighteen-year-old Emilie Bardach, either or both of whom may have served as models for Ibsen when he was writing *Hedda Gabler* and *The Master Builder*. At the end of the summer Ibsen wrote in Emilie's album:

Sublime, painful fortune—to struggle for the unattainable! °

Henrik Ibsen

To Emilie Bardach

Gossensass, September 27, 1889

To the May sun of a September life—in Tyrol.

Henrik Ibsen

Ibsen inscribed a photograph of himself with these words on the last day he and Emilie were together.

° All the letters to Emilie Bardach and Helene Raff are written in German.

To Helene Raff

Munich, Late Friday night,
September 30, 1889

Ibsen saw Emilie Bardach only during that summer in Gossensass, but he continued to see and talk to Helene Raff, who lived in Munich, from the fall of 1889 to the summer of 1891 when Ibsen moved to Norway. An amateur painter and the daughter of a composer, Helene knew many of Ibsen's friends, and she and the playwright frequently took strolls together. She kept an "Ibsen Diary" in which she jotted down notes on their conversations. In November Ibsen began jotting down notes for *Hedda Gabler*.

Dear Child, How kind, how lovable of you to visit us yesterday. My wife is so truly, cordially fond of you. And I too. As you sat there in the twilight and told us various things so thoughtfully and understandingly, do you know what I thought then, what I wished? No, you do not know. I wished—alas, if I only had such a dear and lovely daughter.

Come and see us again real soon. But in the meantime you must keep busy at work artist-like in your atelier. There you must not be disturbed for the present.

Blessings on your dear head.

Yours devotedly,
Henrik Ibsen

To Emilie Bardach

Munich, October 7, 1889

With all my heart I thank you, highly esteemed Fräulein for your exceedingly kind and dear letter, which I received the day before the last of my stay in Gossensass and which I have read again and again.

There in the summer resort during that last week, everything looked gloomy—or at any rate that is how it appeared to me. No more sunshine. Everything gone—lost. The few guests still left could, of course, not offer me any compensation——for the brief and beautiful Indian summer of life.

I took a walk every day in Pflerschthal. That is the perfect place for an idyllic talk. But our bench was unoccupied and I walked by without sitting down.

The big hall was also desolate and dreary to me. The guests, the family Pereira and the professor with his wife, appeared only at mealtimes.

Do you remember the big, deep bay window to the right of the verandah? It was such a beautiful corner. The overwhelmingly fragrant flowers and plants were still standing there. But——how empty——how lonely——how deserted!

So now we are again here——at home——and you are in Vienna. You write that you feel more secure now, more free and happy. How glad I am to hear it! I do not want to say any more.

A new work begins to dawn in me. I shall work on it this winter and try to transfer the bright mood of summer to it. But it will end in sadness. That is my nature. I once told you that I write letters only in telegraphic style. So take this letter for what it is. At least, try to understand it.

With a thousand greetings,

Yours devotedly,

Dr. H. I.

To Emilie Bardach

Munich, October 15, 1889

I received your dear letter with a thousand thanks—and have read it and read it over and over again.

Here I am sitting as usual at my desk.

I would like to work. But I cannot.

My imagination is certainly stirring. But it always strays and wanders. To places where it should not wander during working hours. I cannot repress my memories of summer. Nor do I want to. What I experienced then, I experience over and over——and over again. To recast all that into the form of a play is impossible at present. At present?

Will it ever be possible? And do I really wish that it would be possible?

At least, for the present, it is impossible—or so I believe. I feel it—I know it.

And yet it must happen. It absolutely *must*. And yet, nevertheless, will it really?

Can it really?

Oh, dear Fräulein—forgive me! You write so delightfully in your last—no, no, God forbid—in your *previous* letter you wrote so delightfully: "I am not Fräulein to you." Very well—dear child—for *that* you certainly are to me—tell me—do you recall our conversation about stupidity and craziness? Or rather,—I said all sorts of things about it, and you, dear child, you took the part of the teacher and remarked in your soft, melodic way, and with your faraway look, that there is always a difference between stupidity and craziness. Now, of course, I've always been aware of that. But this episode—like all the rest, nonetheless sticks in my memory. I constantly brood over this: was our meeting stupidity or was it craziness? Or was it stupidity as well as craziness? Or was it neither?

I think the last possibility is the only one that holds good.

It was simply a necessity of nature. But it was also fate. Now you brood over this, if you find it necessary.

But I do not think you will. I assume that you will understand it from beginning to end.

Thousand times good night.

Yours ever devotedly,
H. I.

To Moritz Prozor, translator

Munich, October 25, 1889

Dear Count Prozor, I have had the great pleasure of receiving your esteemed letter of the 20th inst. I signed and forwarded at once the enclosed letter to Mr. Roger of Paris [director of Société des auteurs et compositeurs dramatiques].

I am unable to express all the gratitude I feel for what you have done for me.

The introduction of my dramatic works into France has long been my dream. But I dared not think seriously of it, as it seemed to me impossible and unattainable.

I had no connections in that country to speak of. And I was already so fully engaged attending to my literary business in Scandinavia, Germany, Austria, England, America, and elsewhere, that it was quite beyond my power to attempt to extend my field of operations to that great and inaccessible city, Paris, or what in matters literary is the same thing—to France.

And now you, sir, have already done so much for me. The start has been made, and getting started is the hardest part. Attention and interest have been aroused in influential circles. The wheels are rolling.

All this I owe chiefly to you. My earnest request to you is that you will continue to take charge of my French affairs and everything connected therewith. If you do, I can hope for good results.

But whether my plays succeed in Paris or not, I beg you, dear sir, to believe that I shall always gratefully acknowledge and appreciate all that you have tried to do for me. Of course I will sign an agreement with the greatest pleasure that your translation and no other is the one I wish to be accepted, if you will only be kind enough to send me the declaration as you wish it to appear.

My thanks for the copy of the translation which I received yesterday. It is a very handsome volume, better got up than I have as a rule been accustomed to here in Germany.

And for the money order, too, please accept my thanks. I had no real right to payment in this case.

I have had a very friendly letter from Count Snoilsky. May I take the liberty of asking you to give him my kindest regards and best thanks when opportunity offers.

Assuring you of my profound esteem, I am, sir,

Yours respectfully and gratefully,

Henrik Ibsen

To Emilie Bardach

Munich, October 29, 1889

Every day I have had the intention of writing you a few words. But I wanted to enclose the new photo. However, it is still not ready. So this letter, too, has to be sent off without a picture. From your own experience you know, of course, that taking one's picture can entail certain difficulties. In your previous letter you mention that.

How beautifully you write! Please continue to write me a few lines, whenever you have a free half hour when you are not doing anything.

So you let my letters lie unopened until you are alone and completely undisturbed. Dear child! I will not express my thanks for that. That would be superfluous. You understand.

Do not be upset because I am unable to create for the time being. Actually, I am creating all the time, or at any rate I am dreaming about something which, when it comes to bloom, will reveal itself as a play.

I am being disturbed. Cannot write more. Next time a longer letter.

Yours with true devotion,
H. I.

To William Archer, English translator
Munich, November 3, 1889

As early as 1880 Archer's adaptation of *The Pillars of Society* had been performed in London. In 1889 his translation of *A Doll's House*, the third English version of the play, was published. During 1890 and 1891 Archer edited and translated *Ibsen's Prose Dramas* in five volumes. This formed the basis of the *Collected Works of Henrik Ibsen* (1906–08), through which a whole generation of English readers were to become acquainted with Ibsen.

Dear Mr. W. Archer, I have this moment received, with very great pleasure, your kind letter of the 1st inst., which I hasten to answer.

I shall always feel that I owe you a great debt of gratitude for all that you have done, and are still doing, to introduce my works into England. . . .

The beautiful and valuable edition of *A Doll's House* [a limited edition of only 115 copies] reached me in good condition. For this gift, too, I send you my sincere thanks. I should have done so long ago. I keep the book always lying on my table, and it is greatly admired by all who

see it and are able to appreciate works of art in the typo-
graphical line. I do not deny being proud that a work of
mine should have appeared in your great country in such
a garb. . . .

To Emilie Bardach

Munich, November 19, 1889

At last I can send you the new picture. I hope you will
find it a better resemblance than the previous one. Within
a few days a German biography of me will appear and
you will receive a copy at once. Read it at your convenience. You will get to know the whole story of my life
—that is, up to the end of last year.

Sincerest thanks for your dear letter! But what can you
think of me for not having answered it until now? However, you know that you are always and will always be in
my thoughts. A lively exchange of letters is an impossi-
bility from my side. I have already told you that. Take me
as I am.

I would actually have quite a lot to tell you about my
creative experiences and their "results" lately. But that
must be postponed for now. Right now I am preoccupied
with preparations for my new play. Sitting almost the
whole day at my desk. Go out only a little in the evenings.
Dream and recollect and create further. To create is beautiful; but to live in reality can now and then be much more
beautiful.

Yours in deep devotion,

H. I.

To Emilie Bardach

Munich, December 6, 1889

Two dear, dear letters have I received from you and
have answered neither up to now! What can you think
of me? But I cannot find the necessary peace and quiet to
write you something sensible and detailed. Tonight I have
to go to the theater to attend a performance of *An Enemy
of the People.* The very thought of it pains me. And fur-

thermore I have to do without your photo for the time being. But it is better that way rather than to receive a picture which is not satisfactory. Besides, how vividly your lovely, serene features appear in my memory! For I still believe in an enigmatical princess who hides behind them. But the enigma itself? Of course, one can dream all sorts about that and read many beautiful things into it. And that is what I do. It is, after all, a small substitute for the unattainable and—unfathomable reality. In my imagination I see you always adorned with pearls. You love pearls so much. There is something deeper—something hidden in your love of pearls. But what really? I brood over that quite often. And sometimes I think I have found the connection. But then again not. Some of your questions I shall perhaps try to answer next time. But I have myself so many questions to ask about you. And I am always asking them—in my heart—constantly.

Yours devotedly,

H. I.

To Emil Stang

Munich, December 11, 1889

Emil Stang was the leader of the Conservative Party in Norway.

. . . I cannot rid myself of the feeling that the course of action adopted by the Department of Foreign Affairs, now after five years have passed, of obstructing the advance of my son's diplomatic career on the ground that he has not taken his law degree in Norway—that this course of action is obviously motivated by a desire to hurt someone besides the one who is the immediate target.

But I cannot bring myself to believe that the Norwegian government is entirely powerless in a case like this, or entirely without means to intervene in the matter, assuming that it feels there is cause to do so.

It is only natural that I should concern myself mostly with the personal aspects of the affair, and I ask your Excellency to consider what is at stake for me and those who are close to me. I do not know what other official career in Norway is open to my son now that Sweden has closed its doors on his diplomatic career, to which he felt strongly inclined and for which he had spent five years preparing himself.

Living in Norway, I could never have achieved that position in world literature that is now mine. Living in Norway, I would never have been granted the good fortune of bringing more credit to the Norwegian nation than any other Norwegian has hitherto done in the field of literature—or in any other field, for that matter.

I believe I may say this without overestimating my present position.

Next January I shall be able to look back on forty years of uninterrupted work as a writer. On occasions such as that it is customary for one to receive some token of merit from the nation to which one belongs. Early next year those things that matter most in life for my son and for me will have to be settled once for all. It would indeed be an extraordinary irony of fate if this decision—coming precisely at this moment in my life—would result in the greatest sorrow and disappointment that could ever be mine.

If the case were to come before a public court, there is nothing I could do to prevent it. I am happy to say that I have many dear friends among the Swedes, and my relations with Sweden have up to now been the very best. I need not therefore remind your Excellency how indescribably painful it would be to see my name drawn into distressing controversies, the far-reaching and violent effects of which it would be impossible to predict.

That is why I beg you again, and most urgently, Mr. Minister, and through you the entire Norwegian government, to intervene on behalf of my son and myself to do all that can be done to remove the obstacles raised by the Foreign Affairs Department against my son and his diplomatic career. . . .

To Emilie Bardach

Munich, December 22, 1889

How shall I thank you for your dear, delightful letter! I simply cannot. Not in the way I would like to. As I have already told you, writing letters is not my line. And you must have noticed it in any case.

In the meantime, I read your letter over and over because in that way the mood of those summer days comes so wonderfully to life again. I see, I re-experience what we experienced.

I got to know you as a lovely summer apparition, dear princess. As part of the season of butterflies and wild flowers.

How I would like to see you again in the winter season!

In my imagination I am completely with you. I see you in the Ringstrasse, light, quick, gliding along, gracefully wrapped up in velvet and furs.

I see you also at soirées and parties—and particularly at the theater, leaning back, with a somewhat tired expression in your enigmatical eyes.

I would also like to see you at home. But I cannot quite succeed in doing that since I do not have the necessary facts to go by. You have told me very little about your family life—no, no, your home life. Almost nothing tangible.

Frankly speaking, dear princess—in many definite respects we are strangers to each other.

In one of your earlier letters you have said almost the same thing in regard to my writings since they are not accessible to you in the original language.

Let us not think about it.

Your studies in music—I hope you continue them uninterrupted? I should especially like to know about that.

But above all I should now like to see you at Christmas Eve, in your own home, where I suppose you will spend the evening. How that is celebrated by you I have no clear idea. I only imagine all kinds of things.

And then I have the strange feeling that you and Christmastime do not go very well together.

But who knows? Perhaps they do!

At all events—please accept my heartfelt wishes—accompanied with a thousand greetings!

As always, your devoted

H. I.

To Emilie Bardach

Munich, December 30, 1889

Your beautiful, charming picture with its striking likeness has given me an indescribable joy. I thank you for it—a thousand times and straight from my heart!

In the middle of winter you have brought before my imagination those short, sunny, summer days!

I thank you just as warmly for your dear, dear letter. From me you must expect only a few lines today. Nowadays I am especially lacking the necessary peace and solitude to write you in the way I would like to. My wife received your kind Christmas card with great pleasure. I hope she will herself thank you for it later. She is not feeling quite well these days.

My son is presently visiting us. Whether he will return to Vienna or will be sent somewhere else is not yet decided.

And please accept my most heartfelt good wishes for the New Year. And similar greeting to your dear mother.

With thanks once again for your marvelous gift, I am

Yours always devotedly,

H. I.

To Emilie Bardach

Munich, January 16, 1890

Please accept my sincerest thanks for both your letters, which up to now I have not answered. Since New Year's I have been quite wretched and have hardly been able to hold my pen in my hand. It has most likely been some kind of nasty influenza. However, now I am feeling considerably better.

How sorry I was to learn that you have been really ill. Can you imagine, I had a distinct misgiving about it! In my imagination I have seen you lying in bed, pale, feverish—but irresistibly beautiful and lovely as always.

A thousand thanks for the dainty flowers that you have painted for me! I believe you possess quite an excellent gift for flower painting. You should seriously cultivate this talent. Perhaps you do, too. But you must save your dear voice—for the time being at least. How grateful I am to you that I possess your charming picture! No more for now. I will never become a good letter writer. I live in the hope that you have now recovered completely, and send your esteemed mother my sincere regards.

Yours ever, from

Your devoted

H. I.

To Emilie Bardach

Munich, February 6, 1890

Long, very long, have I let your last dear letter lie— read it and read it again—but without answering it. Receive today my sincerest thanks in a few words. From now on, until we see each other in person again, you will hear from me only a little, and indeed very seldom. Believe me, it is better so. It is the only right thing. I feel it is a matter of conscience to break off my correspondence with you, or at least limit it. You must, for the present, have as little to do with me as possible. You have other tasks to pursue in your young life, other aims to devote yourself to. And I—as I have already told you personally —I can never be satisfied with a relationship through letters. To me that seems like doing things by halves; there is something untrue in it. I find it distressing that I cannot surrender myself fully and wholly to my mood. However, it is my nature. It cannot be changed. You are so sensitive, you instinctively see through things. You will understand what I mean by all this. And when we meet again, I shall explain it to you more fully. Until then you will always remain in my thoughts. And even more so when we are rid of this disturbing, tiresome, halfway measure of corresponding with each other.

Thousand greetings.

Yours,

H. I.

To Carl Snoilsky

Munich, June 29, 1890

Dear Friend, You probably wonder why I have not yet answered the letter I had the pleasure of receiving from you nearly two weeks ago. The reason for my silence is that I wished to be able to tell you whether or not we are certain to be here about the middle of next month.

Our intention has all along been to spend the summer in the Tyrol again. But circumstances are against our doing so. I am at present engaged upon a new dramatic work [*Hedda Gabler*], which for several reasons has made very slow progress; and I do not wish to leave Munich until I can take the completed first draft with me. There is little or no prospect of my being able to complete it in July.

We shall therefore probably have to stay here in town until well on in autumn, and it will give us great pleasure to see you at the time you mention.

The effect produced by *Ghosts* in Paris [see notes to letter of January 23, 1891] was very satisfactory to me. But I was exceedingly sorry that Count Prozer's translation was not used. I have no idea why it was not; but, I often blame myself, when I think of the matter, for not having made a formal protest, even though it might have been to no purpose. My reason for not doing so was that Count Prozor himself wrote to me that he did not wish it. But I should be deeply grieved if the matter were to cause any ill feeling toward me when I owe so much to him. If you have an opportunity, will you be good enough to tell him this. Our very kind regards to you and Countess Snoilsky. We hope soon to bid you welcome here.

Yours most sincerely,
Henrik Ibsen

To Hans Lien Braekstad

Munich, August 18, 1890

The August 13, 1890, issue of the London *Daily Chronicle* contained a report by its Berlin correspondent of an interview in which Ibsen denied that he or his plays sought to

promote the Social Democratic Party or its principles. Braek-
stad was a Norwegian man of letters living in London.

I have had my attention called to a letter from Berlin
relating to myself in the *Daily Chronicle* of August 13;
and as several of the statements in this letter seem sus-
ceptible of misconstruction—have, in fact, already been
misconstrued in the Scandinavian papers—I shall be very
much obliged if some of the expressions attributed to me
could be corrected. It appears to me that some of them
are not exact and complete reproductions of my utterances to the correspondent of the paper.

I did not, for instance, say that I have never studied
the question of socialism. The fact is that I am much
interested in the question and have endeavored to the
best of my ability to acquaint myself with its different
aspects. I only said that I have never had time to study
the extensive literature dealing with different socialistic
systems.

Where the correspondent repeats my assertion that I do
not belong to the Social Democratic Party, I wish that he
had not omitted what I expressly added, namely, that I
have never belonged, and probably never shall belong, to
any party whatsoever.

I may add here that it has become an absolute necessity
to me to work quite independently and to pursue my own
course.

What the correspondent writes about my surprise at
seeing my name put forward by socialistic agitators as a
supporter of their dogmas is particularly liable to be
misunderstood.

What I really said was that I was surprised that I,
who had made it my chief business in life to depict human
character and human destinies, should, without consciously aiming at it, have arrived at some of the same
conclusions as the social-democratic moral philosophers
had arrived at by scientific processes.

What led me to express my surprise (and, I may add,
my satisfaction) was a statement made by the correspondent to the effect that one or more lectures had lately been
given in London, dealing, according to him, chiefly with
A Doll's House. . . .

Bernard Shaw, who in the mid-1880's had been introduced
by his friend William Archer to the works of Ibsen, had

delivered a lecture on Ibsen and socialism to the Fabian Society on July 18, 1890. Ibsen began to win notoriety in England after the three weeks' run of *A Doll's House* in June, 1889, with Janet Achurch as Nora. In the controversy that followed, Shaw defended Ibsen vigorously. Consequently his Fabian lecture was devoted mainly to *A Doll's House,* but from it grew *The Quintessence of Ibsenism,* printed in 1891, the first book in English about the Norwegian playwright.

To Emilie Bardach

Munich, September 18, 1890

Fräulein Emilie, It was with the sincerest sympathy that I read your very sad letter. You may be assured that I have been with you in my thoughts and felt for you deeply during this time that is so difficult for you and your mother. Your sorrow over the loss of your father has found such a soul-stirring and moving expression in your letter, I was deeply affected.

And so suddenly, so unexpectedly, and without any preparation have you been hit by this heavy blow of fate! To offer consolation in such a case is of course impossible. Only time will be able to heal your wounded soul. And we can hope that that will happen, even if it will only happen gradually.

I understand very well how deeply you must regret that you were not at your father's side during his last hours. But I think perhaps it was better so.

I hope this letter will find you still in Alt-Aussee. May your stay there have a really salutory effect upon you!

My wife and my son are presently in Riva am Gardasee and will probably be there up to the middle of October or still longer. So I am living quite alone here and cannot get away. For the new lengthy play with which I am now preoccupied will most likely not be ready until November, although I am working daily, and even almost all day long.

Give my best regards to your esteemed mother—and please accept, by way of friendship, a thousand heartfelt greetings

From your eternally devoted
Henrik Ibsen

To Karl Hals

Munich, October 30, 1890

Together with his brother, Karl Hals had started a piano factory in Christiania in 1847. In November, 1890, the factory was to celebrate the manufacture of the ten thousandth piano.

Dear Mr. Hals, Please accept my thanks for your kind invitation to the festivities of November 3.

I am sorry that I shall not be able to be present—and, of course, you were not counting on it. But I send you my heartiest congratulations and good wishes on this occasion.

I dare not affirm positively that I saw you working on piano No. 1. But it was certainly one of the very first of the enormous number that you and your brother Peter were busy with when we met for the first time. That was in the autumn of 1850, and it was Ole Schulerud who took me to see you. You and your brother were living at that time in Cappelen's house, where your little workshop also was. I remember that you both personally took a hand in the work. Your assistant was Thornam, afterward an actor at the Christiania Theater.

Your brother Peter was very dear to me. He left us long ago. But his fine, noble presence is still large as life in my memory.

And so forty years have passed since we made each other's acquaintance! Neither of us possessed many of the good things of life at that time. I certainly did not. But in the meantime we have both done fairly well, each in his own line.

Early in life you learned to love work. It was not until much later that I understood the happiness it gives. But when I learned that lesson, I learned it thoroughly.

At present I am utterly engrossed in a new play. I have not had one leisure hour for several months. Besides the play, there is an oppressively large correspondence that also has to be attended to.

But all this shall not prevent my being with you in

thought, in your festive circle, on the evening of November 3.

Yours in sincere friendship,
Henrik Ibsen

To Moritz Prozor

Munich, November 20, 1890

Dear Count Prozor, Please accept my warm and sincere thanks for the letter I received yesterday. I herewith return the power of attorney duly signed. It gives me a great sense of security to hand over the care of pecuniary matters to the French literary society; and the terms seem to me to be very fair and advantageous.

My new play is finished. The manuscript went off to Copenhagen the day before yesterday. According to the agreement made when you were here, the galleys will be sent to you straight from the printer. If there is anything in the play requiring explanation, I should be most willing and grateful to help in any way I can.

It gives me a curious feeling of emptiness to find myself suddenly separated from a work that has occupied my time and thoughts for several months to the exclusion of everything else. But on the other hand it is good to have done with it. Living every moment of my life with these fictitious characters was beginning to make me more than a little nervous. . . .

To Julius Elias

Munich, November 27, 1890

Julius Elias was a German critic. Before he moved from Munich earlier in 1890, he had seen Ibsen frequently.

Dear Dr. Elias, Please accept my thanks for your telegram and letter. Since some of the matters referred to are already taken care of, and since the rest do not demand immediate attention, they are not the reason for writing to you today.

The object of this letter is to make you aware of the present sad and serious mental condition of Professor Hoffory. He arrived here from Weimar about two weeks ago and put up at the Hotel Roth, where he is still staying. It struck me at once that his thought processes and his ability to express himself were affected. He had difficulty in finding the right words and especially in remembering the names of persons, even those with whom he is most closely connected.

His condition has grown worse day by day. [Otto] Brahm* saw him and spoke to him a few days ago and can give you the whole story. I can only add that since Brahm left, Hoffory has become still more unlike himself. Yesterday I tried hard to persuade him to return to Berlin immediately. But it was quite in vain. He talked foolishly about some love affair which kept him here and said he could not leave until this had been finally settled one way or another. I believe that his will power has been weakened to such an extent that he cannot make up his mind to pack, or to ask for his bill, or to go to the railway station. I consider him quite incapable of taking care of his money. Both last night and the night before at the Café Maximilian, where I witnessed it myself, he wanted to pay his bill over and over again.

I think there is no doubt whatever that he ought to leave here. But I cannot imagine how he is to be induced to do it. Will you talk over the matter with Erich Schmidt, who lives not far from you and for whom Hoffory has very much respect? Perhaps an earnest request from him might induce H. to return and allow himself to be treated by the doctors who know the history of his illness. It is absolutely imperative that he should do this. There is no one here to give him advice—at least no one to whom he will go. And the consequence is that he is growing rapidly worse day by day.

I know from personal experience how ready you are to devote both time and labor to the service of your friends. Hence I turn to you in this sad predicament. The future of a human being, possibly his very life, is at stake.

* German critic and theater director who founded the Freie Bühne in Berlin. The theater opened on September 29, 1889, with a production of *Ghosts* that inaugurated a new era in the German theater.

With our kindest regards to yourself and Mrs. Elias, I remain

> Yours sincerely,
> Henrik Ibsen

Julius Hoffory (1855–97), the original of Løvborg in *Hedda Gabler,* was taken to a sanitarium at the end of November. He was subsequently released, but his mental illness broke out again in 1893 and he died insane. In 1891 Hoffory sent Ibsen a deed of gift bequeathing his entire estate to him.

To Moritz Prozor

Munich, December 4, 1890

Dear Count Prozor, I shall not let a moment go by before replying briefly to the letter I have just had the pleasure of receiving from you.

The title of the play is *Hedda Gabler.* My intention in giving it this name was to indicate that Hedda as a personality is to be regarded rather as her father's daughter than as her husband's wife.

It was not really my intention to deal in this play with so-called problems. What I principally wanted to do was to depict human beings, human emotions, and human destinies, upon a groundwork of certain of the social conditions and principles of the present day. When you have read the whole, my fundamental idea will be clearer to you than I can make it by entering into further explanations.

Before these lines reach you, you will probably have received forty-eight pages more from Copenhagen. And a few days later, the last sixty-four pages, together with the title page and the list of characters, will come to hand. . . .

Hedda Gabler was published on December 16 in a first printing of 10,000. The first performance was given at the Residenz-Theater in Munich on January 31, 1891. Neither this nor the subsequent productions that opened in Berlin on February 10 (which Ibsen attended), in Stockholm on February 13, in Copenhagen on February 25, and in Chris-

tiania on February 26 were successful as far as the audiences
were concerned. Whistling and laughing constantly interrupted the performances.

To Hans Schrøder

Munich, December 27, 1890

Schrøder was still head of the Christiania Theater.

. . . Hedda should undoubtedly be played by Miss
Bru[u]n, whom I trust will take pains to express the demoniacal basis of the character. I saw Mrs. Heiberg five years
ago at the Bergen theater and at that time I received a
very strong impression of her natural talents. But both
for the sake of my play and herself I feel it would be
desirable that she not be assigned to a task that she
could not, at the present time, handle satisfactorily in
several essential areas. . . .

To Emilie Bardach

Munich, December 30, 1890

I have duly received your dear letter. Also the bell with
the beautiful picture. I thank you from the bottom of my
heart for them. My wife thinks the picture very pretty.
But I beg you: for the time being, please do not write
me. When circumstances have changed, I will let you
know. I shall soon send you my new play. Receive it in
kindness—but in silence! I should like to see you again
and talk to you! Happy New Year to you and to your
mother.

Your ever devoted

H. I.

To Kristina Steen

Munich, January 14, 1891

Kristina Steen was an actress at the Christiania Theater.

Dear Miss Steen: You have been good enough to send my wife a letter, which on one particular point concerns me and therefore I personally have wished to answer briefly.

Mrs. Wolf wishes to be released from playing the maid, Berte, in my new play and feels that this part could be handled by any other actress at the theater.

She is mistaken. There is no one else up there who could play Berte in the way I want to have her represented. Mrs. Wolf is the only one who can do it. But apparently she has not taken the trouble to read the play through attentively. Otherwise it seems to me that she would have understood this herself.

Jørgen Tesman, his old aunts, and the faithful servant Berte together form a picture of complete unity. They think alike, they share the same memories and have the same outlook on life. To Hedda they appear like a strange and hostile power, aimed at her very being. In a performance of the play the harmony that exists between them must be conveyed. And this could happen if Mrs. Wolf takes the part. But only if she does.

Out of regard for Mrs. Wolf's good judgment I cannot seriously believe that she considers it beneath her dignity as an artist to portray a maid. After all, I have not considered it beneath my dignity to *create* this good-natured, simple, oldish person.

Here in Munich this unassuming individual is represented by one of the foremost actresses of the Court Theater. And she embraces her task with love and interest. For besides being an actress, she is also an artist. I mean, she does not pride herself on "acting parts" but in creating real people from these fictitious roles.

An Enemy of the People is now being performed at the Burgtheater in Vienna. Among the many subordinate characters of the fourth act, there is a drunkard with only a few lines to say. This character, who disappears in the

play, is portrayed by the great Gabillon,* well known
throughout Europe. . . .

To Moritz Prozor

Munich, January 23, 1891

Ibsen's fame spread gradually to the Latin countries. In
Italy a translation of *A Doll's House* by the realist writer
Luigi Capuana appeared in a theatrical journal in January,
1891. Eleonora Duse wanted to use this version for her
production of the play, provided the ending was changed,
but she eventually gave in on this point. In France André
Antoine, the founder of the Théâtre Libre, introduced Ibsen
to the Parisian public by staging *Ghosts* on May 30, 1890,
and *The Wild Duck* on April 27, 1891. Prozor had translated Ibsen into French several years earlier (see letter of
October 25, 1889).

Dear Count Prozor, Mr. Luigi Capuana has, I regret to
see, given you a great deal of trouble by his proposal to
alter the last scene of *A Doll's House* for the Italian stage.

I do not doubt for a moment that the version you suggest would be distinctly preferable to that which Mr.
Capuana proposes. But the fact is that I cannot possibly
directly authorize any change whatever in the ending of
the drama. I might honestly say that it was for the sake
of the last scene that the whole play was written.

And, besides, I believe that Mr. Capuana is mistaken in
fearing that the Italian public would not be able to understand or approve of my work if it were put on the stage in
its original form. At any rate the experiment ought to be
tried. If it fails, then let Mr. Capuana, on his own responsibility, use your adaptation of the closing scene, but without any formal approval or authorization on my part.

I wrote to Mr. Capuana yesterday, briefly expressing
my views on the subject, and I hope that he will ignore
his misgivings until he has proved by experience that they
have some basis.

When *A Doll's House* was quite new, I was obliged to
give my consent to an alteration of the last scene for

* Ibsen neglected to mention, or perhaps did not know, that Ludvig
Gabillon made a career of playing "bit" parts. In forty-two years he
played 320 roles.

Frau Hedwig Niemann-Raabe, who was to play Nora in Berlin. At that time I had no choice. I was entirely unprotected by copyright law in Germany, and could consequently do nothing to prevent it. [See letters of February 17 and 18, 1880.] Besides, the play in its original, uncorrupted form was accessible to the German public in a German edition that was already printed and published. With the altered ending it had only a short run. In its unchanged form it is still being played.

I have answered the enclosed letter from Mr. Antoine, thanking him for his intention to produce *The Wild Duck* and urging him to make use of your translation. Of course I cannot tell what he will decide. But as the Théâtre Libre is really a private club, it is probably not possible to procure a legal injunction, and, besides, there are reasons which would make such a step inadvisable. However, I leave the decision of this question entirely to you, assured that you will act in the best way possible. . . .

To Victor Barrucand, French translator

Munich, March 6, 1891

. . . I also want to say that on principle I am opposed to any translation undertaken by two or more working in collaboration. Moreover *The Wild Duck* presents great difficulties, since one must have an intimate knowledge of the Norwegian language in order to appreciate how thoroughly each person in the play has his own special, individual way of speaking, by means of which his degree of education or learning can be noted. When Gina, for example, is speaking, one can immediately hear that she has never learned any grammar and that she is a product of the lower classes. And similarly in various ways for the other characters. Hence the task of the translator is not an easy one. . . .

To Hedvig Stousland

Munich, March 13, 1891

Fires destroyed large sections of Skien, Ibsen's birthplace, in 1854 and 1886. When the town had been rebuilt after the last fire, a celebration was held in 1891.

Dear Sister, I thank you very warmly for the letter which I received last month and which I must no longer delay answering.

I was very glad indeed to learn that Skien, too, is now to have its Public Festival Hall. It is sure to be a large and fine one, up to date in every respect and worthy of the modern town.

And you go on to say that a variety of entertainments will be given to celebrate the opening of this hall.

I wish very much that I could have been present at them. I suppose I would have met only a very few of my childhood acquaintances. I would have been surrounded by a new generation, all strange to me. But perhaps not altogether a stranger. For through all these long years of absence I have always had a feeling that I still belong to my native town.

Had these festivities taken place some years ago and I had been told of them, I would have written a song or a poem and sent it home. I hope and trust that it would have met with a kind reception there.

But I no longer write poems and songs of the kind required. So this is out of the question. And yet I wish with all my heart that I could take part in some way.

And therefore I wish that you would have this letter read aloud, so that everyone present may know that I am with you in thought on this festive occasion, as I have many a time been with you before, both in your sorrows and in your hopes of brighter days to come.

It was in 1850 that I was last in Skien. Not long afterward the town began to pass through a period of spiritual storms, which spread from there over a wider area.*

* In the 1850's Skien was the center of an independent church movement under the clergyman G. A. Lammers. The movement brought strife into many homes, including Ibsen's. His mother, his sister Hedvig, and his younger brother Ole left the state church to join Lammers' group. Lammers was certainly one of Ibsen's models for Brand.

I have always loved stormy weather. And, although I was absent, I went through this tempestuous period with you. That I did take part in it—some of my writings bear witness to that.

Then great calamities befell the town, devastating it again and again. The house where I was born and where I spent my earliest years, and the church—the old church with the angel of baptism under the raftered roof—were burned down. All the things to which my earliest recollections were attached have been burned—every one of them.

So you can understand how impossible it would be for me not to feel myself deeply and personally affected, together with you all, by the blows that struck our common home.

But I beg of you also to believe that it gave me a keen pleasure to read of the rebuilding of the town in a handsome and beautiful style, of the growth of the town, and of its progress in many directions.

It seems to me that gladness and hope must fill your hearts when you think of the future of our town.

I wish I could have said this and much more to you personally. But, in my own way, I am with you in spite of the distance that separates us.

And if I come to Norway again, as I hope I shall, then I will come and see my home again, the old and yet new home.

Dear Hedvig, this is what I particularly wanted to say to you today. I shall do my best to let you hear from me soon. Farewell! Remember me to your own family and to other relatives.

> Your affectionate brother,
> Henrik Ibsen

To Suzannah Ibsen

Vienna, April 10, 1891

In April, 1891, Vienna feted Ibsen with a series of banquets and performances of his plays that rivaled the festivities in Berlin two years before.

Dear Suzannah, Just these few lines to let you know that all is well. An excellent apartment was reserved for me.

But everything is expensive. Yesterday [Thursday], first
dress rehearsal [of *The Pretenders*]. Today, an extra rehearsal. The performance will be masterly.

Am overrun by journalists and other visitors. After the
performance tomorrow, festivities at the Kaiserhof. On
Sunday, great dinner at Director [Max] Burckhard's. Monday at Richard Voss's. Monday or Tuesday, première of
The Wild Duck at the Deutsches Volkstheater with [Frie-
drich] Mitterwurzer as Hjalmar.* On Wednesday, at the
Burgtheater, *An Enemy of the People,* and on Thursday
I hope I shall be homeward bound. All details must wait
till I can tell them by word of mouth. Only this: the interest in literature is much greater here than I had expected. I hope you are both well, and would like to hear
something from you.

Many greetings.

Your devoted
Henrik Ibsen

Ibsen did not return directly to Munich. He went on to
Budapest where he remained from April 19 through April
23, attending a production of *A Doll's House*, being hailed
by the public and the critics, greeted by a procession of
students, banqueted by dignitaries, and in general being
lionized as no playwright before him.

Upon his return to Munich, he began to make preparations
for settling permanently in Norway. His twenty-seven-year
exile was to come to an end. Having no more worlds to
conquer, he may have felt it was time for the hero to return
home. Perhaps he felt that he could bear life in Norway if
he lived there on his own terms. Perhaps he felt more keenly
than ever the truth of the remark he made in his Berlin
speech, January 11, 1887, that he would always be "a
stranger in the great house of Germany."

* Actually *The Wild Duck* did not open until Thursday, the sixteenth.

To Georg Brandes

Christiania, October 25, 1891

Brandes' first book, *Dualism in Our Latest Philosophy,* had been published at the end of October in 1866. (See notes to letter of June 26, 1869.)

[Telegram] IN FRIENDSHIP AND GRATITUDE I SEND YOU THIS DAY MY WARMEST CONGRATULATIONS FOR YOUR 25 YEARS' PIONEERING WORK IN THE CAUSE OF MAN'S SPIRITUAL FREEDOM.

To Helene Raff

Christiania, March 30, 1892

An amateur painter, Helene Raff sent Ibsen at least two of her works, one a painting of the sea, sent shortly before this letter, and the other a sketch of a young girl's head, which Ibsen named "Solveig," sent in 1890.

Dearest Miss Raff: Allow me to send you my warmest, my most heartfelt thanks for your kind letter, which reached me on my birthday, and also for the wonderfully beautiful picture that I had the indescribably great pleasure of receiving a few days ago. It is now hanging in a good place in my study, so that I may constantly satisfy myself with the view out over the broad, open sea—and constantly increase my desire to meet the dear, dear lovely

305

young girl who created this beautiful work of art. And who, while she worked on it, thought of me from afar. Oh—if I might only have the opportunity to thank you in person, as I should like to. I love the sea. Your picture carries me in thought and feeling to what I love. Yes, you have surely enriched my whole life by giving me this. Now little Solveig shall be hung beside the sea picture. Then I will have you wholly and altogether before me—and within me.

Such warm recollections of Munich arose in me when I received those remembrances in words and colors from you. How I should like to be down there again now. For in my heart I belong there. But then there are so many things in life which inhibit a man's wishes and desires.

You have acquired an incredible ability in handling the Norwegian language. Do you ever think of making a summer trip up here? To dream a bright fleeting summer night's dream among the mountains or out by the sea?

Give me an answer to that sometime, dearest Miss Raff. Will you? It would make me indescribably happy to receive again a few lines from you—of course at your convenience.

Yours sincerely and gratefully,
Henrik Ibsen

To Jacob Hegel

Christiania, July 5, 1892

After Frederik Hegel's death, his son Jacob became president of Gyldendal's publishing house in Copenhagen.

. . . Right now there is a great deal of excitement brewing in the political arena here. The party papers are trying to outdo each other in abuse and accusations. Speeches are being held, parades and processions are being planned. Today the Conservative Party is to greet the King with a procession to the palace. The conservatives are in town in an absolute majority. I expect, therefore, with things as they are, that the parade today will be exceptionally magnificent; all the more so since the left-wing procession in honor of Premier Steen last Sunday far surpassed my expectations. I find it very interesting to observe all this at close range. I do not let myself get involved personally; that would be against my nature. And everyone up here understands that. Since my return [to Norway] last year, I have been in the fortunate position of knowing and experiencing daily that both the Right and the Left are for me. . . .

To Jacob Hegel

Christiania, November 10, 1892

. . . I trust you have received the impression from a reading of the manuscript [*The Master Builder*] that Christiania agrees with me as a place in which to work. The parts can be exceptionally well cast at the Danish Royal Theater. And is it not fortunate, in view of certain recent events in Copenhagen, that it does not end with a suicide! . . .

Twenty years ago when the sixth printing of *Brand* was about to appear, we and the Falsens were staying in Dresden. At that time I could never imagine that there would be a twelfth printing of the poem, and I promised Dorothea [Mrs. Falsen] that if there ever were, I would give her half the royalties. Well, now it has happened. She has arrived on the scene and, like Hilde in my play, demands that I fulfill my promise. Would you please be good enough to send the amount due her directly to her, that is, not through me? . . .

To August Lindberg

Christiania, January 6, 1893

The Master Builder, the first play that Ibsen wrote upon his return to his home country, was published on December 12, 1892. During the next month it was staged throughout Scandinavia, with the première taking place in Trondhjem. The Swedish producer August Lindberg began negotiating for the rights, and the following letters show Ibsen at work as his own agent.

Dear Mr. Lindberg: It distresses me that I have no other course than to refuse your latest offer for the rights to

The Master Builder. I cannot grant these rights on any
other conditions than the ones I set forth in my last letter.
The matter should be settled immediately. If it is not, I
shall consider myself free to reach agreements with other
Swedish theater companies and directors.

My business relations have grown by degrees to such an
extent that I am now forced to demand unconditionally
that the royalty be paid in advance before I grant any
director performance rights to my plays. . . .

To August Lindberg

Christiania, February 13, 1893

Dear Mr. Lindberg: It distresses me deeply that I can
not comply with your request for a postponement in the
payment of the balance of the royalty that is due me. I
was counting on your acceptance of all terms of the contract. I was absolutely certain that you would accept the
contract in its entirety. Counting on your acceptance, I
sent a large sum of money last week to Copenhagen for
the purchase of bonds, with the result that I am now very
short of cash. Consequently no postponement is possible. . . .

A Hilde who is absolutely right in all respects is essential to the play.

Yours sincerely,
Henrik Ibsen

To August Lindberg

Christiania, March 4, 1893

[Telegram] I FORBID THE PERFORMANCES IN STOCKHOLM
BECAUSE OF BREACH OF CONTRACT. IF NECESSARY I SHALL
APPEAL TO THE NORWEGIAN PREMIER TO INTERVENE.

IBSEN

To August Lindberg

Christiania, April 4, 1893

I have on this day received 1,000 kroner [$268] from Assistant Police Commissioner Mossin on behalf of August Lindberg.

Henrik Ibsen

To Suzannah Ibsen

Christiania, December 11, 1894

On more than one occasion in the 1890's Mrs. Ibsen left Norway to seek relief from the pains of her gout. Ibsen remained in Christiania while his son Sigurd accompanied Mrs. Ibsen to Germany and Italy. Sigurd had married Bjørnson's daughter Bergliot in 1892, and she helped to look after the Ibsen home while Sigurd and Mrs. Ibsen were away.

Dear Suzannah, I have received your telegrams and just now I got your letter. How happy and reassured I am to hear that so far everything has gone well! I hope it will continue to do so. Everything is fine here. Miss Blehr's cooking suits me perfectly. And there's plenty of it, so we have more than enough for the evening if I feel like having something later on. But then I prefer herring and those heavenly warm potatoes which Lina cooks on the new machine. She takes care of all my needs with the greatest possible attentiveness. Bergliot had dinner with me Sunday. Otherwise no one has been here. The evenings are lonely, but I sit and read at the dining table. In the morning I have my coffee which is served in my room at precisely eight o'clock. Everything is going like clockwork, exactly as if you were here. Every morning Augusta brings me a small plate with bread for the birds. Lina is nice to her and gives her some of all that food that is left over.—Today the new play [*Little Eyolf*] will be published simultaneously here and in Berlin and in London. The English royalties from Heinemann came yesterday, and I shall have Hegel invest 10,000 kroner

[\$2,680] for us. Later, I hope, 4,000 more, without our running short of funds. I am overburdened with correspondence, as you can well imagine. But I express myself as briefly as possible, and in that way I'll get through it. Say hello to Sigurd for me. I'm looking forward to seeing his new book soon, and that makes me very happy. Say hello also to the Grønvolds, and Miss Klingenfeld and Miss Raff. And I mustn't forget Clemence, if she is in town. And thank the last two many times for the beautiful pictures. And I hope that you and Sigurd will have a really pleasant time in the old, familiar places! Please write soon.

Affectionately,

H. I.

To Suzannah and Sigurd Ibsen

Christiania, December 20, 1894

Dear Suzannah, Even though I don't know if this letter will reach you in Munich, I still want to write to you today, hoping that it will reach you in one place or another. You can well imagine what a busy time I've had since December 11 when my play appeared. It has been greeted with a storm of unanimous enthusiasm, like nothing before it. The first printing [10,000] is already sold out and the second printing will appear the day after tomorrow. Mr. [Albert] Ranft has bought and paid for the Swedish performance rights for 3,000 kroner [\$804]. The same for the Christiania Theater. The English royalties have been paid. I am about to invest *17,000* kroner [\$4,556] and that will still leave us plenty to do with as we wish. The Royal Theater in Copenhagen has accepted the play. Also the Burgtheater [in Vienna] and the Deutsches Theater [in Berlin]. And certainly many other German theaters that I haven't heard from as yet. . . .

To Suzannah Ibsen

Christiania, January 13, 1895

Dear Suzannah, Many thanks for your last letter from Bozen. I hope that these lines will reach you at your next stopover and that you will be comfortable there. Can only write briefly since I am completely taken up with theater rehearsals. Opening night day after tomorrow [at the Christiania Theater]. Looks very promising; the actors are exerting themselves to the utmost. Am enclosing a letter from my sister. Everything as usual here. Many greetings to you and to Sigurd from

Your affectionate

H. I.

Yesterday [world] première at the Deutsches Theater. Great success. Telegrams pouring in.

To Georg Brandes

Christiania, February 11, 1895

This letter must be read against the background of Ibsen's attachment to a young lady he met in Christiania and who evidently played an important part in his life up to 1900. Her name was Hildur Andersen. She was the daughter of an old friend of Ibsen's, the granddaughter of Mrs. Sontum, Ibsen's motherly landlady in his Bergen days, and also a relation of Ibsen's personal physician. Ibsen saw her frequently, and, whether she knew it or not at that time, she sat as model to him while he was writing *The Master Builder*. Like Hilde in the play, Hildur had just come from a hiking trip when the master playwright met her. The extent of Ibsen's devotion to her may be indicated by the fact that he gave her a diamond ring inscribed with the date September 19—the very day that Hilde suddenly appears to claim her kingdom from Solness—and that Ibsen gave her, in November, 1894, the manuscript of *The Master Builder*, which, interestingly enough, was finished on September 19, 1892.

Dear Georg Brandes, I cannot resist sending you my special thanks for your "Goethe and Marianne von Willemer" [an article in *Tilskueren*, January, 1895]. I was not acquainted with this episode from Goethe's life. Perhaps I read about it long, long ago in G. H. Lewes' *Goethe*, but I must have forgotten about it because it had no personal interest for me at that time. Now the case is quite different. When I think of the character of Goethe's works during those years, the rebirth of his youth, it seems to me I should have known that he must have been blessed with something as wonderful for him as meeting this Marianne von Willemer. Now and then fate, chance, providence can indeed be rather kind and well disposed toward one.

All best wishes.

Sincerely,
Henrik Ibsen

To Suzannah Ibsen

Christiania, March 12, 1895

Dear Suzannah, Your latest letter came yesterday just as I was about to write to you. Your letters have always been coming through, and when you say I don't mention the things you write about, you must be referring to political matters. But Sigurd took it upon himself to keep you up to date on that. He is much better informed in that field than I am.— Well, as you must have read in the papers, Mrs. Collett is dead. During her illness no one but her children were allowed to see her. But nearly every day I met her son Robert on the street, and he said that she lay and talked constantly about [J. S.] Welhaven and about us and about the times she spent with us abroad. The services took place yesterday in the chapel. On top of the casket, in addition to a wreath from the Queen, there lay a magnificent bouquet from you with long white silk ribbons on which were printed in gold letters: "To Camilla Collett from Mrs. Suzannah Ibsen." From me, a large laurel wreath with ribbons in the national colors. And there were huge quantities of flowers and wreaths.— On that horrible day of March 20 [Ibsen's birthday] Bergliot will be free to do just exactly as she pleases, since that's the way you want it. And I shall receive everybody, even the spies, as politely as I possibly can. I hope Falsen won't come. Dorothea and Magdalena [Falsen] are down with influenza; so they won't make it. Besides, from what I hear they have moved to Park Street. Herman has twisted his foot and can't go out. And now I can tell you that the *third* impression of *Little Eyolf* is being printed and will probably appear next week. Tomorrow night will be opening night in Copenhagen. Hegel has commissioned Eilif Peterssen to do a large portrait of me, which I am sitting for at present. There is a widespread epidemic of influenza in the city. But so far I haven't felt any effects of the disease. Yesterday evening there was a fire upstairs in Mrs. Bjørn's boardinghouse. Somebody had put too much fuel in a lamp which naturally exploded. The fire brigade rushed to the scene, and there was a lot of noise and commotion on the stairs, but the fire was soon put out. At the big art exhibit I bought a masterly painting by Christian Krohg. It's actually a portrait of Strindberg, but Sigurd calls it "The Revolution," and I call it "The Outbreak of Madness." It was Sigurd who pressed me into buying it for the unbelievably low price of 500 kroner [$134]. At present everything is well at Sigurd's. Bergliot has been so kind as to give me some aged cheese and some pickled herring and some wonderful spareribs, which I revel in during the evenings.— I hope that you too are having a really good time down there. Many greetings from your affectionate

H. I.

To Suzannah Ibsen

Christiania, April 3, 1895

Dear Suzannah, I have been waiting a long time to hear from you. But since Sigurd tells me he received letters from you last week, I hope that everything is going as well as can be expected. I know I haven't written as frequently as I used to do. The reason is that Eilif Peterssen is here every day to work on my portrait. But he is just about finished now, and then my letter writing will be back on its old schedule. Here at home everything is going its usual way with the exception that we have begun to cook meals at home. Miss Blehr's cooking got worse from day to day until it was nearly inedible. Lina, on the other hand, prepares quite exceptional dishes, just the kind of things that she knows I prefer—a lot of fish with those wonderful potatoes. . . . Sigurd was here last night and we sat and talked together until late in the night—mostly about his literary plans but also about politics, which is getting more and more messy. Today the King is leaving here, quite unexpectedly, with his whole family to return to Stockholm. A new government has not been formed and the present one does not want to remain. . . . The Falsens still have influenza. Now Henrik Anton is down with a fever. But I met old Falsen on the street yesterday. He is fully recovered, but he said Norwegian politics is making his head turn gray.— If I'm going to mail this letter today, I must stop here. Write soon! Greetings and all best wishes from your affectionate

H. I.

To Suzannah Ibsen

Christiania, Easter Eve
April 13, 1895

. . . Sigurd and Bergliot were here in the evening the day before yesterday, and we had a pleasant time. Sigurd now wants to have a professorship in sociology established for him at the university. But I think he understood that this could not be managed without the support of the Conservative Party, and he asked me to intervene on his behalf with Professor Hagerup and others. I'd be extremely happy to do so; but with the government's position as uncertain as it is at the present moment, it isn't very likely that any such plan can be put into effect in the near future. In any case, Sigurd will certainly write you in more detail about it. . . .

To turn to our own business affairs, I can tell you I've invested a full 24,000 kroner and that I hope to invest another 6,000, so that the increased investment will come to 30,000. That means we shall be getting the income from a total of 166,000 kroner [$44,488]. I think I may be allowed to say "well done!" . . . Next time you write tell me more about how you are getting along down there. Up here we have a few beautiful spring days now and then, but the spring really hasn't come as yet.— Don't misunderstand what I wrote about Sigurd's plan. His idea is to win the support of both the Left and the Right; otherwise he cannot get it through.— Enjoy yourself and write soon to your affectionate

H. I.

To Suzannah Ibsen

Christiania, May 7, 1895

The rumor that Ibsen was keeping Hildur Andersen company and might even be contemplating divorce reached Mrs. Ibsen in Italy, through her stepmother Magdalene Thoresen.

Dear Suzannah, It has distressed me deeply to read your latest letter, dated May 1. I hope that afterward, when you had had time to consider the matter carefully, you regretted that you had sent it to me. Once again it is your stepmother, that damned old sinner, who has gone around trying to stir up trouble between us. But it is easy to see who put those notions into her poor crazy head. It is naturally her dear daughter, who is still gadding about the streets here and who is undoubtedly furious with me because I duck into a side street whenever I catch sight of her. I've actually done this a couple of times. And now she's trying to take her revenge in her own way. But how can you let yourself be fooled by things like that?!

I don't understand your stepmother's crazy way of talking and all her supposedly deep remarks. Never have understood them. But when she writes something about my wanting "a separation no matter what it costs" I can solemnly declare to you that I have never seriously thought or intended anything of the sort and that I never shall think or intend it. Whatever I may have blurted out when your moods and temperamental fits drove me to momentary desperation has no bearing on anything else and is not worth considering. But my earnest advice to you is that if you want to keep your peace of mind, which is necessary for the sake of your health, you should break off all correspondence with that dizzy-brained stepmother of yours. It's quite possible that she means well and wants to do all she can for you. But her interference in every matter or situation has always proved fatal. If you don't want to tell her so, then I shall. But first I have to have your consent. And that's all on that subject for today.

And now for the second topic in your letter. You insist that I rent another apartment. [The dampness of the present apartment aggravated Mrs. Ibsen's gout or rheumatism.] And naturally, since you so absolutely insist on it, I shall do as you wish. But in your letter you reproach me with not having consulted you when I rented our present apartment. (At that time you were in Valders and in such a mood that I could scarcely think of asking your advice.) When you come home this time and find the new apartment rented and furnished, you must bear in mind that I have acted according to your explicit demands and that once again I have not been able to consult you. And it will not be an easy task to find something that satisfies you in every way. Do you remember how Sigurd and Bergliot had to look and look before they finally paid through the nose for something decent? Now the difficulties are even greater. You won't live on the ground floor because of the cold floors, and you won't live on the upper floors because of the steps. But, as I said, your wishes shall be satisfied. A new apartment will be rented.

I neither can nor wish to write about other things today. And in regard to myself, there is nothing to say. [Erik] Werenskiold is here every morning to paint for an hour. And everything is going its usual, regular way in the house. Sigurd and the newspapers must be keeping you in touch with political matters.

And let me soon hear from you that you have been reassured, so that I shall be reassured. And above all, keep those witches away from you! That is the best wish and advice I can send you. Warmest greetings!

Yours affectionately,

H. I.

To Suzannah Ibsen

Christiania, June 21, 1895

. . . I see you have already begun to take the water cures [in Monsummano]. I realize it is still too early to notice if they have had any beneficial effect. But if, on the other hand, you should notice the opposite effect, I hope you will break off in time. Tell me more about your rooms, the food, and how everything else is down there—

and what kind of people are staying there. I am especially interested in hearing about that. I suppose that they are about the same as up at the Brenner spa.

I have now given notice on the apartment at Victoria Terrace and have rented a second-floor apartment in the new building that the Hoff brothers are putting up at the corner of Arbins Street and Drammensvejen. It was Sigurd and Bergliot who suggested it, and I think you will find it satisfactory. I will have a large study opening directly off the entrance hall, so that whoever wishes to see me will not have to go through any other room in the apartment. That means you will have entirely at your disposition a large corner room with balcony, and next to this a living room of nearly the same size, leading to a dining room which can accommodate twenty to twenty-two people and with a niche for a sideboard that I shall purchase. From the dining room you can go directly into the spacious library, and from there into your bedroom, which is considerably larger than my present one here on Victoria Terrace. My bedroom is next to yours and has a balcony. You don't have to use the hallway at all except when you want to take a bath. Naturally there is a large, bright kitchen, pantry and serving room, and many built-in cupboards. As I said, I think you will find it satisfactory. . . .

To William Archer

Christiania, June 27, 1895

Herbert Beerbohm Tree, actor-manager at the Haymarket Theatre in London, produced *An Enemy of the People* there beginning June 14, 1893. The play was also in the repertory during part of 1894.

Little Eyolf, published on December 11, 1894, and first performed at the Deutsches Theater in Berlin on January 12, 1895, had its Scandinavian première at the Christiania Theater on January 15. The play was performed in the other principal Scandinavian theaters during February and March. Paris saw the play in the spring. In writing of this production in the *Journal des Débats,* the French critic and dramatist Jules Lemaître revealed that he had misunderstood a crucial point in the play by thinking that Asta Almers had revealed herself as Alfred Almer's half sister instead of no relation at all. If Lemaître was too eager to read incest into *Little Eyolf*, it may have been because he had erred in the opposite way when he first read *Ghosts*. Only on a second reading did he see that Mrs. Alving very clearly says she would acquiesce in the incestuous union of Regina and Osvald. (See Lemaître, *Impressions de théatre*, Vol. V, Paris, 1900, pp. 25–6.)

Dear Mr. William Archer, Permit me to offer you my thanks for the two checks received. I am enclosing the receipt for Mr. Tree, duly signed, and also the two letters.

I knew of your discussion with Jules Lemaître because the Norwegian papers gave an account of it, quoting from both sides. You came off victorious from that encounter, and it seems to me that your French opponent acknowledged his mistake about Asta in a very generous and pleasant manner. I am exceedingly obliged to you for having straightened out the French literary world on this matter. Unfortunately, too many mistakes still remain uncorrected.

I hope that I shall be able to write a new play next year; but I cannot yet be certain. So many other things demand my time and attention. The state of my wife's health obliged her to spend the winter at Meran in the Tyrol. Now she has gone to Italy to take the baths at Monsummano. My son is with her. I shall have the pleasure of sending her the kind messages in your letter the next time I write.

I regret more and more that I neglected at the proper time to learn to speak English. Now it is too late. If I were conversant with the language, I would go to London at once. Or, to be more correct, I would have been there long ago. I have been turning many ideas over in my mind lately, and, among other things, I have become quite convinced that my Scottish ancestry has left very strong traces in me. But this is only a feeling—perhaps only a wish that it were so. I lack experience and knowledge to know for certain.

With respectful regards to Mrs. Archer, I remain

Yours most sincerely,

Henrik Ibsen

To Hildur Andersen

Christiania, July 29, 1895

Hildur had visited Skien, Ibsen's birthplace, on a hiking tour.

. . . You should have seen more of Skien and *heard* more of it. Because Skien is the town of the storming, streaming, seething waters. At least, that's how I remember it. . . .

It is not without reason that I was born in the town of the rapids. . . .

To Jonas Collin

Christiania, July 31, 1895

Lugné-Poë, who is mentioned in this letter, perhaps did more for Ibsen in France than anyone else. Formerly an actor with Antoine at the Théâtre Libre, Lugné-Poë organized in 1893 his own Théâtre de L'Œuvre, which was oriented toward the symbolistic and poetic drama. During the last decade of the century, Lugné-Poë staged a number of Ibsen's Plays: *Rosmersholm,* October 6, 1893 (revived in 1898); *An Enemy of the People,* November 8, 1893 (revived in 1894 and 1899); *The Master Builder,* April 3, 1894 (revived in 1898); *Little Eyolf,* May 8, 1895; *Brand,* June 22, 1895; *Pillars of Society,* June 17, 1896; *Peer Gynt,* November 12, 1896; *Love's Comedy,* June 23, 1897; and *John Gabriel Borkman,* November 9, 1897. In October, 1894, Lugné-Poë's young troupe came to Christiania and gave an inspired performance of *The Master Builder.* Completely gripped by the performance, Ibsen declared, "This was the resurrection of my play."

Dear Mr. Jonas Collin, Thank you deeply for your kind letter, and I hope that you will excuse my sending only a few words in reply.

I have already received the poster you write about from M. Lugné-Poë, together with other printed matter belonging to it. And I have received a great many other things —much more than I can handle. There is, of course, a certain satisfaction in becoming so famous in one country after another. But it gives me no sense of happiness. What is it all worth—really? Well—!? Kindest regards from

Yours very sincerely,

Henrik Ibsen

To Suzannah Ibsen

Christiania, August 9, 1895

Dear Suzannah, Please thank Sigurd for his letter of July 31. I see from it that your cure is over, but I hope that these lines will find you at the same address. When you leave there, I hope you will let me know in sufficient time where I should write in case something important arises. That is not the case today. Quite the contrary. Here everything is going smoothly and quietly with dismal, cold, rainy weather that looks as if it will never let up.

Mr. Lugné-Poë is in town, and tomorrow there is to be a banquet for him. Unfortunately I cannot get out of going to it—I have no desire to go.

Another famous person has been to see me and I have been very much interested in talking to him. He has gone by now. That was the Serbian prince Boyidar Karageorge-vich, whose father reigned until the present dynasty came to power. I wish that Sigurd could have met him. . . .

There have also been an unmanageable number of tourists this year, and they have really plagued me. But that can be rather pleasant, nevertheless. . . .

In an Autograph Album

Christiania, November, 1895

The absolutely imperative task of democracy is to make itself aristocratic.

To Georg Brandes

Christiania, April 24, 1896

Dear Brandes, Yes, you are right: I never did answer your letter of last December 16, although it has been lying on my desk the whole time, constantly reminding me to write you and thank you. I had hoped that Hegel would send me your big work [Brandes' work on Shakespeare, which appeared in three volumes in 1895–96] when it was completed. But I have not yet received it from him, and I have not wanted to tell him to send it to me. So I am most grateful to you for your offer to intervene in the matter. I assure you there is no book I am so eager to immerse myself in as this new book of yours.

You suggest in your last letter that I should visit London. If I knew enough English, I might consider it. But since that is not the case, I have to give up the idea altogether. Besides, I am busy with the plans for a major new work, and I don't want to put it aside any longer than necessary. A roof tile might very easily fall on my head before I "find time to write the last verse." And then what?

Best wishes.

Yours sincerely,
Henrik Ibsen

To Hildur Andersen's Year-Old Niece

Christiania, April 28, 1896

This was inscribed in a copy of *Brand*.

To Little Eldrid:

Like a perfect poem, may your life express
The reconciliation of duty with happiness.

To Georg Brandes

Christiania, October 3, 1896

Dear Brandes, You know by experience what an incorrigibly bad correspondent I am, and therefore you will understand the real reason why I have not written—not even to you.

I have not only read the whole of your monumental work on Shakespeare but it has absorbed me as scarcely any other book I can remember. I feel as if Shakespeare and his age and you yourself lived and breathed in this brilliant work. A thousand thanks for the enrichment you have given me with this book. . . .

I am hard at work on a new play [*John Gabriel Borkman*], which must be completed as soon as possible.

Therefore I must ask you to be satisfied with these few lines from your faithful and devoted friend,

Henrik Ibsen

To Georg Brandes

Christiania, October 11, 1896

Jules Lemaître, in an article on the influence of Scandinavian literature (reprinted in his *Les Contemporains*, Vol. VI, Paris, 1896, pp. 225–70), had argued that Ibsen had no other ideas than those that were to be found in the early novels of George Sand and in the plays of Alexandre Dumas. Brandes sent an inquiry to Ibsen before writing his reply, "Henrik Ibsen en France," which appeared in the January, 1897, issue of *Cosmopolis* (Vol. V, pp. 112–24).

Dear Brandes, Let me answer your questions briefly:

1. I declare on my honor and conscience that I have never in my life, neither in my youth nor at any later period, read a single book by George Sand. I once began to read *Consuelo* in a translation but put it aside immediately, as it seemed to me to be the work of an amateur philosopher not of a poet. But as I read only a few pages, I may be mistaken.

2. The above makes an answer to this question unnecessary.

3. To Alexandre Dumas I owe nothing as regards dramatic form—except that I have learned from his plays to avoid several very awkward faults and blunders of which he is not infrequently guilty.

My best thanks to you for taking the trouble of disabusing the French of their illusions!

Yours ever,
Henrik Ibsen

To Peter Hansen

Christiania, December 17, 1896

John Gabriel Borkman was published on December 15, 1896, in an unprecedented first printing of 15,000. It was first produced in Helsinki on January 10, 1897, and first in Germany at Frankfurt am Main on January 16. In Norway the play was first staged by the Swedish troupe of August Lindberg, who brought his production to a town near Christiania on January 19, a week before the Christiania Theater was to give its production of *Borkman*. The following letter concerned the casting of the play at the Christiania Theater.

My dear Friend, Thank you for your letter. What Mr. Hennings alleges in regard to his conversation with me here is sheer nonsense. I told him explicitly, in the presence of Mr. Schrøder [the head of the theater], that there was no leading role for Mrs. Hennings in my new play, but maybe a minor part. I was thinking of Frida. For the part of Ella I wanted to suggest Mrs. Oda Nielsen. An actress who can play Rita [in *Little Eyolf*] should also be able to play Ella. And besides, she will be believable as the twin sister of Mrs. Eckardt, who naturally will have to play Gunhild.

Yours sincerely,
Henrik Ibsen

To Georg Brandes

Christiania, June 3, 1897

Dear Georg Brandes, Not until I received your letter did I learn that the illness from which you are suffering is that troublesome and tedious old Capitoline ailment of yours, phlebitis. It was mentioned for the first time in the *Politiken* which I received yesterday. I had imagined that it was merely some unimportant infection of the throat that was preventing you from lecturing. How could anything else have occurred to me, seeing that you have published in these last few weeks long articles on Helge Rode's new play [*Sommeræventyr*] and his writings generally, on Victor Hugo's monument, and on other subjects? Truly your productive power is inexhaustible. I have not been able to follow all the details of the great controversy into which you were led by your French essay on me, and therefore I shall postpone talking about it and thanking you, until we meet again.

When I write of our meeting, I am not making use of an empty phrase. Can you guess what I am dreaming about, and planning, and picturing to myself as so delightful? Settling down near the Sound, between Copenhagen and Elsinore, on some free, open spot, from which I can see all the seagoing ships starting on and returning from their long voyages. I cannot do that *here*. Here all the straits are closed, in every sense—and all the channels of communication are blocked. Oh, dear Brandes, a man does not live for twenty-seven years in the wider, liberal and liberating, cultural world without suffering the consequences. Up here by the fjords is my native land. But—but—but—where am I to find my *home*land? It is the sea that draws and attracts me most.

In the meantime I go about in my loneliness planning something new in the way of a play. But I have no distinct idea yet what it will be.

Now, in the first place, see that you get well again, with as little trouble as possible. And then—to our next meeting in the new home with the Sound spreading out before me.

Your faithful and devoted friend,

Henrik Ibsen

To Suzannah Ibsen

Christiania, June 13, 1897

Mrs. Ibsen had to leave Norway again in 1897 for her health, and while she was away the question of Sigurd Ibsen's professorship at the University of Christiania came to a head. It was obvious that a bill to offer such a professorship to Sigurd Ibsen had no chance of passing the Norwegian Storting where the Conservative Party was in a distinct majority. Instead the Storting was asked to grant Sigurd the opportunity of delivering a series of lectures on social science on the basis of which a specially selected committee would consider his qualifications as a professor. During the term of 1896–97 Sigurd delivered these lectures to huge audiences, with Ibsen regularly present. On April 29, 1897, the *ad hoc* committee declared that Sigurd Ibsen could not be entrusted with a professorship. Sigurd left immediately to rejoin his mother in Italy.

. . . There is a strong feeling of indignation in wide circles about the committee's findings sent to the government. Professor Blix came and talked to me about the matter, called it a scandal and a blunder, and confided to me that he and several others would take united action before the matter came up in the Storting. The paper *Intelligensen,* of which I have become a subscriber, as well as the [Norwegian] *Dagblad* have published articles against the committee.

Does Sigurd receive those papers daily? If not, I shall forward them to him whenever they contain anything of interest. The conservative press has so far maintained silence; I have not seen one word in defense of the committee's findings in any of the papers I have read, and I doubt if there has been anything in any of the others. . . .

Here in the house everything is going smoothly with everything in its place—you need not worry about that. The hydrangea is putting out just as many buds as last year. I have had to order a dozen new shirts with French cuffs because the ones I took with me from Munich are completely worn out. As far as food is concerned, I have exactly what I like: ham, scrambled eggs, a great deal of smoked salmon prepared in different ways, salads, and other good, healthy summer dishes. I am feeling exceptionally good—and in my solitude a new play is beginning to sprout forth and to hatch out. I can already sense the basic mood, but so far I can see only one of the characters. But don't worry, the other ones will come forth.— Write soon so that I may know you have reached the grotto and that everything is as you desire.

Affectionately,

H. I.

To Bjørnstjerne Bjørnson

Christiania, June 15, 1897

Dear Friend, My sincere thanks for your invitation to visit you at Aulestad.

Unfortunately it is impossible for me to get away nor have I the peace of mind to do so. What the newspapers write about a proposed journey to Denmark is a complete misunderstanding. Should I leave here, I would leave for good and all. And if all roads are barred to Sigurd in Norway I don't see that I have anything more to do here.

And I have many places to which I can retreat. In Munich I have lived long enough to be naturalized as a Bavarian; there I can be sure of being well received. In Italy likewise.

I must say Norway is a difficult country to belong to.

More about this when we meet.

Again many thanks and cordial greetings to you and your wife.

Your devoted
Henrik Ibsen

To Julius Elias

Christiania, June 20, 1897

The German critics Julius Elias and Paul Schlenther, the latter being one of the founders of the Freie Bühne in Berlin, had convinced the publisher S. Fischer of the desirability of issuing a German edition of Ibsen's collected works. They sent their detailed plan to Ibsen on June 14, 1897.

Dear Elias: It was a great pleasure to receive and study your and Dr. Schlenther's plan for a new collected edition of my literary works. In all essentials I approve of it. But I wish to make one or two remarks. The table of contents for Vol. I includes poems and prose writings. Of the last mentioned I have written none suitable for translation into German. And I would suggest that my poems should form part of the last volume rather than the first, since they were written singly during the course of my whole literary career. Besides, a satisfactory translation could hardly be made by the time the first volume ought to be published. . . .

[*Midsummer Eve (Sancthansnatten)* and *Olaf Lilje-krans*], which I wrote in my youth, I have never wanted to publish, and I do not wish to have them translated. . . .

After entering into a few more particulars, I hope to come to an agreement with Mr. Fischer. I shall write to him very soon about one or two little things that I should like to have more plainly stated in the contract between us.

To save myself the trouble of writing in a foreign language, I am not sending a letter of thanks direct to Dr. Schlenther. But I ask you to consider this letter as addressed to both of you.

Yours sincerely and gratefully,
Henrik Ibsen

To Suzannah Ibsen

Christiania, July 2, 1897

Dear Suzannah, I have waited now for several days for a letter from you, but in vain. I hope that everything is going well with you, and, for my part, I won't wait any longer to send you a few lines. The papers keep you informed about public affairs, so I shall confine myself to household affairs, all of which are in good order. Last week we had quite a spectacle here when my study was cleaned from top to bottom. The paintings were taken down to be cleaned, and they now shine and sparkle so that it is a joy to look at them. The curtains have also been washed and so have the walls. The floor was scrubbed and then varnished, so that it is hard to recognize it. It had to dry for six days, and during that time the furniture was down in the yard being thoroughly beaten. I used the red room in the meantime. Now it is the blue room's turn, where the floor will also be varnished as well as the dining room. I can eat in the library. It's good that we have enough rooms; and Mina is very good; she has had a charwoman to help her a couple of days.— I am now busily corresponding about the German edition which will fill nine thick volumes. Already there is a mass of tourists here, and yesterday a flock of reporters arrived from the congress in Stockholm. Most of them left their cards with me, or else talked with me at home or in the hotel. I feel wonderfully good, and I don't see how I could have it better anywhere else in the summertime. And I've begun to think about a new play! And consequently I'm taking longer walks, going every day first to Skillebæk and back again—and then down into town. I'm thriving on it. But the main thing is how the spring waters agree with you this year. You must give me full details on this in your next letter. You should throw away that tincture of iodine which didn't agree with you in Labers and get yourself a new bottle. Let me also hear how Sigurd is making out. There can hardly be any possibility of a new competition or a new committee. I sent a telegram to Bergliot on June 16. I am right in thinking that is her birthday, am I not? As for *yours*, I know that Mrs. Lie has written to you, and she sent beautiful flowers here to the house. Miss Cappelen was also here with some wonderful roses. Now I have scribbled down everything fast and furious, but I felt I had to write you today. We're having the most wonderful summer weather, the air is so easy to breathe. Now enjoy yourself; I wish you all the best.

Affectionately,

H. I.

To Count I. Milewski

Christiania, Summer, 1897

When Count Milewski, a collector of autographs, visited Christiania in his yacht, the following was written in German in his album.

The development of the human race went off the track from the start.

The dear children of men should have evolved as creatures of the sea.

To Julius Elias

. . . Today I am sending you *The Warrior's Barrow* [*Kjæmpehøjen*], which I was finally lucky enough to find a copy of. After reading it through, I find that there are several good things in this little youthful work of mine, and I sincerely thank you for insisting that it be included in the collected works. . . .

To Julius Elias

Dear Dr. Elias: I hereby declare once and for all that I neither wish to, nor have the right to, allow the play *Midsummer Eve* to be included in a collection of *my* works. The play is a miserable product that really did not come from my hands. It is built on a careless, clumsy outline that I once got from a student friend [Theodore Bernhoft], reworked and signed my name to, but I cannot now possibly recognize it as mine.* Therefore I must urgently beg you and Dr. Schlenther not to insist any more on the publication of this mess. Far from shedding light on my other works, this play has no connection whatsover with them. Consequently I have for years now regarded it as having never been written and as nonexistent. . . .

To Emilie Bardach

The silence between Emilie Bardach and Ibsen (see letter of December 30, 1890) was broken by Emilie when Ibsen's

* Compare this view of the origin of *Midsummer Eve* with that in the petition of March 10, 1863.

seventieth birthday was about to be celebrated. Ibsen's reply was his last letter to her.

Sweetest, darling Fräulein—!

Accept my deepest thanks for your letter. The summer in Gossensass was the happiest, the most beautiful of my whole life.

I scarcely dare to think about it. And yet I *must,* always. Always!

Your truly devoted
Henrik Ibsen

To the Reader

Christiania, March, 1898

As part of Ibsen's seventieth-birthday celebration, the first volumes of his collected works were published simultaneously in German and Danish editions in March, 1898. For the Danish edition Ibsen wrote a special prefatory note, which was later included in the German edition.

When my publisher was kind enough to suggest the publication of a collected edition of my works in chronological order, I realized immediately the great advantages this would offer for a better understanding of my plays.

Simultaneously with the production of my works another generation of readers has grown up, and I have often noticed with regret that their knowledge of my more recent works was considerably more detailed than of my earlier ones. Consequently these readers lack an awareness of the mutual connections between the plays, and I attribute a not insignificant part of the strange, imperfect, and misleading interpretations that my later works have been subjected to in so many quarters to this lack of awareness.

Only by grasping and comprehending my entire production as a continuous and coherent whole will the reader be able to receive the precise impression I sought to convey in the individual parts of it.

I therefore appeal to the reader that he not put any play aside, and not skip anything, but that he absorb the plays —by reading himself into them and by experiencing them intimately—in the order in which I wrote them.

According to Bergliot Ibsen, the German publisher Fischer paid 5,000 marks [$1,190] for each play in the collected edition, while Gyldendal, Ibsen's old publishers in Copenhagen, paid 200,000 kroner [$53,600] for the exclusive publishing rights to all of Ibsen's plays. Of the German collected works at least 40,000, and perhaps 80,000, copies were printed. (See Bergliot Ibsen, *The Three Ibsens,* New York, 1952, pp. 130–32.)

Speech at the Banquet in Christiania

Christiania, March 23, 1898

The celebrations attendant on Ibsen's seventieth birthday were without parallel. No Norwegian personality had ever been so honored, nor has anyone since.

In addition to the publication of his collected works in Danish and German editions, the theaters in the Scandinavian and German-speaking countries put on a series of Ibsen's plays. On March 20, his birthday, two theaters in Copenhagen, three in Stockholm, six in Berlin, and four in Vienna were performing his plays. In Christiania the Central Theater staged *Ghosts* while the Christiania Theater produced *The Feast at Solhaug* plus some scenes from *Peer Gynt*. The next evening, March 21, Ibsen attended the production of *The Master Builder* at the Christiania Theater. The following day the university students honored him with a procession, and on March 23 an official banquet brought the Norwegian festivities to a close.

Just now when I struck my glass for silence, it became so quiet all around. At least so it seemed to me. But if you have been expecting me to respond fully to all those warm, kind words that have been addressed to me, you are mistaken. I can express my most cordial thanks for them only in a general way. And likewise for all the honor and homage being shown me here today.

Or perhaps you have been expecting that I would make a speech about my books? I could not do that. For in that case I would have to bring my whole life into the discussion. And that would make a mighty thick book all by itself.

And, furthermore, I now really intend to write such a book. A book that will link my life and my writings together into an explanatory whole. Yes, for I think that I have now attained so ripe an age that I might be permitted to allow myself some little breathing time—take a year's vacation—for such a book would indeed be a vacation compared to the exciting and exhausting work of writing plays. And I have never really had a vacation since I left Norway thirty-four years ago. I think I may need it now.

But, ladies and gentlemen, you must not on that account think that I definitely intend to lay aside my dramatic quill. No, I intend to rely on that and to hold to that until the very last. For I still have various crazy ideas in stock that I have not so far found opportunity to give expression to. Only when I have well rid myself of *these* will it be time to put a stop. And how easy it would be to stop *then* as compared to the time when I was still beginning! How silent and empty it was around one then! How one's fellow combatants stood scattered, each by himself, without relating to one another, without joining one another! Many a time it seemed to me—when I was away—that I myself had never been here. Nor my work, either.

But now! Now there are people everywhere. Young forces, confident of victory, have come on the scene. They do not any longer have to write for a narrow circle. They have a public, an entire people to whom they may speak and to whom they may direct their thoughts and feelings. Whether they meet with opposition or sympathy—that is immaterial. It is only deliberate hardness of hearing and being snubbed and ignored that is evil. That is something I have felt.

I sincerely regret that I have come in such little contact with many of those in this country who are to continue the work. Not because I would, if such were the case, attempt to exert any pressure, but because I myself might reach a deeper understanding. In particular I would have used that closer relation to remove a misconception that has in many ways been a hindrance to me—the misconception that there should be a feeling of absolute happiness connected with that rare fairy-tale fate I have had: gaining fame and fortune yonder in foreign lands. And it is true I have won warm, understanding hearts out there. That first and foremost.

But the true inner happiness—that is no lucky find, no

gift. It must be earned at a price that may often seem high enough. For here is the point: he who wins a home for himself in foreign lands—in his inmost soul he scarcely feels at home anywhere—even in the country of his birth.

But perhaps that may come yet. And I shall regard this evening as a starting point.

For here I behold something that resembles a united group. Here all views, all divergent opinions have been collected around one single thought. I no longer have here the painful feeling of being regarded as the poet of a party. Of either one or the other. A poet must have his entire people around him—either in sympathy with him or in opposition against him. And then the idea of unity can march on toward larger aims and higher tasks. That is my hope and my belief.

Therefore, ladies and gentlemen, I ask you to accept my most cordial thanks for all your kindness and friendliness!

Speech at the Banquet in Copenhagen

Copenhagen, April 1, 1898

The birthday celebrations continued in Copenhagen where Ibsen, arriving on March 30, was promptly decorated with the Grand Cross of the Dannebrog Order. The first Norwegian writer to be accorded this honor, Ibsen was in good spirits during the first part of his stay in Denmark. On March 31 he attended a performance of *The Wild Duck* at the Royal Theater and was greeted by a procession of university students. His mood seemed to change the next day, perhaps because the celebration came at an inopportune time of the year. Many people prominent in the theater and in Danish public life could not attend the official banquet either because of the impending national elections or the sudden change of program at the theater. After two men who had been asked to deliver the encomium to Ibsen declined, Professor Peter Hansen, an old friend of Ibsen's, had to improvise a speech, which he did in a pleasantly ironic and humorous way. Ibsen was obviously a little irritated when he rose to thank him, whether because of the attendance at the banquet, or because Hansen's speech forced him to modify his prepared reply, is hard to say.

Professor Hansen's speech has confused me and ruined my reply. I must now extemporize and kindly ask for your

attention. Today is the first of April. On the same day in
the year 1864 I arrived in Copenhagen for the first time.°
That is now thirty-four years ago. Remember the date and
the year! I traveled southward, through Germany and
Austria, and passed through the Alps on the ninth of
May. On the high mountains the clouds hung like great
dark curtains, and we rode underneath these and through
the tunnel until we suddenly found ourselves at Miramare,
where the beauty of the South, a wonderfully bright gleam
shining like white marble, suddenly burst upon me and
placed its stamp on all my future writings, even though
everything in them is not beautiful.

This feeling of having escaped from the darkness into
the light, from the mists through a tunnel out into the
sunshine, this is a feeling I re-experienced the other morning when I gazed the length of the Sound. And then I was
greeted here by loyal Danish faces. It seemed to me then
that these two journeys acquired an inner relationship.
And for this I give you my most cordial thanks.

The day after this banquet Ibsen had an audience with King
Christian IX and later attended banquets given by the
Women's Literary Society and by the Students' Society of the
University of Copenhagen. On Sunday, April 3, he attended
a performance of *Brand* at the Dagmar Theater, which put
him in a better mood. On April 6 he left for Stockholm.

Speech at the Banquet of the Swedish Society of Authors

Stockholm, April 11, 1898

Ibsen spent the first two days of his stay in Stockholm
viewing the city. Then on Saturday, Holy Saturday of that
year, he had a five-minute audience with King Oscar, who
decorated him with the Order of the North Star, and later
in the evening he had dinner with the King. On Monday,
April 11, he was feted by the Swedish Society of Authors.

Ladies and Gentlemen: I wish to thank you cordially
for this evening. It has been a rather peculiar experience

° Not quite true. Ibsen first came to Copenhagen in 1852, and when
he passed through there again in 1864 on his way to Italy, it was after
April 5.

for me to be present here. I do not know that I have ever belonged to any association, and I almost think that this is absolutely the first time I have been present at a meeting of one. It is true that there is a society in Christiania which is of somewhat the same nature as this one, but there I am a member for appearance's sake only, and for several reasons never take any part in its meetings. Here for the first time I have appeared at a club, and so it is something new to me. The fact of the matter is that a society does not suit my temperament. And in a certain sense it would seem as if organizations were least of all made for authors; for authors must go their own wild ways— Yes, as wild as they might ever wish, if they are to fulfill the missions of their lives. I think, however, that such a club as this may after all in certain respects have its tasks to perform. Real cultural tasks. One of these tasks is this, that authors jointly protect themselves against outer forces, something which may many times be of great necessity. Then there is another task that I think is of no less importance, and that I cannot fail to stress here. It is unfortunately true that playwrights must be translated; but the Scandinavian peoples—for I really cannot give up my old idea of a united Scandinavia as a cultural unity— should they not be able to agree to avoid as much as possible reading each other in translation? Whatever we read in translation is always in danger of being more or less misunderstood, since unfortunately translators themselves are too often somewhat lacking in understanding. I think that if we would read each other in the original we should reach a far more intimate and deeper understanding of the content. To work for improvement in this direction is one of the finest tasks of this club.

In conclusion I would like to say that I always feel so good here in Sweden. I have found here an old established culture, founded on a strong tradition—stronger than in many other countries—and which goes deeper than many think. And then I have met here so many good and hearty people. I do not easily forget such people when I have once learned to know them.

I shall always hold in imperishable memory this evening and all those who have shown me the honor of wishing to be here with me. My cordial thanks to you!

Speech at the Banquet in Stockholm

Stockholm, April 13, 1898

Tuesday evening there was a gala performance of *The Pretenders* at the Vasa Theater, and on Wednesday, three days after Easter, the official banquet honoring Ibsen was held at the Grand Hotel.

It seems like a dream, my visit here in Stockholm. And indeed it is a dream. The first figure that met me in the dream was His Majesty the King. He bestowed upon me the greatest honor that could have been accorded me. I was astonished. I who came here to express my gratitude was given still more to be grateful for. And then I was invited to this splendid and brilliant gathering here, so representative in every way. When His Majesty the King did me such a great honor, it all seemed to me like an ingenious royal eccentricity. And I feel something similar here too. I do not see in the homage that is here paid me a pure and simple personal homage. I see in it a sanctioning of literature as a cultural power, approved by the Swedish people. And what effect this may have on me I am sure you can imagine. My life has been like a long, long Holy Week, and now, in the real Passion Week, my life is transformed into a fairy play. I, the old dramatist, see my life recreated as a poem, a fairy tale. It has been transformed into a midsummer night's dream. Thank you, thank you for the transformation!

The following day Ibsen received a deputation of students from the University of Uppsala and invited them to lunch. In the evening he attended a gala performance of *Lady Inger of Østraat* at the Royal Dramatic Theater, with King Oscar present in the royal box.

Ibsen's stay in Stockholm was extended beyond his original schedule in order that he might accept the invitation extended by two feminist societies, the Fredrika Bremer League and the New Idun, to a banquet in his honor on Saturday the sixteenth. Ibsen apparently came to regret his acceptance, for he seemed irritable and tired at the banquet. But afterward he was enlivened by a group of young girls who performed a number of Swedish folk dances. Ibsen was much happier talk-

ing to them—especially to one of them, Rosa Fitinghoff—than
addressing the feminists. The next day he left for Norway.

Speech at the Banquet of the Norwegian League for Women's Rights

Christiania, May 26, 1898

A month after the official birthday celebrations were over,
Ibsen and his wife were invited to a banquet in his honor
given by the leading Norwegian feminist society.

I am not a member of the Women's Rights League.
Whatever I have written has been without any conscious
thought of making propaganda. I have been more the
poet and less the social philosopher than people generally
seem inclined to believe. I thank you for the toast, but
must disclaim the honor of having consciously worked for
the women's rights movement. I am not even quite clear
as to just what this women's rights movement really is. To
me it has seemed a problem of mankind in general. And if
you read my books carefully you will understand this. True
enough, it is desirable to solve the woman problem, along
with all the others; but that has not been the whole purpose. My task has been the *description of humanity*. To be
sure, whenever such a description is felt to be reasonably
true, the reader will read his own feelings and sentiments
into the work of the poet. These are then attributed to the
poet; but incorrectly so. Every reader remolds the work
beautifully and neatly, each according to his own personality. Not only those who write but also those who read are
poets. They are collaborators. They are often more poetical
than the poet himself.

With these reservations, let me thank you for the toast
you have given me. I do indeed recognize that women
have an important task to perform in the particular directions this club is working along. I will express my thanks
by proposing a toast to the League for Women's Rights,
wishing it progress and success.

The task always before my mind has been to advance
our country and to give our people a higher standard. To
achieve this, two factors are important. It is for the
mothers, by strenuous and sustained labor, to awaken a

conscious feeling of *culture* and *discipline*. This feeling must be awakened before it will be possible to lift the people to a higher plane. It is the women who shall solve the human problem. As mothers they shall solve it. And only in that capacity can they solve it. Here lies a great task for woman. My thanks! And success to the League for Women's Rights!

To Georg Brandes

Christiania, September 30, 1898

Dear Georg Brandes, I have received your letter, and I am very grateful to the Bohemian composer [Zdenko Fibich] for having induced you to break your vow never to write to me again. But I am still more grateful to you for your letter, such as it is.

You tell me about your illness—as if I did not know all about it! Each day during the critical period I read with eager anxiety the bulletins published in the newspapers.

The newspapers said that you were not allowed to receive any visitors. Did you expect me to force my way in with a scrap of a letter every now and then to the very bed where you lay ill? I cannot possibly imagine that, in the condition you were in, you were very anxious to hear from me. I believe you are deluding yourself now in thinking that you were. In your place, I would have asked for peace and quiet in order to get well again—and no disturbing visitors.

Then you know, only too well, my inveterate aversion to writing letters.

And what good would writing have done? You surely know with how much gratitude I acknowledge all that you have done for me very recently. And if you did doubt it— would a written assurance from me make any difference? Good heavens! you know how easy it is to put together a kind of French Staff letter.

Taking everything into consideration, I cannot admit that my crime of silence justifies you in addressing a friend of many years' standing as "Honored Sir," or something to that effect. And I think that it ought to be beneath the dignity of a man like you to behave that way because of one or two letters that have not been written—by a man whose chief passion is certainly not correspondence, even with his best and dearest friends. . . .

To Georg Brandes

Christiania, December 30, 1898

In 1898 Brandes published two works, *Poems of My Youth* and *Julius Lange: Letters Written in His Youth,* which he sent to Ibsen after he had received Ibsen's last letter. On December 27, Brandes' mother died.

Dear Georg Brandes, The newspapers have informed me of the loss which you and your family have suffered; and I well know the feeling of bereavement and emptiness that oppresses you, for you were unusually close to your mother. My thoughts have been very much with you these last few days, I can assure you.

And now you must let me thank you for the dear present you were so extremely kind and generous to send me— immediately after receiving my last letter, which certainly didn't encourage such a friendly answer. Thanks, many thanks for it! I am reading and rereading your fine, ardent and soulful poems, and I understand now why you no longer write verse. You have been pouring the same poetical gifts into your grand epic on Shakespeare, in your creative works on Disraeli and Lassalle, and in all others. No matter how historical the material may be, it is permeated with latent poetry, with your own poetry of the days when you wrote these youthful verses.

The work on Julius Lange I found most engrossing while I was reading it, and consequently it has stayed in my mind afterward. But it has not given me any warmer feeling for Julius Lange. He still seems to me a little too academic, a little too correct, and much too irritating with his troubled conscience. But then your own letters are missing. I very much wish they had been printed too, for it does not help one to understand a dialogue if one hears only one side of it and is obliged to guess at the other. The friendship between you and Julius Lange was never very comprehensible to me. Did you not sometimes, without really intending to, exercise a terrorizing influence on his style? While writing these letters to his friend, did he not think about how they would be received? I don't believe such considerations are in the spirit of a true friendship.

But, good gracious, here I have unintentionally trespassed on other people's land. So—*Schwamm darüber!* [Forget it!]

Thank you for all you have been to me and done for me during the past year. All best wishes to you and yours, and may everything go as you wish in the coming year.

Your faithful and devoted
Henrik Ibsen

To Edvard Brandes

Christiania, March 1, 1899

Dear Dr. Edvard Brandes, Today I write to you as a kind of petitioner, although not directly on my own account.

The matter concerns a young countrywoman of mine, Miss Hildur Andersen, the pianist, whom you probably know by name. She has been asked to come to Copenhagen in the beginning of March to assist at a Palais Concert. She is a pupil of Leschetizky and enjoys a very good reputation as a performer in this country, but she has a certain, not unnatural, dread of Copenhagen, where she has not as yet appeared.

Obviously it is not my intention to try to influence in any way the criticism which will be published in your paper, but simply to ask that she be received in a kindly spirit. She is an intimate friend of mine—a good, wise, and faithful friend; and I am greatly indebted to her relations, in whose house I lived when I was a young man in Bergen. That is my reason for writing to you.

I must avail myself of this opportunity to thank you very sincerely for what you did for me by initiating the idea of a complete edition of my works. It is turning out to be a very satisfactory undertaking as far as I am concerned.

Yours most sincerely,
Henrik Ibsen

To Rosa Fitinghoff

Christiania, April 17, 1899

Rosa Fitinghoff was apparently the last of the young girls in whose company Ibsen sought rejuvenation. He had met her the previous April 16 (not April 11 as this letter has it) during his stay in Stockholm, where she had been one of the girls who entertained the playwright with a group of folk dances.

Dearest Miss Rosa, You are more than kind to send me the little blue flower—*die blaue Blume* that is so full of significance and so seldom found or earned.— And many thanks for giving me a thought or two for April 11 last year. That day will always remain in my memory. Be assured of that.— Your letters live in their own little room in my desk, and when I go to work in the morning, I always look in on them and say, "Hello, Rosa." Warmest greetings.

H. I.

To Julius Elias

Christiania, January 3, 1900

Ibsen's last play, *When We Dead Awaken,* which he called an epilogue to his previous works, was published on December 22, 1899, in a first printing of 12,000. It was sold out before it reached the bookshops, and a new printing appeared immediately. Apart from readings to secure the copyright, the first performance of the play was given by the Court Theater in Stuttgart on January 26, 1900. In Scandinavia the play was staged at the Royal Theater in Copenhagen on January 28, at the Swedish Theater in Helsinki on January 29, at the newly built National Theater in Christiania on February 6, and at the Swedish Theater in Stockholm on February 14.

Dear Dr. Julius Elias: I cannot undertake a plain and simple explanation of what I meant. Irene's hints must rather be considered as a kind of *"Wahrheit und Dichtung."*

In my list of characters I have "A Lady Tourist" while in the German text this has been "improved" to read "Irene." I am certain that my splendid, sensitive, and understanding translator [Christian Morgenstern] is not to blame. It must be the printer or one of his assistants. I hope he is kept under watchful eye in the future. . . .

To Gunnar Heiberg

Christiania, c. February, 1900

In a conversation with Heiberg, the Norwegian critic and playwright, Ibsen had said that Irene in *When We Dead Awaken* was twenty-eight. Heiberg said that was impossible.

Dear Gunnar Heiberg: You are right. I am wrong. I have looked in my notes. Irene is about forty years old.

Yours,

Henrik Ibsen

To Moritz Prozor

Christiania, March 6, 1900

Dear Count Prozor, Permit me in the first place to express the sincere pleasure it gives me to know that Countess Prozor has bravely and successfully undergone the operation and is making a good recovery. I have been with her daily in my thoughts.

Please accept my thanks for the check for 1,000 francs [$190] which I received yesterday. I hope I may expect to see your translation in book form in the near future.°

I cannot say yet whether or not I shall write another play, but if I continue to retain the vigor of mind and body that I enjoy at present, I do not think I shall be able to keep away from the old battlefields permanently. However, if I do appear there again, I shall appear with new weapons and in new armor.

You are quite right when you say that the series which ends with the epilogue really began with *The Master*

° The French translation of *When We Dead Awaken* first appeared in *La Revue de Paris*, January–February issue, 1900.

Builder. However, I am reluctant to say more on this subject.

I leave all commentaries and interpretations to you.

With kindest regards, I remain

Yours sincerely and gratefully,

Henrik Ibsen

To August Lindberg

Christiania, May 5, 1900

In March Ibsen was stricken with erysipelas and was seriously ill.

Dear Mr. Lindberg: As you have probably read in the papers, I have not been feeling well since March, and the doctors have forbidden me to write. That is the reason for my silence.— I do not think my new play is suitable for a traveling troupe, since it requires unusual sets. But perhaps you can get them from Mr. Ranft [Stockholm theatrical producer]. As for royalties, I must ask 600 kroner [$161], to be paid immediately, as I cannot concern myself with business matters later this summer when I shall be staying at a sea resort.

Friendly respects,

Henrik Ibsen

To Suzannah Ibsen

Sandefjord, June 13, 1900

While Ibsen was being treated for his illness at a seaside resort, Mrs. Ibsen was preparing to go to Italy again for her health.

Dear Suzannah, Thanks for the letter which I just now received. Everything is going well. I sleep well. Have a ravenous appetite at each meal. I get a massage every day and it agrees perfectly with me. Not a trace of pain. Already I can walk as far as I wish without feeling tired in my foot.

This is the last letter I shall send you before you leave. I got Sigurd's letter yesterday.

The apartment must not be locked up without giving Helga access to the key. This is for the sake of the insurance. Be sure you remember this! Otherwise I won't have a moment's peace here.

And now I want to wish you with my whole heart a pleasant and successful journey. The anniversary dates of June 18 [their wedding anniversary] and 26 [Suzannah's birthday] I shall celebrate here quietly. May you have as good results from the mineral springs as I have had from the massages.

Many greetings to Sigurd.

Yours affectionately,
H. I.

To Anna Stousland

Sandefjord, August 11, 1900

Anna Stousland was the only daughter of Ibsen's sister Hedvig Stousland.

My dear little Anna, Thank you for your good and lovely letter. It warmed my heart to read it, and I wish you were here with me. Of course you may call me your "Sun God." All the fires of my youth are still burning in me.

I am rather well and am taking long walks.

Your "Sun God"

To Hildur Andersen

Christiania, September 19, 1900

After the death of Ibsen and his wife, Hildur Andersen let it be known that she had no intention of releasing to the public the letters that Ibsen had written to her in the 1890's. The only part of this correspondence that was published was a section of the letter of July 29, 1895, which Hildur allowed to be printed in a journal. After her death the Ibsen scholar Francis Bull prevailed on Hildur's maid to disclose what she could remember about the Ibsen correspondence. The two brief notes that follow are based on her recollection. (See

Francis Bull, "Hildur Andersen og Henrik Ibsen," in *Edda,* Vol. 57 [1957], pp. 47–54.)

The first note accompanied a set of Ibsen's collected works; the second was written on a card that came with a bouquet of flowers. (For the significance of the date September 19, see letter of February 11, 1895.)

Hildur, These twenty-five twins belong to us together. Before I had found you, I seeked and searched as I wrote. I knew that you were somewhere in this big, wide world; and after I had found you, I wrote only about princesses in one form or another.

H. I.

Nine red roses for you, nine rose-red years for me. Take the roses as thanks for the years.

The story of Hildur Andersen might have ended with these brief notes but for an announcement in 1962 that Ibsen's letters to her were indeed extant and in the hands of a private collector. Unfortunately the present editor was not able to secure permission to print any of these letters; nor have they been printed elsewhere as of this writing.

To Cornelius Karel Elout

Christiania, December 9, 1900

During the course of an interview on November 24, 1900, Ibsen had his say about the South African war between the Boers and the British, which had broken out in 1899. Said Ibsen:

My sympathy with the Boers is somewhat divided. Remember that the Boers took their lands in an unrightful way and that they chased the original inhabitants away. And furthermore, the Boers came there as a half-civilized people and had no intention of spreading civilization. And Boers have for a long time held back the progress of civilization. And now a more civilized nation arrives on the scene—the English—and wants to force its way in. That is no worse—in fact, it is not as wrong as what the Boers themselves have done. The English are only taking what the Boers have stolen. Now it's the Boers' turn to put up with it. They have previously chased people out in just the same way, both in the east and in the west. They have been brave and courageous, and they have also had good places where they could stand their ground.

This interview was published in *Ørebladet*, No. 276. The Dutch journalist Cornelius Karel Elout, editor of the *Algemeen Handelsblad*, replied to it. In an open letter, published in the Danish *Politiken*, December 7, he challenged Ibsen either to offer proof for his statements or to withdraw his words. The book referred to in the letter is Elout's *Der Kulturkampf in Südafrika, Ein Versuch zur Prüfung der Krügerschen Kulturpolitik*, published in 1901.

My dear Sir, You have done me the honor of writing me an open letter in *Politiken*, and I take the liberty of sending you a brief open answer in the same paper.

In the field of politics I am, as you perhaps know, a man of peace; and nothing was further from my thoughts than the possibility of my being entangled in the South African war. In the quarrel between the Boers and the English, I have kept myself as carefully in the background and as neutral as the great Dutch colonial power itself.

And my aphoristic utterances in the Norwegian *Øreblad* were most certainly not intended to injure the Boers in the great world of politics.

You write of a book that has not yet appeared, but which will have the power of convincing me that the Boers did not acquire their territory unrightfully, and that the English have done no more for the cause of civilization in South Africa than the Boers.

We shall see.

If this promised book or pamphlet succeeds in convincing me of all this—which would be equivalent to revolutionizing my present views—I shall honestly acknowledge it.

I owe a deep personal debt of gratitude to your nation, Mr. Editor. But you cannot expect me to be ready to pay off part of this debt by doing violence to my convictions.

You conclude by saying that the Dutch are the natural defenders of the Boers in Europe.

Why did your countrymen not choose a more useful place in which to defend them while there was yet time?

I am thinking of South Africa.

And as to defending your kinsmen with books and

pamphlets and open letters—are there not, Mr. Editor, more effective weapons than these?

I am thinking of—.

> Yours respectfully,
> Henrik Ibsen

To Rosa Fitinghoff

Christiania, January 15, 1901

Dear Miss Rosa, What can you think of me for not writing to you in such a long time? But I have been ill. For the first time in my life. During the whole summer I had to stay at Sandefjord resort and have my bad foot massaged daily. But now, fortunately, everything is better.

And then you came to me with the song of little birds and with happy trolls [a reference to a Christmas gift], just like the beautiful young princess in fairy tales. My warmest thanks to you for the beautiful, thoughtful gift. You could have given me nothing better. . . .

Will you soon send another letter to gladden the heart of

> Your devoted
> Henrik Ibsen??

Later in 1901 Ibsen suffered his first stroke, from which he made a fairly good recovery. But a second stroke in 1903 left him unable to walk or write. He died in the afternoon on May 23, 1906.

INDEX

DRAMABOOKS